“双一流”建设高校专业核心课程教材 新形态教材

公司金融

（中英双语版）

CORPORATE FINANCE

周 静 赵 元 高 笛/主编

西南财经大学出版社

中国·成都

图书在版编目(CIP)数据

公司金融:中英双语版/周静,赵元,高笛主编.
成都:西南财经大学出版社,2024.9. --ISBN 978-7-5504-6282-3
Ⅰ. F276.6
中国国家版本馆 CIP 数据核字第 202489CC69 号

公司金融(中英双语版)
GONGSI JINRONG(ZHONGYING SHUANGYUBAN)

周静 赵元 高笛 主编

策划编辑:何春梅
责任编辑:肖 翀
助理编辑:徐文佳
责任校对:周晓琬
封面设计:墨创文化
责任印制:朱曼丽

出版发行	西南财经大学出版社(四川省成都市光华村街 55 号)
网　　址	http://cbs.swufe.edu.cn
电子邮件	bookcj@swufe.edu.cn
邮政编码	610074
电　　话	028-87353785
照　　排	四川胜翔数码印务设计有限公司
印　　刷	四川五洲彩印有限责任公司
成品尺寸	185 mm×260 mm
印　　张	16.25
字　　数	370 千字
版　　次	2024 年 9 月第 1 版
印　　次	2024 年 9 月第 1 次印刷
印　　数	1— 2000 册
书　　号	ISBN 978-7-5504-6282-3
定　　价	42.00 元

前言

习近平总书记在党的二十大报告中明确指出:“高质量发展是全面建设社会主义现代化国家的首要任务。发展是党执政兴国的第一要务。”在2023年中央金融工作会议上,习近平总书记再一次强调:“坚定不移走中国特色金融发展之路。”没有坚实的物质技术基础,就不可能全面建成社会主义现代化强国。显然,社会主义现代化国家不仅需要“物质”基础,还需要“技术”基础,而中国金融必须为奠定这“两大基础”提供坚实有力的保障。中国金融的长期稳定发展,不仅关系到国内大循环内生动力和可靠性的发展,还对中国的跨国企业参与国际金融活动,提升国际循环质量和水平起到了关键作用。改革开放以来,我国金融业发展取得了历史性成就。同时也应看到,我国金融业的市场结构、创新能力、服务水平还不适应经济高质量发展的要求。伴随金融市场的深度变革与金融工具的巨大创新也出现了诸如财务丑闻、垃圾债券、内幕交易等问题。由此,在金融实践的快速变化形势下,理论教学也应顺应时代发展趋势。当前,西方金融理论在中国新兴市场不适用的问题仍然突出,深化金融学教育改革,立足祖国大地,紧跟时代步伐,探索中国特色金融发展之路,创新中国公司金融理论体系,是金融学科教育工作的重要目标。

公司金融作为金融学专业的必修课程和重要分支学科,用于考察公司如何有效地利用各种融资渠道获得最低成本的资金来源,并形成合适的资本结构。其内容包括企业投资、利润分配、运营资金管理及财务分析等,同时也涉及现代公司制度中的一些诸如委托-代理结构的金融安排等深层次的问题。作为一门具有很强操作性的微观金融课程,公司金融在实践中具有广泛的应用性和涉外性,非常适合双语教学。但在教学实践过程中还存在如下问题：①学生所使用的教材大多是英文原版教材，或者是中文译本。在理论学习过程中只能依据西方已有的理论体系搭建知识框架，中译本也容易造成中文翻译后的理论与外文原版理论的偏差，无法使学生真正理解公司金融理论的基本内涵。②案例分析缺乏系统设计。中国金融市场发展相对较晚，但金融相关的问题是快速变化的，不能照搬外文书上的典型案例。案例应不断适应新时代的公司治理和资本市场变化，需要结合中国金融实践进行严密清晰的分析，并使案例建设规范化。③双语教学或全英文教学对学生提出了巨大考验。学生个体外语水平差距较大，对于理论知识的吸收程度不一，学生个体在听、说、读、写、算等各个方面都难以做到应用自如，这对于学生掌握知识体系具有影响。

因此，撰写公司金融双语教材一方面有助于学生了解中国特色金融理论体系、培养英文文献阅读能力、强化专业素养并打开国际视野，另一方面也为课程的双语或全英文课堂实践教学奠定了良好的教学基础。本书紧紧围绕公司金融的核心问题，按照公司金融的实践活动安排教材内容。在各章内容中，充分突出中国元素，并且结合新时代经济发展的特点，将数字经济和数字金融融入公司金融的教学内容中，有助于学生理解中国企业在新时代进行金融活动时面临的机遇和挑战。每章都总结了重点和难点，并提供了配套的习题。本书的特点主要表现在：

第一，思政引领。本书内容充分体现了理论性、政治性、思想性和实践性的高度统一。党的十八大以来，习近平总书记在领导全党全国各族人民推进党和国家事业的实践中，立足世界百年未有之大变局和中华民族伟大复兴战略全局，着眼民族复兴伟大梦想，提出了一系列有关教育改革发展的新理念、新思想、新观点，形成了新时代中国特色社会主义教育理论体系。在习近平新时代中国特色社会主义思想指导下，本书积极探索专业课教学与课程思政相结合的途径和方法，力争在课程教学目标中，既能使学生掌握传统公司金融中的投资决策、融资决策和营运资本管理等主要内容，又能在教学中加入中国元素，从中国公司发展的实践背景出发，结合中国金融制度改革的特点，讲述中国金融制度在支持实体经济发展中所起到的关键作用，以及在新形势下中国公司参与社会金融活动的具体实践，帮助学生理解中国特色金融发展之路。这是财经院校的高等教育教学改革顺应时代发展潮流，切合中国国情，讲清楚经济发展脉络、历史渊源、基本走向、价值理念，在本科生培养中实现“立德树人”根本目标的重要手段，也是将一流学科建设与课程思政有机结合的重要结合点。

第二，系统性。本书以公司金融的核心问题为主体，以价值评估为主线，按照“估值基础—投资决策—融资决策—营运管理决策”的思想脉络，系统介绍了公司金融的基本理论和实用技术。全书共分为四篇。第一篇为基础篇，在阐述了公司金融的主要问题及目标、财务分析的基础上，介绍了货币的时间价值的基本理论和估值技术。第二篇为投资决策篇，分别介绍了投资决策的评价方法和资本预算的估值方法，以及证券价值评估和定价的基本理论与技术。第三篇为融资决策篇，主要介绍了资本成本、资本结构以及股利分配的基本理论与方法。第四篇为营运管理决策篇，包括短期财务计划、现金管理以及信用和存货管理的基本理论与实用技术。各篇既独立又相互联系，以满足教师教学与学生自主学习的多元化需求。

第三，新颖性。本书在总体把握全章节内容的基础上，通过案例分析和课后习题的设计突出知识要点，突显内容设计的新颖性，以加深学生对知识点的理解和掌握。首先，本书将现代公司金融的理论与案例分析相结合。在内容设计上，根据每章的讲授内容，配以案例分析或延伸阅读加深学生对理论和方法的理解和掌握，力争做到理论阐释与案例分析的有机结合。其次，章节后还总结了每章的重点和难点内容，并提供了配套的客观题和主观题供读者练习，且学生可以扫描二维码获得习题答案。

第四，应用性。本书将现代公司金融理论与我国公司的金融实践活动相结合，为学生提供一种具有国际化视野的公司金融决策思路或导向。本书主要作为全英文课程“公司金融”的配套教材，在双语的选择上，每章的学习目标、重点难点、基本理论和评价方法以英文形式呈现，力求与国际接轨；每章的案例以我国上市公司的真实财务数据和金融实践为基础，以中文形式呈现，并将各章的重点概念、理论和财务术语用中文加以总结，以加深学生或读者对公司金融本质的理解和对知识点的运用，充分发挥双语教学的优势，获得更好的学习效果。

本书既可作为公司金融、财务管理、会计等专业的本科教材，也适合非金融、财务、会计专业的本科学生使用。同时，对公司金融感兴趣的社会各界人士也可以在阅读本书的过程中获得收益。

全书框架由周静教授设计。本书由周静教授担任主编，赵元副教授和高笛讲师担任副主编。各章具体分工如下：第一章、第三章、第四章和第五章由周静教授撰写；第六章至第九章由赵元副教授撰写；第二章、第十章至第十三章由高笛讲师撰写。最后由周静教授对全书进行修改和总纂。

本书在编写过程中，参阅了大量国内外公司金融领域专家、学者的著作和研究成果，他们的观点和思想对本书的完成极为重要。书中引用的观点或案例内容尽可能标注了相应的出处，以反映专家和学者的贡献，在此一并致谢。感谢西南财经大学出版社的支持，感谢出版社的徐文佳老师、何春梅老师在本书编辑出版过程中付出的辛勤劳动。

在本书写作过程中，虽然作者极尽努力追求高质量，但由于时间和作者水平有限，难免会存在一些疏漏和不当之处，我们真诚希望各位同行专家和读者提出宝贵的修改意见。你们的批评和建议将是本书不断修订和完善的重要依据。

周静

2024 年 4 月

CONTENTS

Part One　Foundations of Corporate Finance
(公司金融基础)

Part Two　Investment Decision
（投资决策）

Part Three　Financing Decision
(融资决策)

Part Four　Short-Term Finance Management Decision
(短期营运管理决策)

Part One Foundations of Corporate Finance (公司金融基础)

Chapter 1 Introduction（导论）

Learning Objectives

● Learn the forms of business organizations.

● Learn three main questions corporate finance aims to address.

● Learn the goal of financial management.

● Understand agency problems and ways to solve them.

Corporate finance is an important part of finance. It studies how enterprises operate, obtain funds, and allocate funds for the purpose of realizing their existence. Among them, the investment decisions, financing decisions and working capital management decisions are important parts of corporate finance. Through the study of this chapter, you can understand the basic forms of business organizations, be familiar with the main contents of corporate finance, the classic financial management objectives, as well as the principal-agent relationship and agency problems.

1.1 The Corporate Firm

A company is a corporate entity established and registered in accordance with the Company Law for the purpose of profit. Due to the different requirements of company laws in different countries for establishing a company, the legal concept of a company also varies. The corporate form of business is the standard method for solving the problems encountered in raising large amounts of cash. However, businesses can take other forms, like the following:

● The Sole Proprietorship(个人独资企业), which is a business owned and run by an individual. It is the easiest business type to start and operate.

● The Partnership(合伙制企业), which is an unincorporated business entity formed by two or more people, including the General Partnership and the Limited Partnership. The owners of a partnership are called partners who put their joined efforts and resources to start the business.

●The Corporation(公司), which is a business owned by shareholder(s). A board of directors is selected to oversee the organization's activities.

Table 1-1 shows the comparison of business forms.

Table 1-1 A Comparison of Business Forms

	Sole Proprietorship	Partnership	Corporation
Liquidity	Subject to substantial restrictions	Subject to substantial restrictions	Shares can be easily exchanged
Taxation	The owner pays taxes on distributions	Partners pay taxes on distributions	Double (corporate income taxes and individual income taxes)
Reinvestment and dividend payout	All cash flows are distributed to the owner	All cash flows are distributed to partners	Broad latitude
Liability	The owner needs to afford unlimited liability	general partner takes unlimited liability while limited partner takes limited liability of the business.	Shareholder takes limited liability
Continuity	Limited life	Limited life	Perpetual life

1.2 What Is Corporate Finance?

Finance is a discipline that studies how individuals, businesses, and governments allocate resources and time in uncertain environments. There are two characteristics that distinguish financial decision-making from other resource allocation decisions: ①The costs and benefits of financial decision-making are distributed over time; ②neither decision-makers nor anyone else can clearly know the result of decision-making in advance. According to its different research scope, the finance discipline is divided into macro finance and micro finance. Macrofinance is a discipline that studies the allocation of funds within a country or globally, including Macroeconomics, Monetary Banking, and Financial Market. Microfinance is a discipline that studies how individuals and corporates allocate resources and price financial assets, including Investment and Corporate finance.

Corporate Finance addresses the following three questions:

● What long-term investments should the firm choose?

● How should the firm raise funds for the selected investments?

● How should short-term assets be managed and financed?

By answering the three questions, we can also define the main financial decisions of corporate finance, which are Investment Decision (Capital Budgeting Decision), Financing Decision (Capital Structure Decision), and Short-Term Asset Management (Net Working Capital Management Decision).

1.2.1 Investment Decision(投资决策)

From the left side of the balance sheet, the fixed assets of company are generally formed by its investment activities. Managers first seek investment opportunities and then raise funds. The scale and yield of investment opportunities determine the financing strategy. The success of investment is the key to the survival of company.

1.2.2 Financing Decision(融资决策)

From the right side of the balance sheet, the company's short-term liabilities, long-term liabilities and equity form the company's financing activities, that is, the capital structure. The company can obtain funds from different channels, and the financing costs and risks of different channels are also different. When making financing decisions, the company needs to pay attention to the financing costs, the reasonable arrangement of financing structure, and closely cooperate with the actual needs of investment to achieve timely and appropriate funds

1.2.3 Short-Term Asset Management(短期资产管理)

From the top of the left and right sides of the balance sheet, we can make a comparative analysis of current assets and current liabilities, which constitutes the company's short-term asset management problem, that is, the net working capital management decision. For a company, because the value of highly liquid assets such as cash and accounts receivable often change, and accounts payable, taxes payable, and matured debts must be paid on time, the company must pay attention to current assets and current liabilities. Net working capital management needs to reasonably adjust the structure of current assets and current liabilities to improve the turnover efficiency of current assets.

1.3 The Goal of Financial Management

The goal of corporate finance refers to the goals that enterprises aim to achieve in their financial activities. It determines the basic direction of corporate financial management. The most representative views on corporate financial goals currently include the following.

1.3.1 Profit Maximization(利润最大化)

Profit can refer to the current year's profit or the expected profit during the project evaluation process. The results of all financial activities of a company are ultimately reflected to a certain extent in the level of profit. Maximizing profits is the theoretical foundation of Microeconomics, and western economists used to analyze and evaluate corporate behavior and performance based on maximizing profits. This viewpoint holds that enterprises are profit-oriented economic organizations, and it is reasonable to prioritize maximizing profits as their goal. But there is also criticism believing that the goal of maximizing profits overlooks time value, risk, social responsibility, and long-term benefits, etc.

1.3.2 Earnings Per Share Maximization(每股收益最大化)

This view suggests that the company's profits should be linked to the capital invested by shareholders, and the goal of corporate finance should be summarized using earnings per share to avoid the shortcomings of profit maximization. But this view does not take into account the timing and risk of obtaining earnings per share.

1.3.3 Enterprise Value Maximization(企业价值最大化)

Maximizing enterprise value is a widely recognized view in the financial industry, and the financial goal of a corporate is thus defined as maximizing corporate (enterprise) value or shareholders' wealth. Managers should operate the firm's resources with the goal of increasing its market value. Enterprise value is the present value of the expected future cash flows that a corporate can create. This goal reflects the potential or expected profitability and growth ability of the enterprise, and its advantages are reflected in:①considering the time value of cash flows and investment risk;②reflecting the requirements for the preservation and appreciation of enterprise assets;③beneficial for overcoming one-sidedness and short-term behavior in management;④beneficial to the rational allocation of social resources.

1.3.4 Stock Price Maximization(股价最大化)

The main advantage of maximizing stock price is that:①it takes into account risk, and usually the stock price responds more sensitively to risk;②considering the timeliness of cash flows, which avoids to pursue short-term profits;③stock price is an objective indicator that is easy to quantify. However, the goal of maximizing stock price can only be applied to listed companies, and under nonefficient market conditions, stock prices are easily influenced by other factors. The goal of stock price maximization emphasizes shareholders' interests and overlooks other stakeholders.

Which is the correct goal then? Normally, to maximize shareholders' wealth outperforms other goals which are to some extent unilateral. For example, the goal to maximize current profits may be at the expense of future profits, thereby hindering the long-term growth of the firm. The Financial Manager's primary goal is to increase the value of the firm by selecting value creating projects and making smart financing decisions. However, at present, we need to ask a question of why only shareholders' interest is considered? How the interest of other stakeholders is ensured, likewise creditors, government, employees, customers, suppliers, communities, environment, managers, alliance partners, etc?

延伸阅读 1-1 《股东至上还是利益相关者价值最大化?》

很多实证都支持公司治理应该采用利益相关者模式。如 1992 年哈佛大学的课题组在很长的时间里研究了两类公司的业绩:一类公司比较注重利益相关者价值;另一类则只重视传统的股东价值。结果他们发现在 11 年的时间里前一类公司的价值平均增长了 682%,而后一类只增长了 166%(金海平,2007)。但这些研究还不足以推翻股东主导的单边治理模式的有效性,因为类似的计量研究给出了完全相反的结论。以英美为代表的股东至上模式表现出迅猛的发展势头,更给利益相关者理论提出了这样一个问题:如何解释这种现象?这就必须从理论到实证都要有合理的证明和诠释。以前的实证研究虽表明多数情况下采用利益相关者治理模式的公司的经营绩效更好,但实证中所做的假设有些是不严格甚至是经不住推敲的。尤其是在以下几个方面:

(1)利益相关者的界定问题。企业为谁服务首先要解决的问题是企业是谁的。采用利益相关者治理模式就意味着在公司治理中各个层面的利益都要被考虑进去。那么就存在这样一个问题：利益相关者的边界在哪里？它是包括所有人和物，甚至空气在内的一个广义概念，还是一个特定的范围？尽管目前对其有各种各样的界定，如：广义的利益相关者和狭义的利益相关者、现实的利益相关者和潜在的利益相关者、关键利益相关者和非关键利益相关者等。但总的来说，每一种界定方法都能找出它的缺陷，即使对于非主流企业理论的经济学家来说，目前对利益相关者的界定也还未达成一致的结论，这无疑会给利益相关者理论的体系构建带来制约，也容易使其成为股东至上理论的攻击目标。另外，企业的边界也是不断变化的，例如战略联盟和虚拟企业就是这种状况。这样利益相关者的范围就在不断扩展。因为联盟前的企业和联盟后的企业，其利益相关者的范围是不一样的，这又给利益相关者的界定带来了新的问题。

(2)利益相关者的绩效评价问题。支持公司治理应采用利益相关者模式的理论其实有个隐含的前提，那就是采用利益相关者治理模式的公司的绩效要比采用股东至上治理模式的公司的绩效要强。不同的利益相关者参与企业决策的实践对企业实际绩效的影响很难计量，因为影响企业绩效的因素很多，无法把它们有效地分离，因而也就不能提出真正有说服力的计量检验结果。在前文中，我们可以看到，并非所有的实证都支持利益相关者治理的绩效性，这就给利益相关者治理模式提出了一个挑战：既然采用利益相关者治理方法无法改变企业的绩效，我们为什么还要采用利益相关者治理模式？这有三种可能：一是确实如这些实证所言，利益相关者治理和企业绩效本来就没有明显的正相关性；二是这些实证采用的方法可能有问题，但实际中有些国家的例子却证明非利益相关者治理确实也是有绩效的；三是对绩效的定义可能有问题，这里的绩效应该是社会绩效而不单纯是财务上的绩效，但社会绩效到底怎么去衡量目前仍然是个难题，这也给利益相关者理论留下了问题。

(3)基于利益相关者的公司治理模式。利益相关者理论的归宿实际上是提出一套适用的公司治理模式(陈宏辉，2004)。在传统的设计中，无论是“资本雇佣劳动”模式还是“劳动雇佣资本”模式都会有明确的责任人和清晰的委托-代理关系。在理论上思路清晰，在操作上也明了可行。但这种单边治理模式一直不被研究利益相关者理论的学者看好。在指出其缺陷后，他们提出了基于利益相关者理论的公司治理模式，把利益相关者而不仅仅是股东作为企业的最高权力机关，企业的经营目标不再是单纯的盈利最大化，同时还必须承担相应的社会责任（杨瑞龙、周业安，2001）。这在理论上没有问题，但在实践中怎样实施就遇到了两个问题。一是不是所有利益相关者都能参与到企业治理中，如果所有利益相关者都参与公司的日常治理，那极有可能达成“谁都负责结果谁都负不了责”的局面。如果是部分参与，到底哪部分利益相关者才能参与？利益相关者对公司治理一方面通过政府立法间接规范竞争秩序，为公司的良好运转创造条件，另一方面让一部分利益相关者通过直接介入公司的决策机构参与公司的战略制定，从而保障自身的利益。或者根据成本收益原则，哪些利益相关者能直接进入董事会等决策机构，要取决于这种直接介入能否带来企业利益的增加。反之，如果不让某些利益相关者加入就必然遭受企业整体利益的明显或潜在的损失，那么让其进入就是有效的。但这些只是理论上的，现实中到底让哪部分利益相关者参与公司治理没有定论，处理得不好又可能回到“股东至上”的老路。二是企业的社会责任问题。现有的问题都强调企业要承担社会责任，并且已有大量文献证明企业承担社会责任有可能和企业绩效正相关，但企业怎样做才是承担了社会责任的表现，在利润目标和社会责任发生冲突时是不是放弃利润就算实现了社会责任？现有文献涉及很少，也未就此问题达成一致。这也给利益相关者理论的可接受程度提出了挑战。

资料来源：周翼翔，郝云宏.从股东至上到利益相关者价值最大化：一个研究文献综述[J].重庆工商大学学报(社会科学版)，2008(5)：20-26.

1.4 The Agency Problem of Corporation

The separation of ownership and control rights is an important symbol of modern companies, leading to achieving the corporate goal of being bigger, stronger, and longer. However, the separation of two rights can also bring about principal-agent problems. This agency problem arises from the agency relationship that exists in a corporation where stockholders (principals) hire managers (agents) to run the company. The interest of agents is not always aligned with principals. For instance, the owners' goal is to pursue the maximization of shareholder wealth, while the managers' goal is to maximize personal compensation (including the equivalent use of monetary and non monetary income for on-the-job consumption). As such, the managers may harm the owners' goals in order to achieve their own goals. The typical form is called the owner - manager conflict, including moral risk and adverse selection. Therefore, in order to minimize the agency problem, the owners must provide effective incentives and constraints to the managers.

Corporate governance is the way to minimize the agency problem. It refers to a mechanism of supervision and balance between owners and managers, which is to reasonably allocate the rights and responsibilities between the two through a system arrangement, in order to achieve the company's goal of maximizing shareholder wealth. Corporate governance includes internal and external mechanisms. The internal mechanisms of corporate governance include decision-making mechanism, supervision mechanism, and incentive mechanism, while the external mechanisms include legal environment, capital market, product market, managers market and corporate control market.

1.4.1 Internal Mechanisms of Corporate Governance

1. Decision-Making Mechanism(决策机制)

The board of directors is the decision-making body for corporate governance. On the one hand, the board of directors is responsible to all shareholders and exercises its power within the authorized scope of the shareholders' meeting; On the other hand, the board of directors entrusts specific affairs to the executing agency, forming a second layer of commission agency relationship. Therefore, the quality of the board of directors is directly related to the success of corporate governance, while the composition of directors is directly related to the efficiency and effectiveness of the board of directors. Independence is a necessary condition for the efficient functioning of the board of directors. To ensure the independence of the board of directors, it is necessary to be independent of both major shareholders and the management team, such as establishing independent directors.

2. Supervision Mechanism(监督机制)

In order to avoid the board of directors representing the interests of owners from pursuing their own interests and damaging the interests of the company, shareholders, creditors, and employees, it is necessary to restrict and supervise the board of directors through certain institutional arrangements. At the same time, for the agency relationship between the board of directors and the management, it is also necessary for the board of directors to supervise the managers they hire, in order to avoid managers from pursuing their own interests and harming the company's interests. Therefore, the supervision mechanism is the institutional design by which the owners effectively review and control the management's decision - making behavior, including internal and external supervision mechanisms. Internal supervision mechanisms refer to shareholder meetings and supervisory board, while external supervision mechanisms refer to media and intermediary agencies.

3. Incentive Mechanism(激励机制)

Incentives can be used to align the interests of management and shareholders. The incentives need to be structured carefully to make sure that they achieve their intended goal. The core of motivating managers is to transform their pursuit of maximizing personal utility into the pursuit of company's goal. In the process of modern company operation, the incentive for managers is mainly reflected in equity incentives. Equity incentive is a form of economic rights granted to managers by acquiring company's equity. By doing so, they can participate in corporate decision-making, share profits, and take risks as shareholders, thus diligently and responsibly serving the long-term development of the company.

1.4.2 External Mechanisms of Corporate Governance

1. Legal Environment(法律环境)

To achieve good corporate governance, there must be a legal system to protect investors. If a country has a high level of investor property protection, investors are willing to invest in stocks and bonds, and the capital market will be highly developed. The high degree of investor property protection can avoid conflicts of interest between investors and managers, ensuring that the majority of the company's cash flow is repaid to investors in the form of dividends and stock repurchases.

2. Capital Market(资本市场)

Good corporate governance cannot be achieved without effective capital markets. An effective capital market can quickly provide signals to all shareholders about the company's operating conditions, thereby transmitting bad behavior by the management to the stock price. For instance, managers' opportunistic behavior can cause a decline in the stock price. If the company's stock price is lower than that of its competitors, shareholders can choose to sell the company's stock, raise inquiries at shareholders' meetings, or directly take over the control of the company. Under the pressure of such a supervisory mechanism, the board of directors and management can only fulfill their responsibilities to ensure the realization of shareholders' interests.

3. Product Market(产品市场)

In a competitive and customer-oriented industrial environment, if a company's products or services are popular with customers, its market share will increase. If the company's products or services cannot occupy a certain market share, shareholders will pay attention to the company's business management status. Although the appointment and removal of managers are determined by the board of directors, shareholders can use their rights to influence the board of directors and encourage them to punish incompetent managers.

4. Managers Market(经理人市场)

In an effective managers market, information about managers' business acumen and sense of responsibility is publicly known. Irresponsible or incompetent managers may find it difficult to get satisfactory jobs after being fired, and can only receive low positions and low salaries. Diligent and capable managers will receive high positions and superior compensation. The loss of status and personal income after business failure, as well as the competition for control of the company in the capital market, can serve as a warning to managers who attempt to slack off or pursue excessive compensation.

5. Corporate Control(公司控制)

Due to the free transfer of company stocks through the securities market, hostile acquirers may choose companies with poor performance or insufficient potential growth capabilities to acquire their stocks, thereby achieving control over the company. The corporate control market forces managers to fully utilize their operational abilities, otherwise their personal interests may be affected, as managers of merged companies are often replaced or downgraded. Thus, the threat of a takeover may result in better management.

Burkart et al. (2003) demonstrate that in the United States and United Kingdom, some of the largest publicly listed firms, such as Wal-Mart Stores and Ford Motor, are family controlled. In effect, except for the United States and United Kingdom, the concentrated ownership structure rather than diffused ownership, is found to be the prominent characteristic of large publicly traded companies around the rest of the world, such as Western Europe, South and East Asia, Latin America, the Middle East, and Africa. In particular, ownership and control rights over the company are often maintained in the hand of a group of individuals who are usually combined through family. Even in the United States, where ownership is dispersed at its highest, founders or families are found to exercise a substantive extent of control over most of public corporations. Publicly traded family firms accounted for 34% of China's listed companies, while the Small and Medium Enterprises board (SME) in the Shenzhen Stock Exchange (SZSE) was almost entirely constituted by family firms at the end of 2018.

For those listed firms above, is the owner-manager conflict considered as the main agency problem? What are the other concerns for agency problems? To ease these agency problems, what else can be done besides the internal and external mechanisms of corporate governance?

Key Concepts and Skills

1. Three forms of business organizations and their advantages and disadvantages.

2. Three main questions that corporate finance aims to address.

3. The goals of financial management.

4. The formation and resolution of agency problems.

本章重点与难点

1. 企业的三种组织形式及各自的优缺点。
2. 公司金融要解决的三个主要问题。
3. 公司金融的目标。
4. 代理问题的形成及解决。

Self-Test Questions

Ⅰ. True (T) or False (F) Questions

1. Compared with sole proprietorships or partnerships, the greatest advantages of corporations are limited liability, easy transfer of equity, and easy access to external capital. ( )

2. If capital markets are fully efficient, share prices can truly reflect the value of shareholder' wealth. ( )

3. The shareholders' claim to the company's profits is fixed. ( )

4. In order to ensure that the financial objectives of the business are met, the owners' dismissal of managers is the best option for shareholders to reconcile their own objectives with those of managers. ( )

5. The biggest disadvantage of a corporation compared to a sole proprietorship or partnership is the limited size of the company. ( )

6. The criterion for determining whether a financial decision is feasible is net present value, not accounting profit. ( )

7. The theory of valuation is about intrinsic value, net added value and valuation models, which is the most fundamental theory of corporate finance. ( )

8. Moral risk and adverse selection are the main manifestations of managers' deviation from financial objectives. ( )

9. The main reason for the principal-agent relationship between shareholders and managers is the separation of ownership and management. ( )

10. In a corporation, shareholders have unlimited liability for the assets and a residual claim to the firm value. ( )

Ⅱ. Short Answer Questions

1. What are the three basic questions Financial Managers must answer?
2. What are the three major forms of business organization?
3. What is the goal of financial management?
4. What are agency problems, and why do they exist within a corporation?

本章习题答案

Chapter 2 Financial Analysis （财务分析）

Learning Objectives

- Know how to compute and interpret important financial ratios.
- Know how to compute and interpret important financial ratio systems.
- Be able to develop a financial plan using the percentage of sales approach.

The financial statement is the key element of the corporation. In this chapter, we introduce the basis of financial analysis, and the useful ratios in the practice of financial analysis, which helps the beginners form a systematic method to measure the firms' financial status or make the comparison between firms of different sizes. Moreover, not only can we assess different aspects of firms by historical information, but we can also arrange financial planning based on the financial statement. We thereby introduce the percentage of sales approach, to summarize the projected future financial status of a company in the form of pro forma financial statements.

2.1 Financial Ratio Analysis

Owing to the different sizes, we could not directly compare between two companies when we get their financial statements. To avoid the problems involved in comparing companies of different size, one of the most important measures is to calculate and compare financial ratios. Financial ratios are traditionally grouped into the following categories: ①Short-term solvency or liquidity measures; ②Long-term solvency ratios; ③Asset management or turnover measures; ④Profitability measures; ⑤Market measures.

2.1.1 Short-Term Solvency Measures

Short-term solvency ratios measure the firm's ability to pay its bills over the short run without due stress. The group of ratios focuses on one firm's current assets and current liabilities, sometimes called liquidity measures.

1. Current Ratio(流动比率)

The current ratio is the ratio of the current assets to current liabilities. It measures the ability of one firm to translate its current assets into cash to pay its current liabilities off. Normally, a current ratio is expected to be 1~2. A lower-than-1 current ratio means bad short-term liquidity because that net working capital (current asset less current liabilities) is negative, while a higher-than-2 one means good short-term liquidity, but it depends on the specific industries.

$$\text{Current ratio} = \frac{\text{Current assets}}{\text{Current liabilities}}$$

2. Quick (or Acid-Test) Ratio(速动比率)

Compared with the current ratio, the number of inventories isn't taken into consideration in the quick ratio. Because inventory is the least liquid current asset, so the book value couldn't accurately reflect the market value. Moreover, a large bulk of inventories, however, encumber the liquidity of firms in many circumstances. Similarly, the quick ratio is expected to be 1, but it also varies a great deal across industries. However, an extremely high quick ratio is not a good signal, it means too much cash is occupied by other current assets, which encumber the cash turnover.

$$\text{Quick ratio} = \frac{\text{Current assets} - \text{Inventory}}{\text{Current liabilities}}$$

Notice that using cash to buy inventory does not affect the current ratio, but it reduces the quick ratio, again, owning to the weakest liquidity of inventory.

3. Cash Ratio(现金比率)

The cash ratio is the ratio of cash to current liabilities. Normally, it is expected to be more than 20%. Because cash is the most liquid current asset, the very short-term creditor might care about the cash ratio.

$$\text{Cash ratio} = \frac{\text{Cash}}{\text{Current liabilities}}$$

2.1.2 Long-Term Solvency Measures(长期偿债能力比率)

Long-term solvency ratios reflect the firm's ability to meet its obligations in the long run, or its financial leverage, so they are sometimes called financial leverage ratios or leverage ratios.

1. Total Debt Ratio(总负债比率)

The total debt ratio considers one firm's ability to pay off both current liabilities and non-current liabilities, which could be defined as:

$$\text{Total debt ratio}=\frac{\text{Total assets}-\text{Total equity}}{\text{Total assets}}$$

Normally, the lower the total debt ratio is, the easier the firm is to meet the obligation in the long term. And the ratio is expected to be 60% for most firms. Moreover, two variations of it are frequently used.

$$\text{Debt-equity ratio}=\frac{\text{Total debt}}{\text{Total equity}}$$

$$\text{Equity multipier}=\frac{\text{Total assets}}{\text{Total equity}}$$

2. Times Interest Earned(利息倍数)

Times Interest Earned measures how well one firm has its interest obligations covered, it's also called the interest coverage ratio.

$$\text{Times interest earned ratio}=\frac{\text{EBIT}}{\text{Interest}}$$

Normally, the higher the times interest earned is, the stronger ability the firm has to meet the obligations in the long run. The ratio is expected to be 3, and for keeping debt-paying ability, it must be no less than 1.

3. Cash Coverage(现金保障倍数)

The cash coverage ratio measures how well a company has its interest obligations covered. Notice that depreciation and amortization are two accounting concepts but not actual cash flow, but they are deducted from the expense. Actual cash available to pay interest should include the amount of depreciation and amortization, so the cash coverage ratio is defined as:

$$\text{Cash coverage ratio}=\frac{\text{EBIT}+(\text{Depreciation and amortization})}{\text{Interest}}=\frac{\text{EBITDA}}{\text{Interest}}$$

EBITDA(息税折旧摊销前利润) is not only a basic measure of a firm's ability to generate cash from operations but is also used as a measure of cash flow available to meet financial obligations.

4. Other Useful Long-Term Solvency Ratio

Moreover, we could also include notes payable (normally bank debt) and long-term debt in the numerator and EBITDA in the dominator as a long-term solvency ratio:

Interest bearing debt/EBITDA

Values below 1 on this ratio are considered very strong and values above 5 are considered weak.

2.1.3 Asset Management or Turnover Measures (资产管理和周转指标)

1. Inventory Turnover(存货周转率)

Inventory turnover measures how many times the firms sell off their entire inventory in one year. As long as they don't run out of stock and thereby forgo sales, the higher the ratio is, the more efficient the inventory management is.

$$\text{Inventory turnover} = \frac{\text{Cost of goods sold}}{\text{Inventory}}$$

After we know how many times we turn our inventory over during one year, we can figure out how long it took us to turn it over on average:

$$\text{Days' sales in inventory} = \frac{365 \text{ days}}{\text{Inventory turnover}}$$

Day's sales in inventory roughly show how many days inventory sits on before it is sold.

2. Receivables Turnover(应收账款周转率)

Similarly, receivables turnover measures the average times the firms collect their credit accounts and lent the money again in one year, reflecting how fast they could collect the sales account.

$$\text{Receivables turnover} = \frac{\text{Sales}}{\text{Accounts receivable}}$$

And the days' sales in receivable are defined below:

$$\text{Days' sales in receivables} = \frac{365 \text{ days}}{\text{Receivable turnover}}$$

Day's sales in receivables roughly show how many days a firm needs to collect on its credit sales. This ratio is also called the average collection period (ACP).

3. Total Asset Turnover(总资产周转率)

The total asset turnover ratio measures the number of times a company's total assets are turned over in a year. Generally speaking, it reflects how much one unit of asset contribute to the firm. Besides asset management, it's also an important ratio to describe the profitability of one firm. Normally, the total asset turnover is expected to be 80%. Commonly, the ratio is less than 1, especially if a firm has a large number of fixed assets.

$$\text{Total asset turnover ratio} = \frac{\text{Sales}}{\text{Total Assets}}$$

2.1.4 Profitability Measures(盈利性指标)

Profitability measures reflect how efficiently the firm uses its assets and how efficiently the firm manages its operations.

1. Profit Margin(销售利润率)

The profit margin is the ratio of net income to sales. It measures how much net income each unit of sales can generate.

$$\text{Profit Margin} = \frac{\text{Net income}}{\text{Sales}}$$

2. EBITDA Margin(EBITDA 利润率)

The EBITDA margin is another commonly used measure of profitability. Because EBITDA adds noncash expenses back, EBITDA margin directly focuses on operating cash flows rather than net income, regardless of capital structure or taxes.

$$\text{EBITDA Margin} = \frac{\text{EBITDA}}{\text{Sales}}$$

Normally, we expect a higher EBITDA margin, which corresponds to a low expense ratio relative to sales. However, it also varies a great deal across industries. Grocery stores have a notoriously low-profit margin of around 2%, but that for the pharmaceutical industry is about 15%.

3. Return on Assets(资产收益率)

Return on assets (ROA) is a measure of profit per unit of asset contribute to the firm. ROA is usually measured as:

$$\text{Return on Assets} = \frac{\text{Net income}}{\text{Total assets}}$$

4. Return on Equity(权益收益率)

Return on assets (ROE) is a measure of how profit per unit of equity contribute to the firm. Because one firm's final goal is maximizing the benefits of stockholders, ROE is the most important measure of performance for investors. ROE is usually measured as:

$$\text{Return on Equity} = \frac{\text{Net income}}{\text{Total equity}}$$

5. The DuPont Identity(杜邦分析法)

Notice that we can separate ROE into two other ratios, ROA and the equity multiplier:

$$\text{Return on equity(ROE)} = \frac{\text{Net income}}{\text{Total equity}} = \frac{\text{Net income}}{\text{Total equity}} \times \frac{\text{Assets}}{\text{Assets}}$$

$$= \frac{\text{Net income}}{\text{Assets}}(\text{ROA}) \times \frac{\text{Assets}}{\text{Total equity}}(\text{Equity multiplier})$$

Then, we can further decompose ROE by multiplying the top and bottom by total sales:

$$\text{Return on equity(ROE)} = \frac{\text{Net income}}{\text{Assets}} \times \frac{\text{Sales}}{\text{Sales}} \times \frac{\text{Assets}}{\text{Total equity}}$$

$$= \frac{\text{Net income}}{\text{Sales}} \times \frac{\text{Sales}}{\text{Assets}} \times \frac{\text{Assets}}{\text{Total equity}}$$

$$\text{ROE} = \text{Profit margin} \times \text{Total asset turnover} \times \text{Equity multiplier}$$

The last expression of the preceding equation is called the DuPont identity. It's obvious that the ROE is affected by three factors: ① Operating efficiency (measured by profit margin); ②Asset-using efficiency (measured by total asset turnover); ③Financial leverage (measured by the equity multiplier).

【Example 2-1】

Pop Co. has a debt-equity ratio of 0.7. Return on assets is 8.4 percent, and the total equity is $840,000. What is the equity multiplier? Return on equity? Net income?

Answer:

$$\text{Equity multiplier} = 1 + \frac{\text{Debt}}{\text{Equity}} = 1 + 0.7 = 1.7$$

$$\text{ROE} = \text{ROA} \times \text{Equity multiplier} = 0.84 \times 1.7 = 0.1428$$

$$\text{Because ROE} = \frac{\text{Net income}}{\text{Sales}} \times \frac{\text{Sales}}{\text{Assets}} \times \frac{\text{Assets}}{\text{Total equity}}$$

$$= \frac{\text{Net income}}{\text{Assets}} \times \frac{\text{Sales}}{\text{Sales}} \times \frac{\text{Assets}}{\text{Total equity}}$$

$$= \frac{\text{Net income}}{\text{Total equity}}$$

So, Net income = ROE×Total Equity = 0.1428×840,000 = $119,952

2.1.5 Market Value Measures(市场指标)

The group of ratios is not based on the financial statement, but the market information.

1. Earnings Per Sharing Ratio(每股收益)

EPS is the ratio of net income to shares outstanding.

$$\text{EPS} = \frac{\text{Net income}}{\text{Share outstanding}}$$

2. Price-Earnings Ratio(市盈率)

Price-earnings ratio, or PE ratio, is defined as the ratio of price per share to EPS. PE ratio measures how much the investors are willing to pay per share of one firm. The higher PE ratio commonly implies that the investors expect the firm a promising future.

$$\text{PE ratio} = \frac{\text{Price per share}}{\text{Earnings per share}}$$

3. Market-to-Book Ratio (市值面值比)

Market-to-book ratio is the ratio of market value per share to book value per share.

$$\text{Market-to-book ratio} = \frac{\text{Market value per share}}{\text{Book value per share}}$$

Book value per share is an accounting number that reflects historical costs. The market-to-book ratio compares the market value of the firm's investments to its cost, so a value less than 1 could mean that the firm fails to create value for the investors.

4. Market Capitalization(股票市值)

Market capitalization is a commonly used ratio for potential investors to one firm, equal to the firm's stock market price per share multiplied by the number of shares outstanding.

$$\text{Market capitalization} = \text{Price per share} \times \text{Share outstanding}$$

5. Enterprise Value(企业价值)

Enterprise Value measures the market value of outstanding shares of stock of one firm plus the market value of outstanding interest-bearing debt less cash on hand. The ratio could closely estimate how much one investor should spend on buying all outstanding stock of the firm and also paying off the debt. The cash deducted is immediately used to pay the debt or dividend off.

$$\text{EV} = \text{Market capitalization} + \text{Market value of interest bearing debt} - \text{Cash}$$

6. Enterprise Value Multiples(企业价值乘数)

Enterprise Value Multiplies are used to estimate the value of the firm's total business. Notice that even when there are differences in capital structure or interest expense between two companies, we could still use the ratio to compare them.

$$\text{Enterprise value multiples} = \frac{\text{EV}}{\text{EBITDA}}$$

Similar to PE ratios, a firm with high growth opportunities means the investors expect it with a promising future.

案例分析 2-1 《康美药业财务造假》

一、案例背景

康美药业是曾经的千亿市值白马股,但自 2018 年以来屡遭市场质疑,证监会经过 5 个月的调查,证实了康美药业财务造假。2019 年 4 月 29 日晚间,康美药业公告表示,公司从 2018 年 12 月 28 日被证监会立案调查后,对此进行了自查,发现 2018 年之前的营业收入、营业成本、费用及款项收付方面存在账实不符的情况。其中,康美药业对 2017 年财务报表进行重述,货币资金多计 299.44 亿元,营业收入多计 88.98 亿元,销售费用少计 4.97 亿元,财务费用少计 2.28 亿元等。

二、康美药业财务造假迹象

(1)存贷双高。康美药业在有巨额存款的情况下还存在巨额负债,背负负债的同时还承担着高额的财务费用,这本身就不合理,而其闲置存款不购买理财产品也不进行资金管理,利息收入非常低,这一行为违背一般管理者的商业逻辑。由此可以看出其存款可能存在虚构情况。

(2)净经营现金流每年都低于净利润。这可能存在两种情况:一是企业近年来的实际收入和利润都是虚高的;二是应收账款存在坏账。两种情况均证明康美药业存在虚增利润的现象。

(3)应收账款和存货均高于同行业。存货余额共 180 亿元,金额较大,其中还有人参等难以判断存在性的存货。证明其虚构的利润可能放入了存货中。与此同时,消耗性生物资产在市场价格下降的时候不计提跌价准备,在关联方资金往来中其他应收款余额中坏账准备为 0 元。

(4)康美药业主业为医药贸易,毛利率达到 30%,远高于行业平均水平。横向对比说明了康美药业的净利润有虚高之嫌。

(5)账面现金数 377 亿元,基本与有息负债数 400 亿元相同。有息负债融资的资金基本没有用于生产经营,因此,融资现金就无法转化成其他科目,极大可能是被大股东体外占用了,体外占用无法在报表中体现。因此,报表中一直显示有 377 亿元现金,但是依然需要不断增加有息负债。

(6)2017 年利息收入 2.69 亿元,年利息率大约 0.7%。利息收入过低也可以作为资金被体外占用的证据。

(7)股东股权质押比例非常高。截至目前,大股东康美实业持有的康美药业 91.91%的股权已经质押,表明有庄股的嫌疑。

资料来源:王秀珍.康美药业财务造假案例分析[J].经济师,2020(2):98,100.

2.2 Financial Planning and Growth

Another important use of financial statements is financial planning. Pro forma financial statements are frequently used in financial planning to summarize the projected future financial status of a company.

2.2.1 The Percentage of Sales Approach(销售百分比法)

The percentage of sales approach is a simple method to generate pro forma statements, based on the expected growth rate of sales. There is a reasonable assumption that some items of the financial statements increased at the same rate as sales, but for the remains, which are set by the management, it probably isn't. To use the financial planning model based on the percentage of sales approach, it's necessary to follow the steps below.

(1) Separate the income statement and balance sheet accounts into two groups, one of which is relative to sales, but another is not. Then calculate the ratio of the items to sales.

(2) Set the expected growth rate of the sales.

(3) Calculate the expected financial items under the growth rate.

(4) Forecast the increase in retained earnings.

(5) How much should the firm finance to support the predicted sales level?

Here is a simple example, and we separately discuss the income statement and the balance sheet。

2.2.2 Income Statements

Table 2-1 is the most recent income statement for the R corporation and it has projected a 25% increase in sales for the next year. The change is shown in Table 2-2.

Table 2-1 Simple Income Statement for R

Sales		$ 5,000
Costs(80% of the sales)		4,000
Taxable income		1,000
Taxes (25%)		250
Net income		750

Table 2-1(continue)

-Dividends	250	
-Addition to retained earnings	500	

Table 2-2 Pro forma Income Statement for R

Sales		\$6,250(5,000 * 1.25)
Costs(80% of the sales)		5,000
Taxable income		1,250
Taxes (25%)		312.5
Net income		937.5

R set the growth rate as 25%, so the expected sales are $5,000 \times 1.25 = 6,250$, and the cost of the next reporting annual is still 80% of the sales ($6,250 \times 80\% = 5,000$). It's not difficult to notice that the profit margin \$750/5,000 = 15% for R is equal to the profit margin \$937.5/6,250 = 15% of the pro forma statement for R.

Then, we need to project the dividend payment. We can assume R has a policy of paying the dividend at a fixed proportion of net income, which means a constant dividend payment ratio.

$$\text{Dividend payout ratio} = \frac{\text{Cash dividend}}{\text{Net income}}$$

We also introduce the retention ratio (or plowback ratio), equal to 1 minus the dividend payout ratio because all not paid is retained.

$$\text{Retention ratio} = \frac{\text{Addition to retained earnings}}{\text{Net income}}$$

In this case, the retention ratio is $250/750 = 33\frac{1}{3}\%$, and under the ratio, the expected increase in retained earnings is $937.5 \times \frac{2}{3} = 625$.

2.2.3 Balance Sheet

Table 2-3 is the most recent balance sheet for R, and Table 2-4 is the pro forma balance sheet based on Table 2-3. In the balance sheet, we assume some items are relative to sales, but others are not. And we use "n/a" to label if an item isn't relative to sales.

Table 2-3 **Balance Sheet for R**

Assets			Liabilities and Owners' Equity		
	$	Percentage of sales		$	Percentage of sales
Current assets			Current liabilities		
-Cash	900	18%	-Accounts payable	600	12%
-Accounts receivable	1, 100	22	-Notes payable	900	n/a
-Inventory	2, 000	40	Total	1, 500	
Total	4, 000	80	Long-term debt	7, 000	n/a
Fixed assets			Equity		
Net plant and equipment	8, 000	160	- Common stock and paid-in surplus	800	n/a
			-Retained earnings	2, 700	n/a
			Total	3, 500	
Total assets	12, 000	240	total L+E	12, 000	n/a

As we mentioned above, the sales level is projected to be $6, 250 in the coming year, so it's simple to calculate all the relevant items. For example, cash is equal to 18% of sales for this reporting year. Under this planning method, we assume this percentage applies to the coming year. For each unit increase in sales, cash will rise by 0. 18. As for the items set by the management, such as notes payable, long-term debt, and so on, we assume that they keep unchanged in the pro forma balance sheet for R.

Table 2-4 **Pro Forma Balance Sheet for R**

Assets			Liabilities and Owners' Equity		
	Next year	Δ		Next year	Δ
Current assets	$	$	Current liabilities	$	$
-Cash	1, 125(6, 250 * 18%)	225	-Accounts payable	750(6, 250 * 12%)	150
-Accounts receivable	1, 375	275	-Notes payable	900	0
-Inventory	2, 500	500	Total	1, 650	150
Total	5, 000	1, 000	Long-term debt	7, 000	0
Fixed assets			equity		
-Net plant and equipment	10, 000	2, 000	-Common stock and paid-in surplus	800	0

Table 2-4(continue)

			-Retained earnings	3,325 (2,700+625)	625
			Total	4,125	625
Total assets	15,000	3,000	total L+E	12,775	775
			External financing needed	2,225	2,225

In tables 2-4, " Δ " is the projected change in each item. For example, the projected cash for the next reporting annual is 1,125, so $\Delta = 225$, which means an increase of 225 over the previous year. Observing the pro forma balance sheet for R Corporation, we notice a gap between the projected sales increase, and the total liabilities plus equity if the firm refuses any additional financing. We label the gap external financing needed (EFN).

$$EFN=\frac{\text{Assets}}{\text{Sales}}\times\Delta\text{Sales}-\frac{\text{Spotaneous liabilities}}{\text{Sales}}\times\Delta\text{Sales}$$
$$-PM\times \text{ projected sales }\times(1-d)$$

In this formula, the "Spontaneous liabilities" means the liabilities that spontaneously increase and decrease with the sales. And the PM and d represent the profit margin and retention ratio. Meanwhile, notice that there are three parts. The first part is the expected increase in assets, which is calculated using the capital intensity ratio (Assets/Sales). The second part is the increase in spontaneous liabilities. The third part is the projected addition to retained earnings, which is projected net income (PM×projected sales), multiplied by the retention ratio (1-d).

In this case, the spontaneous liabilities are 300; the profit margin and dividend ratios are 15% and 1/3; the total assets and sales are 12,000 and 5,000; so we have:

$$EFN=\frac{12,000}{5,000}\times1,250-\frac{600}{5,000}\times1,250-0.15\times6,250\times(1-\frac{1}{3})=2,225$$

2.2.4 External Financing and Growth

In the previous part, we introduce the calculation of EFN. In this part, we will figure out the connection between the EFN and the growth of sales. It is known that under different growth rates, the projected added retained earnings and the projected debt - equity ratio could be calculated by the percentage of sales approach. So, there is a unique EFN for each growth rate. Here, we assume that there are no spontaneous liabilities and combine the depreciation, interest and expense in balance sheet. For example, R forecast its next year's sales level at 6, 250, so the percentage increase in sales is 1, 250/5, 000 = 25%. Using the percentage of sales approach, we can figure out the projected addition to retained earnings is 625, so the external financing needed, EFN is 3, 000 − 625 = 2, 375. The original EFN for R is 7, 000/4, 000 = 1. 75. We will assume that the R does not wish for the new equity. In this case, the 2, 375 in EFN will have to be borrowed. So the new debt will be 9, 375, the total equity will be 4, 125, and the new debt-equity ratio will increase to 9, 375/4, 125 = 2. 27. Table 2-5 shows EFN for several different growth rates:

Table 2-5　Pro Forma Balance Sheet for R

Projected Sales Growth (%)	Increase In Assets Required	Addition to Retained Earnings	EFN	Projected Debt-Equity Ratio
0	0	500	-500	1. 63
5	600	525	75	1. 76
10	1, 200	550	650	1. 89
15	1, 800	575	1, 225	2. 02
20	2, 400	600	1, 800	2. 15
25	3, 000	625	2, 375	2. 27

There's a direct relationship between EFN and growth. The higher the rate of growth in sales, the greater the need for external financing will be. Figure 2-1 directly shows the connection between them by plotting asset needs and addition to the retained earnings from the results of Table 2-5.

As shown in the Figure 2 - 1, at low growth levels, internal financing (retained earnings) may exceed the required investment in assets. However, as the growth rate increases, internal financing will not be enough, and the firm will have to go to the capital markets for financing (EFN>0). Notice that examining the relationship between growth and external financing required is a useful tool in financial planning.

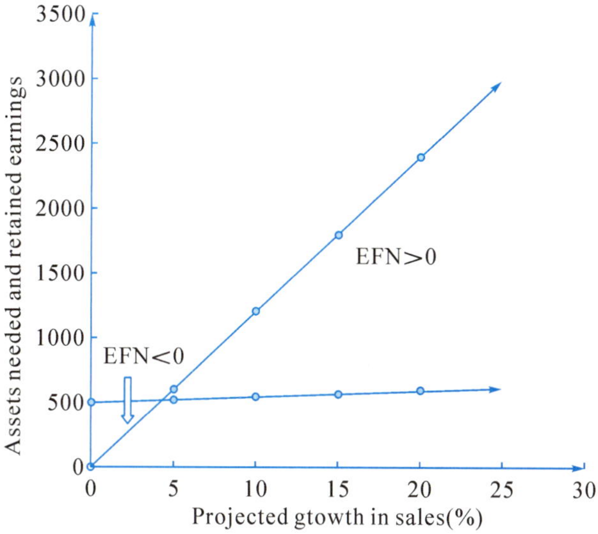

Figure 2-1 **Growth and Related Financing Needed for R**

2.2.5 Financial Policy and Growth

Based on the discussion above, we find that external financing is directly relative to sales growth. In this part, two important growth ratios in long-term planning will be introduced.

1. The Internal Growth Rate(内部增长率)

The internal growth rate is the maximum growth rate that can be achieved without additional external financing of any kind. To maximize the growth, the EFN we discussed above, must be 0. We define the ratio as:

$$\text{Internal growth rate}=\frac{\text{ROA}\times b}{1-\text{ROA}\times b}$$

Notice that b is the retention ratio we discussed before.

2. The Sustainable Growth Rate(可持续增长率)

The sustainable growth rate is the maximum growth rate a firm can achieve without any external equity financing while it maintains a constant debt-equity ratio. "Sustainable" means that a firm's overall financial leverage keeps unchanged.

$$\text{Sustainable growth rate}=\frac{\text{ROE}\times b}{1-\text{ROE}\times b}$$

3. Determinants of Growths

ROE is the key element of a sustainable growth rate. There's no doubt the important factors of ROE are also important determinants of growth.

As we discussed before, the ROE can be separated into three ratios:

ROE = Profit margin× Total asset turnover ×Equity multiplier

Moreover, the retention ratio also plays an important role in deciding the sustainable growth rate. Therefore, we conclude four important determinants of growth: ①Profit margin(operating efficiency); ②Total asset turnover(asset use efficiency); ③Financial leverage(choice of optimal debt ratio); ④Dividend policy (choice of how much to pay to shareholders versus reinvesting in the firm)

案例分析 2-2 《数字经济赋能会计创新》

2016 年，习近平总书记在十八届中共中央政治局第三十六次集体学习时强调：“世界经济加速向以网络信息技术产业为重要内容的经济活动转变。我们要把握这一历史契机，以信息化培育新动能，用新动能推动新发展。”21 世纪以来，随着“大智移云物区”等新技术与新经济、新业态深度融合，人类社会进入了数字经济时代。在会计领域，数字化在推动会计实践深刻变化的同时，也对传统会计观念产生了巨大挑战。比如，在实务界出现了“会计消亡论”的观点，在理论界出现了“会计管理活动论已过时”的声音。会计变革历史和数字经济实践均表明，价值管理活动作为对会计本质问题的认识，不仅代表了会计学术的过去，而且仍然指导着会计学术与实务的现在和未来。在生产力高度发达的数字经济时代，会计愈发凸显其服务于企业价值创造这一本源目标。危机中育新机、变局中开新局，数字经济在对会计提出一系列挑战的同时，也在助推会计更好地服务于企业战略决策和经营管理，为会计管理提供了连接战略与业务的便捷路径。在企业财务数字化转型方面，中国石化集团共享服务有限公司扬州服务部（以下简称“扬州服务部”）发挥重要的领头作用，依托财务共享服务平台的搭建，不断提升企业体验度、业财融合度、决策支持度、财务管理效率及财务运行效能。此案例将对扬州服务部的财务改革措施进行分析，探讨数字化在实务中如何推进传统财务部门转型。

（一）业务数字化转型为会计有效满足差异化服务需求创造了条件

数字经济可以提升数据集成度，丰富数据来源与数据形态。会计部门是企业内外部数据交汇的中心，应通过转变工作模式以满足业务数字化的服务需求：一是转型为多部门协同的财务共享中心，通过整合规范性强、重复度高的业务和依托信息化技术搭建网络平台，为不同成员单位提供财务服务；二是向及时化、定制化的服务模式转变，结合内外部大数据分析，为战略目标和业务过程中的个性化需求提供更加深入全面的分析和建议；三是利用多种分析方法和报告形式，实现对企业内部大数据与非结构化数据的多维度分析，并利用智能报表技术提供更便捷与实时化的报告界面，实现财务数据可视化。这些转变可以提高财务管理流程的标准化水平、运营效率和管控能力，让会计更好地参与到企业数字化转型的战略决策和业务支持的工作中，进而从管理本源的角度挖掘绩效提升的潜力。扬州服务部在中石化共享服务公司的ERP系统上建立了业务、财务数据存储和信息处理中心。企业通过财务共享专业化运营，将分散在各个单元的财务业务及业务数据整合在共享中心，从而提高业务处理效率、降低流程重复率。扬州服务部在中国石化集团共享服务有限公司的统一部署下，加快推动企业取消财务初审节点，从而解决了财务与财务共享对报销业务重复审核的问题。取消财务初审平均节省财务人员8%的工作量，业务处理时效提高20%，促进财务人员从基础性工作中解放出来，投入企业财务转型。此外，扬州服务部还积极探索流程优化，针对共享自助系统提报端口分散、流程节点多、处理效率低的情况，开发了业务情景化提报产品的方法，形成情景化、自动化、一站式的业务提报，释放了企业财务管理人员的压力。

（二）会计数字化转型提升企业业务运行与管理决策效能

随着5G网络、大数据中心新型数字基础设施建设的快速推进，未来企业将朝着由数据驱动的全价值链数字化、网络化、平台化和智能化企业转型方向发展。这股数字新基建浪潮将覆盖企业全业务流程，并促进会计工作流程自动化、决策分析智能化和会计服务共享化。会计作为一个由财务会计与管理会计相结合的开放系统，将依托信息系统的融合，将价值管理活动扩展到价值链的各个环节。利用信息技术手段智能处理价值链系统中的价值信息，从而为企业数字资产生成提供更为可靠的经营和财务状况数据，也为企业未来可持续发展的战略预测和决策提供有力支持。扬州服务部将初始的报账、核算等业务流程，优化调整为采购至付款、销售至收款、总账报表三个财务业务服务流程，实现了企业财务对公司业务各环节的动态化升级，并构建"基础业务服务+业务支持与拓展"二元式组织机构体系，提供高价值的"专业服务+创新型增值服务"，持续创新管理理念和运营模式，将会计角色深化应用于运营管理各环节之中，使其更好赋能企业决策支持。一方面可通过数据分析、内部资源整合与增值，扩大价值链的覆盖范围，协同企业开展经验管理、信息化管理等各种工作；另一方面可与企业互通有无，持续深化前中后台的衔接，打通业务壁垒，实现高效、灵活、集约的财务运营

（三）数字经济突显会计在生产和利用数字化知识和信息方面的独特价值

数字经济以使用数字化的知识和信息作为关键生产要素。"大智移云物区"新技术改变了会计工作中会计部门人力和数据要素的投入产出结构，数字应用边际收益大于人力投入边际收益的工作将逐步由软件与数字设备的组合取代，会计专家服务成为企业战略决定和业务决策中不可替代的中流砥柱。

一是重复性财务工作的自动化，大幅提升企业管理效能。财务工作中的交易、控制、合规、报告四个中间环节可以由人工智能代替进行，实现高效率、无间断工作，完成工作效率跃升。二是管理会计过程控制的全局化，形成更完整的决策支持。数字化信息将战略计划、预算预测、执行控制、分析、绩效考核紧密结合，降低管理成本，增强了会计管理工具的应用效果。三是分析性事务的专家化，让会计成为企业管理的重要一环。扬州服务部大力推动 RPA（财务机器人）项目的开发落地，如研发出审批流自动绘制机器人，将 RPA 应用场景从常规的操作业务系统或处理数据延伸到模拟人工绘图，既实现了流程自动化，提高了财务运营质量及效率，又越来越能够满足企业的个性化需求，为企业财务转型提供了更大可能。

党的二十大报告中，习近平总书记再度强调："加快发展数字经济，促进数字经济和实体经济深度融合，打造具有国际竞争力的数字产业集群。"发展数字经济是把握新一轮科技革命和产业变革新机遇的战略选择，只有推动以会计为代表的传统职能部门的数字化改革，不断做强做优做大我国数字经济，促进数字经济和实体经济深度融合，才能更好地推动经济实现质的有效提升和量的合理增长。

资料来源：

[1]徐玉德.数字经济时代会计变革的反思与逻辑溯源[J].会计研究，2022(8):3-13.

[2]陈磊.财务共享服务助力企业财务转型的探讨[J].财务与会计，2022(22):62-64.

Key Concepts and Skills

1. Current ratio, quick ratio, cash ratio
2. Total debt ratio; equity multiplier; times interest earned; cash coverage
3. Inventory turnover and days' sales in inventory; receivables turnover and days' sales in receivables; total asset turnover
4. Profit margin; return on assets; return on equity
5. The Dupont identity
6. Price-earnings ratio; market-to-book ratio; enterprise value multiples
7. A simple financial planning model; the percentage of sales approach; external financing need
8. Internal growth rate; sustainable growth rate

本章重点与难点

1. 流动比率,速动比率,现金比率
2. 总负债比率,权益乘数,利息倍数,现金保障倍数
3. 存货周转率和周转天数,应收账款周转率和周转天数,总资产周转率
4. 销售利润率, ROA, ROE
5. 杜邦分析法
6. 市盈率,市值面值比,企业价值乘数
7. 财务预测模型,销售百分比法, EFN
8. 内部增长率,可持续增长率

Self-Test Questions

Ⅰ. True (T) or False (F) Questions

1. There is a direct correlation between the level of a company's retention ratio and its operating conditions. Generally speaking, the higher the revenue of a company, the higher the retention ratio of the company. (　　)

2. An increase in inventories will increase the company's current ratio but will not affect the company's quick ratio. (　　)

3. The total asset turnover reflects the profitability of a company by dividing the sales revenue by the average total assets during the accounting period. (　　)

4. Return on assets is the core indicator of the DuPont analysis. (　　)

5. Company A plans to keep a growth rate at 10%. Now, it has a debt-equity ratio that equals 0.5, a dividend payout ratio that equals 20% and the fixed ratio between total assets and sales revenue (1.2:1). To achieve the purpose, company A has to keep a profit margin at 8%. (　　)

Ⅱ. Single Choice Questions

1. Assume that the current ratio of Company Patrick is 1 now, which of the following measures can improve a company's current ratio: (　　)

A. Use cash to purchase the raw materials

B. Increase the long-term debt to pay the short-term debt off

C. Both of the measures will take effect

D. Neither of the measures will take effect

2. The current asset of Company A is \$5,000,000. (including quick asset = \$2,000,000). Company A plan to pay the payables off with the \$1,000,000

cash. What the impacts would the decision have on the company's current ratio and quick ratio: ( )

A. Unchanged; Unchanged

B. Increase; Unchanged

C. Unchanged; Decrease

D. Unchanged; Increase

3. Which of the indicator can't measure company's capacity of asset utilization: ( )

A. Inventory turnover

B. Receivables turnover

C. PBIT

D. Total asset turnover

4. The Sun Bank and Moon Bank both have un total asset of $10 billion, and un ROA of 1%. However, the ROE of Sun Bank is 10% while that of Moon Bank is 16%.Which of the following statement is correct: ( )

A. Moon Bank generates higher returns for shareholders with the same assets, so Moon Bank performs better than Sun Bank

B. Sun Bank has a lower capital multiplier than Moon Bank and is less exposed to insolvency, thus performing better than Moon Bank

C. The performance can't be only evaluated by ROA and ROE. The quality of the assets also matters.

D. Because banks' performance is essentially measured by ROA, these two banks have the same performance

5. Which of the following measures can companies take to increase their sustainable growth rate: ( )

A. Repurchase of shares

B. Increase retained earnings

C. Increase M&A

D. Reduce the debt

Ⅲ. Calculation Questions

1. Company's financial information is as follows:

Total asset	60 million
Current asset/ total asset	0. 4
Inventory/current asset	0. 5
Current ratio	3. 33

Please calculate the net working capital, current ratio, and quick ratio after the following transactions:

(1) purchasing material valued at 0.1 million, $40,000 payments from bank deposit, and $60,000 payments in credit.

(2) purchasing machines and equipment valued at $0.6 million, $0.4 million from bank deposit, the residual money is offset by manufactured goods.

(3) $0.2 8million account receivables are recorded as bad debts and the company increases $0. 8million in short-term borrowings.

2. Please use DuPont Identity to analyze the company's ROE and the accounts for its change.

Item		2021	2022
Sales revenue		280	350
	Sales in credit	76	80
Total cost		235	288
	Sales cost	108	120
	overhead expenses	87	98
	Financial cost	29	55
	Sales expense	11	15
Total profit		45	62
Income tax		(15)	(21)
Net profit		30	41
Total asset		128	198
	Fixed asset	59	78
	Cash	21	39
	Accounts receivable(average)	8	14
	Inventory	40	67
Total debt		55	88

3. The most recent financial statements for Firm A are shown here:

Income Statement		Balance Sheet			
Sales	25,800	Assets	113,000	Debt	20,500
Costs	16,500			Equity	92,500
Taxable income	9,300	Total	113,000	Total	113,000
Taxes(34%)	3,162				
Net income	6,138				

Assets and costs are proportional to sales. Debt and equity are not. A dividend of \$1,841.40 was paid, and this firm wishes to maintain a constant payout ratio. Next year's sales are projected to be \$30,960. What external financing is needed?

本章习题答案

Chapter 3 The Time Value of Money（货币时间价值）

Learning Objectives

● Learn to compute the future value of a single cash flow or series of cash flows.

● Learn to compute the present value of a single cash flow or series of cash flows.

● Learn compounding periods and to compute effective annual rate of return.

● Learn annuities and perpetuities.

● Understand the forms of loan amortization.

Money has time value. The current one yuan is expected to be more valuable than the future one yuan, because if you have one yuan now, you can use it to invest and earn interest. The interest earned is the value generated by owning one yuan as early as possible, that is, the time value of money. In this chapter, we should fully understand the concept of time value of money, and on this basis, master the simple interest and compound interest calculation, as well as the concept and calculation of future value and present value, and also introduce the calculation method of annuities and perpetuities.

3.1 Future Value and Compounding

3.1.1 The One-Period Case

The total amount due at the end of the investment is called the Future Value

(FV).

In the one-period case, the formula for FV can be written as:

$$FV = PV \times (1 + r)$$

Where **PV** is the present value (i.e., the value today), and ***r*** is the appropriate interest rate.

【Example 3-1】

If you were to invest \$10,000 at 4-percent interest for one year, your investment would grow to \$10,400. \$400 would be the interest (\$10,000×0.04), \$10,000 is the principal repayment (\$10,000×1), and \$10,400 is the total due, that is, the future value of \$10,000 investment at the end of one year.

3.1.2 The Multi-Period Case

In practice, we have two kinds of interest:

Simple interest: Interest is earned only on the original principal.

Compound interest: Interest is earned on principal and interest received.

Normally, the future value of the multi-period case is computed on the basis of compound interest. The general formula for the future value of an investment over many periods can be written as:

$$FV = PV \times (1 + r)^t$$

Where

PV is the present value,

r is the appropriate interest rate, and

t is the number of periods over which the cash is invested.

【Example 3-2】

Suppose a stock currently pays a dividend of \$1.20, which is expected to grow at 50% per year for the next six years. What will the dividend be at the end of year six?

Answer:

Simple interest: $\$1.20 + 6 \times [\$1.20 \times 0.50] = \$4.80$

Compound interest: $\$1.20 \times (1.50)^6 = \$13.67$

Obviously, the future value computed on the basis of compound interest is larger than on the basis of simple interest. If the period is long enough, the difference can be very surprising.

3.2 Present Value and Discounting

3.2.1 The One-Period Case

In the one-period case, the formula for PV can be written as:

$$PV = \frac{C_1}{1+r}$$

Where C_1 is cash flow at date 1, and r is the appropriate interest rate. We could also write the formula as:

$$PV = \frac{FV_1}{1+r}$$

【Example 3-3】

If you were to be promised \$10,000 due in one year when interest rates are 4 percent, your investment would be worth \$9,615.38 in today's dollars.

$$\$9,615.38 = \frac{\$10,000}{1.04}$$

The amount that a borrower would need to set aside today to be able to meet the promised payment of \$10,000 in one year is the Present Value (PV). Note that \$10,000 = \$9,615.38×(1.04).

3.2.2 The Multi-Period Case

In the multi-period case, the general formula for the present value of a future investment valued today can be written as:

$$PV = \frac{FV}{(1+r)^t}$$

Where

PV is the present value,

r is the appropriate interest rate, and

t is the number of periods over which the cash is invested.

【Example 3-4】

How much would an investor have to set aside today in order to have \$20,000 four years from now if the current rate is 12%?

Answer:

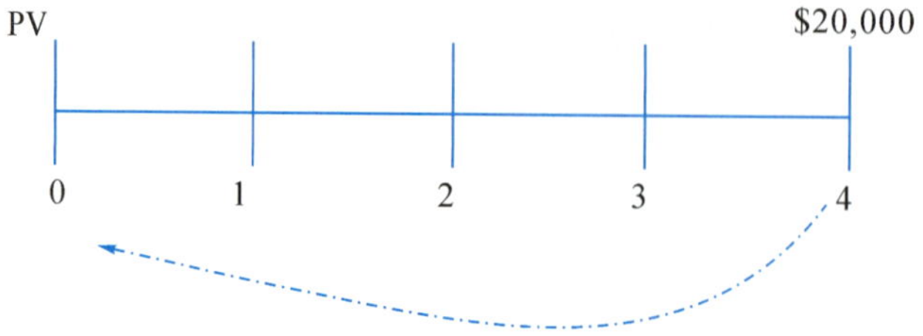

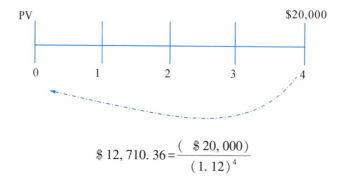

$$\$12,710.36=\frac{(\$20,000)}{(1.12)^4}$$

3.2.3 Net Present Value(净现值)

The Net Present Value (NPV) of an investment is the present value of the expected cash flows, less the cost of the investment.

In the one-period case, the formula for NPV can be written as:

$$NPV = -Cost + PV$$

【Example 3-5】

Suppose an investment that promises to pay \$10,000 in one year is offered for sale for \$9,800. Your interest rate is 4%. Should you buy?

Answer:

$$NPV = \$-9,800+\frac{\$10,000}{1.04}$$

$$NPV = \$-9,800 + \$9,615.38$$

$$NPV = \$-184.62$$

The present value of the cash inflow is smaller than the cost. Since the Net Present Value is negative, the investment should not be purchased. In other words, If we had not undertaken this negative NPV project, and instead invested our \$9,800 elsewhere at 4 percent, our FV would be more than the \$10,000 the investment promised, and we would be better off in FV terms: $\$9,800\times(1.04) = \$10,192 > \$10,000$.

3.2.4 Multiple Cash Flows

Simially, in the case of multiple cash flows, the NPV of an investment equals to the present value of all the future cash flows less the initial cost.

【Example 3-6】

Consider an investment that pays \$200 one year from now, with cash flows increasing by \$100 per year through year 4. If the interest rate is 15%, what is the present value of this stream of cash flows? If the issuer offers this investment for \$1,000, should you purchase?

Answer:

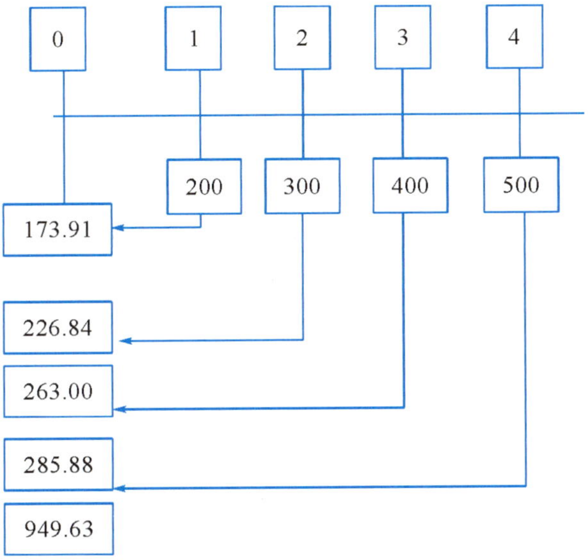

$$(1)PV = \frac{\$200}{1.15} = 173.91$$

$$(2)PV = \frac{\$300}{(1.15)^2} = 226.84$$

$$(3)PV = \frac{\$400}{(1.15)^3} = 263.00$$

$$(4)PV = \frac{\$500}{(1.15)^4} = 285.88$$

173.91+226.84+263.00+285.88=949.63<1,000

Present Value < Cost→Do Not Purchase

3.2.5 What Rate Is Enough?

By answering the question of what rate is enough, we can calculate the interest rate to acheive the future value through a number of years if investing an amout of cash today.

【Example 3-7】

Assume the total cost of a college education will be \$80,000 when your child enters college in 6 years. You have \$40,000 to invest today. What rate of interest must you earn on your investment to cover the cost of your child's education?

Answer:

$$\$80,000 = \$40,000 \times (1+r)^6$$

$$(1+r)^6 = \frac{\$80,000}{\$40,000} = 2$$

$$(1+r) = 2^{1/6}$$

$$r = 2^{1/6} - 1 = 1.1225 - 1 = 0.1225$$

3.2.6 Finding the Number of Periods

This section aims to calculate the number of periods through which an investment can grow to an expected amount of future value.

【Example 3-8】

If we deposit \$5,000 today in an account paying 5%, how long does it take to grow to \$10,000?

Answer:

$$\$10,000 = \$5,000 \times (1.05)^T$$

$$(1.05)^T = \frac{\$10,000}{\$5,000} = 2$$

$$\ln(1.05)^T = \ln(2)$$

$$T = \frac{\ln(2)}{\ln(1.05)} = 15 \text{ years}$$

The rule of 72(72 法则)

The rule of 72 is a quick way to estimate how long it will take you to double your investment?

Period = 72 / r, where r is the appropriate interest rate.

For the above example, based on the rule of 72, the number of periods to double the investment is 72/5 = 14.4 years.

3.3 Compounding Periods

Compounding an investment m times a year for T years provides for future value of wealth:

$$FV = C_0 \times \left(1 + \frac{r}{m}\right)^{m \times T}$$

For example, if you invest \$100 for 4 years at 10% compounded semi-annually, your investment will grow to:

$$FV = \$100 \times \left(1+\frac{0.10}{2}\right)^{2\times4} = \$100\times(1.05)^8 = \$147.75$$

A reasonable question to ask in the above example is "what is the effective annual rate of interest on that investment?"

The Effective Annual Rate (EAR) of interest is the annual rate that would give us the same end-of-investment wealth after 4 years:

$$\$100\times(1+EAR)^4 = \$147.75$$

$$FV = \$100\times(1+EAR)^4 = \$147.75$$

$$(1+EAR)^4 = \frac{\$147.75}{\$100}$$

$$EAR = \left(\frac{\$147.75}{\$100}\right)^{1/4} - 1 = 10.25\%$$

So, investing at 10.25% compounded annually is the same as investing at 10% compounded semi-annually.

Componding an investment m times a year for T years, the general formula to compute the effective annual rate of interest is:

$$EAR = \left(1+\frac{APR}{m}\right)^{m*T} - 1$$

where APR is the annual percentage rate of interest.

Continuous Compounding(连续复利计息)

The general formula for the future value of an investment compounded continuously over many periods can be written as:

$$FV = C_0 \times e^{rT}$$

Where

C_0 is cash flow at date 0,

r is the approprate annual interest rate,

T is the number of years, and

e is a transcendental number which approximately equals to 2.718. e^x is a key on your calculator.

3.4 Annuity and Perpetuity

This section will introduce some special forms of cash flows and a simple calculation method of their value.

3.4.1 Annuity(年金)

Annuity is a stream of constant cash flows that lasts for a fixed number of periods, including Ordinary Annuity（普通年金）, Annuity Due(先付年金), and Deferred Annuity(递延年金).

1. The Present Value of Annuity(年金的现值)

(1)The Present Value of Ordinary Annuity

A constant stream of cash flows with a fixed maturity is presented as follows:

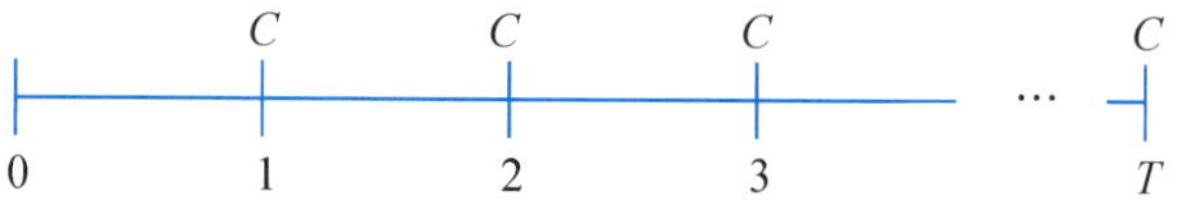

The present value of an ordinary annuity is the sum of the discounted cash flows received or paid annually or monthly for a future period, calculated based on the time value of money at a given investment return rate at the end of the calculation period.

$$PV=\frac{C}{(1+r)}+\frac{C}{(1+r)^2}+\frac{C}{(1+r)^3}+\cdots\frac{C}{(1+r)^T}$$

$$PV=\frac{C}{r}\left[1-\frac{1}{(1+r)^T}\right]$$

【Example 3-9】

If you can afford a \$500 monthly car payment, how much car can you afford if interest rates are 8% on 36-month loans?

Answer:

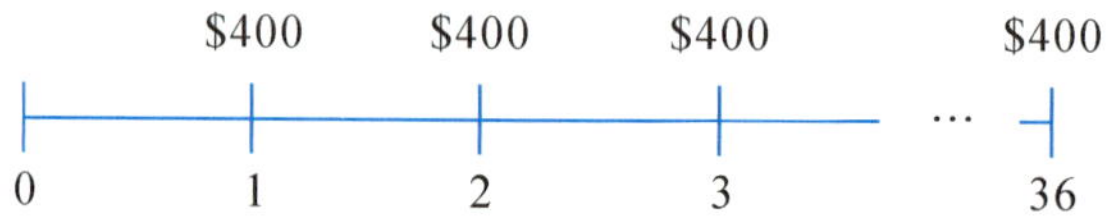

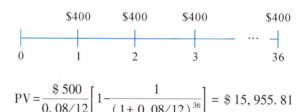

$$PV=\frac{\$500}{0.08/12}\left[1-\frac{1}{(1+.0.08/12)^{36}}\right]=\$15,955.81$$

【Example 3-10】

Suppose you plan to buy a real estate, and now you have \$20,000 to pay the down payment and expenses. The cost of the expenses is about 4% of the loan value. Your annual salary is \$36,000, and the bank can allow you to pay 28% of your monthly income on your mortgage. The loan interest rate is 6%, compounded once a month (equivalent to 0.5% of the monthly interest rate). Loan term is 30 years based on fixed interest rate. How much loan can the bank lend you? How much can you afford a real estate?

Answer:

Monthly income = \$36,000 / 12 = \$3,000

Monthly loan = 0.28(\$3,000) = \$840

PV of loan = \$840[1 − 1/1.005(12 * 30)] /0.005 = \$140,105 = \$840 (P/A, 0.5%, 360)

Expenses = 0.04(\$140,105) = \$5,604

Down payment = \$20,000 − 5,604 = \$14,396

The value of the real estate = \$140,105 + 14,396 = \$154,501

(2) The Present Value of Annuity Due

The present value of an annuity due is the sum of the present value of constant cash flows received and paid at the beginning of each period. The number of payments and receipts for a n-period annuity due is the same as that for a n-period ordinary annuity. However, due to the different timing of payment, the payment for the first period dose not need to be discounted, and the residual payment can be considered as a $(n-1)$-period ordinary annuity. Therefore, the present value of a n-period annuity due is calculated as follows:

$$PV = A + A * (P/A, i, n-1) = A * [(P/A, i, n-1) + 1]$$

(3) The Present Value of Deferred Annuity

The present value of a deferred annuity can be calculated using the formula for the present value of an ordinary annuity (as there are no annuities during the deferred period).

【Example 3-11】

What is the present value of a four-year annuity of \$100 per year that makes its first payment two years from today if the discount rate is 10%?

Answer:

$$PV_1 = \sum_{t=1}^{4} \frac{\$100}{(1.1)^T} = \frac{\$100}{(1.1)^1} + \frac{\$100}{(1.1)^2} + \frac{\$100}{(1.1)^3} + \frac{\$100}{(1.1)^4} = \$316.99$$

$$PV_0 = \frac{\$316.99}{1.10} = \$288.17$$

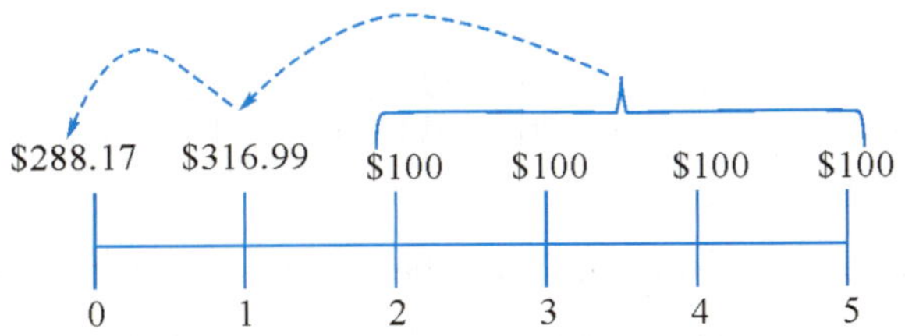

2. The Future Value of Annuity(年金的终值)

(1)The Future Value of Ordinary Annuity

The future value of an ordinary annuity refers to the sum of the future value of constant income or expenses at the end of each period within a certain period.

【Example 3-12】

Suppose you start saving for retirement now, and prepare to deposit $2, 000 annually(at the end of the year). The annual interest rate is 7.5%. How much retirement deposit will you have in 40 years?

Answer:

$$FV = \$2,000(1.075, 40 - 1)/0.075 = \$454,513.04$$
$$= \$2,000(F/A, 7.5\%, 40)$$

(2)The Future Value of Annuity Due

The future value of an annuity due refers to the sum of the future value of constant cash flows received and paid at the beginning of each period within a certain period. In oreder to compute the future value of a n-peirod annuity due, we can add one more payment at the end of its last period. By doing so, this n-period annuity due can be considered as a $(n+1)$-peirod ordinary annuity but less one payment at the end of last period. Therefore, the formula to calculate the future value of a n-period annuity due can be presented as:

$$FV = A * (F/A, i, n+1) - A = A * [(F/A, i, n+1) - 1]$$

3.4.2 Growing Annuity(增长年金)

Growing annuity is a stream of cash flows that grows at a constant rate for a fixed number of periods.

1. The Present Value of Growing Annuity(增长年金的现值)

A growing stream of cash flows with a fixed maturity is shown as:

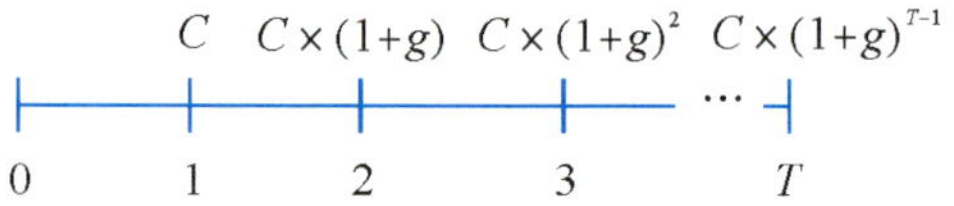

$$PV = \frac{C}{(1+r)} + \frac{C \times (1+g)}{(1+r)^2} + \cdots + \frac{C \times (1+g)^{T-1}}{(1+r)^T}$$

$$PV = \frac{C}{r - g}\left[1 - \left(\frac{1 + g}{(1 + r)}\right)^T\right]$$

【Example 3-13】

A defined-benefit retirement plan offers to pay $20, 000 per year for 40 years and increase the annual payment by 3% each year. What is the present value at retirement if the discount rate is 10%?

Answer:

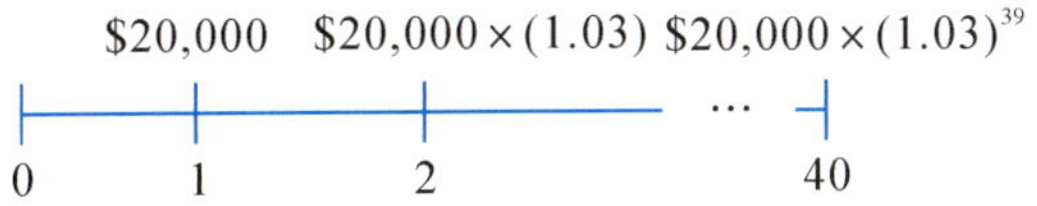

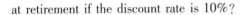

$$PV=\frac{\$20,000}{0.10-0.03}\left[1-\left(\frac{1.03}{1.10}\right)^{40}\right]=\$265,121.57$$

3.4.3 Perpetuity（永续年金）

Perpetuity is a constant stream of cash flows that lasts forever. Its present value can be calculated as follows:

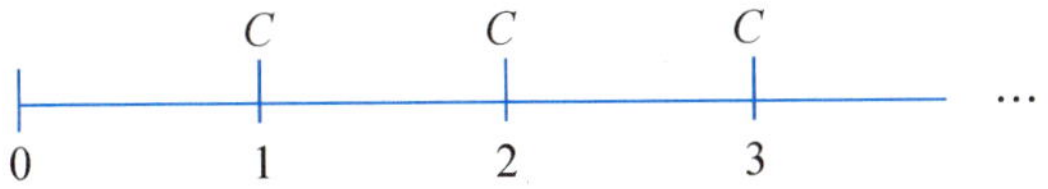

$$PV=\frac{C}{(1+r)}+\frac{C}{(1+r)^2}+\frac{C}{(1+r)^3}+\cdots$$

$$PV=\frac{C}{r}$$

【Example 3-14】

What is the value of a British consol that promises to pay £ 15 every year forever?

The interest rate is 10 percent.

Answer:

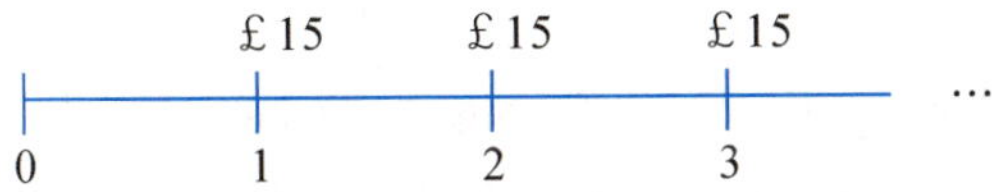

$$PV=\frac{£15}{0.10}=£150$$

3.4.4 Growing Perpetuity（永续增长年金）

Growing perpetuity is a stream of cash flows that grows at a constant rate forever. The present value of a growing perpetuity can be calculated as follows:

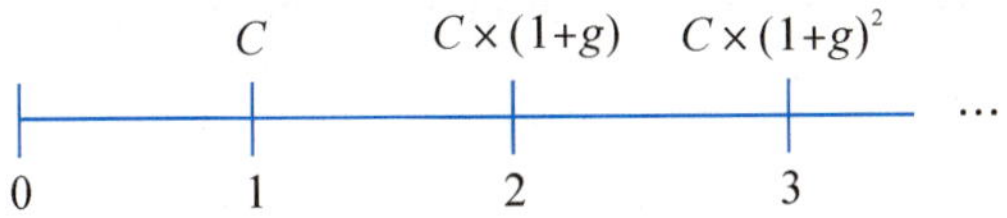

$$PV = \frac{C}{(1+r)} + \frac{C \times (1+g)}{(1+r)^2} + \frac{C \times (1+g)^2}{(1+r)^3} + \cdots$$

$$PV = \frac{C}{r-g}$$

【Example 3-15】

The expected dividend just paid is \$1.30, and dividends are expected to grow at 5% forever. If the discount rate is 10%, what is the value of this promised dividend stream?

Answer:

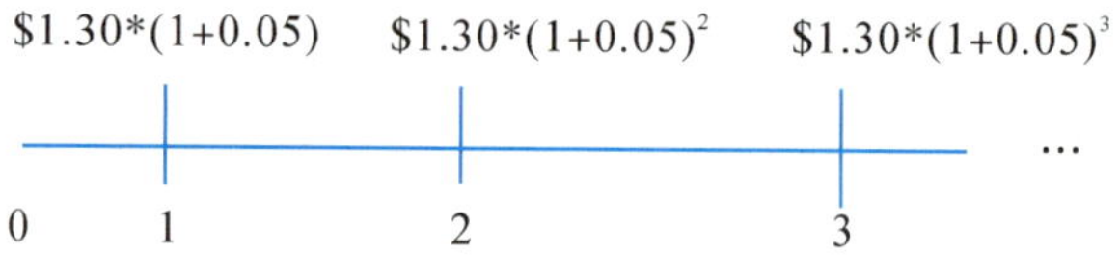

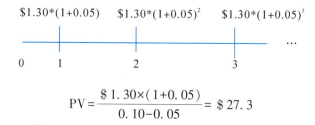

$$PV = \frac{\$1.30 \times (1+0.05)}{0.10-0.05} = \$27.3$$

3.5 Loan Amortization

Pure Discount（纯贴现贷款）: The principal amount is repaid at some future date, without any periodic interest payments. Treasury bills are excellent examples of pure discount loans.

Interest-Only Loans（附息贷款）: This kind of loans requires an interest payment each period, with full principal due at maturity.

Amortized Loans（按揭贷款）

● Amortized Loan with Fixed Principal Payment（等额本金）: The total amount of the loan principal is divided equally during the repayment period. The monthly repayment equals to the same amount of principal and montly interest generated by the remaining principal. Obviously, the monthly repayment amount decreases during the loan periods.

● Amortized Loan with Fixed Payment（等额本息）: The total amount of the loan principal and interest is divided equally during the repayment period. The montly repayment is the same, in which the amount of principal increases and the amount of interest expense decreases during the loan periods.

延伸阅读 3-1 《校园贷风险分析与防范机制研究（节选）》

一、校园贷概念及形式

（一）校园贷的概念

目前，诸多学者对校园贷进行了研究，但并未针对校园贷给出一个统一的界定。有些学者将其笼统定义为“在校大学生在网络平台上开展的互联网金融借贷行为”；也有学者从校园贷的运行机制出发，将其定义为“在网络借贷平台上针对在校大学生开展的贷款服务，主要包括分期购物、信用贷款等，以满足大学生在物质或现金方面的需求”。由此可见，校园贷的主要特点是“大学生+网络借贷”，其不同于银行贷款，不需要实物抵押，只需在借贷平台上按照既定模板填写个人基本信息，支付相应手续费或者预先扣除一部分本金，甚至无须支付任何费用，即可快速拿到钱物。因此，本书认为校园贷是指在校大学生为了满足生活或其他消费需求，从校园金融平台获得无抵押信用贷款的一种金融消费模式。

（二）校园贷的形式

为维护在校大学生的合法权益，避免校园贷带来的不法侵害，党和国家从校园金融产品、校园贷平台、大学生教育管理等方面出发，制定了一系列规范，校园贷形式逐渐发生了变化。目前的校园贷主要有两种类型。一是分期购物。主要是指传统电子商务平台——淘宝、京东等提供的信贷服务，如蚂蚁花呗借呗、京东校园白条等。分期购物不提供现金借贷，消费者从平台获得商品后分期交付约定的钱款。这些平台相对正规，风险较小。二是信用贷款。信用贷款无须抵押物和相关担保，进行申请和简单的身份认证即可放款，其因简单快捷逐渐成为校园贷的主流形式。近年来，一些不法借贷机构为了吸引学生借贷，推出了培训贷、刷单贷、美容贷、游戏贷等新型校园贷，这些校园贷更加隐蔽和复杂，大大增加了国家对校园贷的监管难度。

二、不良校园贷的危害

（一）过高的贷款利率

贷款利率除了受法律规定的最高利率限制，尚无其他限制，利息可按照市场利率、交易方式等因素确定，因此，很多网贷企业倾向于提高利息以获取更高的利润。一些网贷公司利用大学生薄弱的防范意识和社会认知能力，通过文字游戏掩盖其高额利率。“日息最低只要 0.02%，年利率 7%起，实际利率以审批结果为准”等广告信息中的“最低”“起”“以审批结果为准”隐瞒、模糊了实际资费标准，掩盖了其高利率性，诱导涉世未深的大学生陷入债台高筑的困境。

（二）信息泄露风险

一般的借款平台并没有建立健全保障信息安全的规章制度，对收集到的大学生信息并不会进行安全保护，还有可能利用这些学生信息进行电话诈骗、恶意炒作、造谣生事等不法操作，甚至会向第三方机构售卖借款学生信息，通过泄露、曝光、买卖借款学生信息牟利。这些行为不仅会侵害大学生的隐私，还可能使其产生巨大的心理阴影，严重干扰大学生的正常学习生活。

（三）暴力催收风险

贷款之初，借款人详细填写了个人信息，其中不仅有学生本人的信息，还有其父母或其他监护人的信息，甚至有老师和同学的相关信息。大学生一旦不能按时还贷，就会被电话辱骂、信息轰炸、人身攻击等暴力催债手段逼迫还贷，相关联系人也会不断受到骚扰，导致借款学生及相关联系人的人身安全、正常生活受到不同程度的影响，甚至还出现了大学生利用违法所得偿还贷款，从受害者转变成不法加害者的情形，严重影响了在校大学生的正常学习生活。

（四）树立错误的消费观

高校学生来自五湖四海，消费观念和消费水平并不相同，朝夕相处过程中难免会出现攀比的现象。当从父母那里获取的生活费及自己的收入难以满足需求时，部分大学生会寻找其他经济来源。无法从正规借贷平台获得资金的大学生在看到贷款公司发出的要约邀请后，便将“勤俭节约，量入为出”的观念抛诸脑后，参与到校园贷中，逐渐养成从众消费、过度消费、超前消费等错误的消费观。

三、结语

校园贷的出现在一定程度上解决了大学生短期资金紧缺的问题。但是，校园贷具有较大的迷惑性和变异性，加之贷款平台参差不齐，给金融市场的正常运行带来了不可忽视的风险。因此，各高校应引导大学生坚决抵制不良校园贷。具体来说，在大学生提高自身分辨能力的同时，政府、高校、家长等有关方要联动起来，迅速行动，建立政府主导、学校重视、家长参与的协同育人机制，在学校、家庭、社会和学生自身的共同努力下，引导大学生文明消费、理性消费，树立正确的消费观。

资料来源：李庆红，张蕾.校园贷风险分析与防范机制研究[J].中国农业会计，2023，33(16)：101-103.

Key Concepts and Skills

1. The concepts and calculations of future value and present value.
2. The difference between compound interest and simple interest.
3. Calculation of Net Present Value.

4. Calculation of annual percentage rate of interest and effective annual rate of interest.

5. Types of annuities, and calculations of future value and present value of annuities.

6. Types of perpetuities, and calculations of present value of perpetuities.

本章重点与难点

1. 终值和现值的概念和计算。
2. 复利和单利的区别。
3. 净现值的概念和计算。
4. 名义年利率和实际年利率的计算。
5. 年金的种类,以及年金终值和现值的计算。
6. 永续年金的种类,以及永续年金现值的计算。

Self-Test Questions

Ⅰ. Single Choice Questions

1. To deposit $2,000 in the bank at an annual interest rate of 3% and calculate the value of this money in 5 years, we should use ( )

A. Present value coefficient of compound interest

B. Future value coefficient of compound interest

C. Present value coefficient of annuities

D. Future value coefficient of annuities

2. Mr. Wang plans to withdraw $10,000 from the bank in 5 years at an annual interest rate of 3%. To calculate the amount of money he needs to deposit in the bank at present, we should use ( )

A. Present value coefficient of compound interest

B. Future value coefficient of compound interest

C. Present value coefficient of annuities

D. Future value coefficient of annuities

3. Mr. Wang plans to deposit $10,000 into the bank at the end of each year, with an annual interest rate of 3%. The total value of this money in 5 years should be calculated using ( )

A. Present value coefficient of compound interest

B. Future value coefficient of compound interest

C. Present value coefficient of annuities

D. Future value coefficient of annuities

4. Mr. Lee plans to withdraw \$100,000 for his daughter's college tuition fee in 5 years, with an annual interest rate of 3%. To calculate the amount of money he needs to deposit in the bank at the end of each year from now, we should use ( )

A. Present value coefficient of compound interest

B. Future value coefficient of compound interest

C. Present value coefficient of annuities

D. Future value coefficient of annuities

5. A perpetuity pays \$100 at the end of each year at an annual interest rate of 5%. What is the present value of this perpetuity? ( )

A. \$2,000

B. \$1,800

C. \$1,600

D. \$1,400

6. A growing perpetuity just paid \$100 at the end of this year and grows at 2% per year with an annual interest rate of 5%. What is the present value of the growing perpetuity? ( )

A. \$3,400

B. \$3,000

C. \$2,900

D. \$2,800

7. What is the effective annual rate of interest for a bank that pays 5% annual rate per quarter? ( )

A. 4.98%

B. 5%

C. 5.09%

D. 5.30%

8. A company issues a 10-year zero coupon bond with a face value of \$1,000. Discount rate is 4%. What is the issuance price of this bond? ( )

A. \$675

B. \$1,000

C. \$810

D. \$715

Ⅱ. Calculation Questions

1. Compute the following future value of \$1,000 with annual compound interest:

(1) Interest rate is 10% for 5 years;

(2) Interest rate is 8% for 10 years;

(3) Interest rate is 5% for 15 years.

2. Company X estimates that it will pay \$1.5 million pension in 20 years. If the company can invest in projects with an interest rate of 8%, how much should the company invest now to repay the pension in 20 years?

3. What is the future value of a \$1,000 bank deposit in five years? The annual interest rate is 8%, and is:

(1) Compounded annually

(2) Compounded semiannually

(3) Compounded monthly

(4) Compounded continuously

4. You have found three investment options for a three-year deposit: 10% APR compounded monthly; 8% APR compounded semiannually; 6% APR compounded quarterly. Calculate the effective annual rate (EAR) for each of the above options.

5. Your child is in the first grade of a private primary school, and is expected to graduate from high school in 12 years. The tuition for primary school is \$40,000 per year, while 5% more expensive for secondary school (middle school and high school). The tuition will be paid at the beginning of each year. If the annual interest rate is 5%, what is the present value of all the tuition during his education?

本章习题答案

Part Two
Investment Decision
（投资决策）

Chapter 4 Investment Rules（投资决策方法）

Learning Objectives

●Learn to compute the net present value, understanding why it is the best decision rule.

●learn to compute the payback period and the discounted payback period, understanding the advantages and disadvantages of the two methods.

●Learn to compute the internal rate of return and understand its advantages and disadvantages.

●Learn to compute the profitability index and understand its advantages and disadvantages.

A successful investment decision is a decision that can bring a positive net present value to the company and improve the company's market value, which will make a positive contribution to the company's financial performance in the future for a long time. In contrast, a failed investment decision will cost the company dearly. In order to objectively and scientifically analyze whether various investment projects are feasible, this chapter introduces several evaluation methods commonly used in investment decision-making. To choose an evaluation method, the indicators of the investment project should be determined according to the specific situation for reference in decision-making.

4.1 The Net Present Value

When evaluating a capital investment project, the most direct method is to compare the income and cost of the project to see whether the income is greater than the cost. However, the income and cost of investment project often occur at different time points. Due to the time value of money, we need to first discount the income and cost to the same time point, and then make the comparison. The net present value (NPV) method follows this idea. Specifically, NPV refers to the sum of discounted cash flows within the life cycle of the investment project. It can be calculated by the following formula:

Net Present Value (NPV) = Total PV of future CF's + Initial Investment

4.1.1 Selecting Criteria

The principle of using the NPV method to analyze the project capital budget is:

1. Single project(单一项目)

Accept if NPV > 0, suggesting that the expected income of the project is greater than the cost, and this project should be taken.

2. Multiple projects(多个项目)

For Independent Projects(独立项目): accepting or rejecting one project does not affect the decision of other projects, must exceed a MINIMUM acceptance criteria, that is, accept if NPV > 0;

For Mutually Exclusive Projects(互斥项目): only ONE of several potential projects can be chosen, RANK all alternatives, and select the best one, that is, accept the project with highest NPV.

【Example 4-1】

If you want to run a restaurant, the initial investment cost is \$2,000,000. The restaurant is expected to operate for three years and generate annual income of \$500,000, \$1,000,000 and \$1,500,000, respectively. The investor's expected rate of return is 10%. Is this a good investment project?

Answer:

$$NPV = 2,000,000 - \frac{500,000}{(1+0.1)} + \frac{1,000,000}{(1+0.1)^2} + \frac{1,500,000}{(1+0.1)^3} = 407,963.94$$

As the NPV value is positive, this project should be taken.

4.1.2 Why Use Net Present Value?

Accepting positive NPV projects benefits shareholders.

(1) NPV uses cash flows. The company can directly use the cash flows obtained from project. In contrast, profit contains many subjective factors, and it is not cash that can be used directly.

(2) NPV uses all the cash flows of the project. Other investment decision-making methods often ignore the cash flows in a specific period, such as the payback period method, which ignores the cash flows after the payback period.

(3) NPV discounts the cash flows properly. Other methods tend to ignore the time value of money when dealing with cash flows, and may accept projects with negative NPVs, damaging the value of the company.

The NPV method is not a perfect evaluation method, and its advantages and disadvantages mainly include:

1. Advantages

(1) The time value of funds is fully considered, which is conducive to evaluate the timeliness of the project;

(2) The selection of discount rate includes the opportunity cost and risk return rate of the project;

(3) It can reflect the increase of absolute value of shareholders' wealth.

2. Disadvantages

(1) The actual rate of return that the investment project may achieve cannot be revealed;

(2) The difference of investment scale is not considered in the decision-making of mutually exclusive projects;

(3) It is difficult to determine appropriate discount rate.

4.2 The Payback Period

This method aims to answer a question of how long it takes the project to "pay back" its initial investment. That is, the Payback Period equals to the number of years to recover initial costs. If the net cash flows of each year are the same after the project is completed, the calculation formula of the investment payback period is as follows:

$$P_t = K/A,$$

where K refers to the initial costs and A refers to the net cash flows of each year during the investment period.

If the net cash flows of each year are different before the project is completed, the calculation formula of the investment payback period is:

P_t = (The year when the cumulative net cash flows are positive for the first time−1) + Investment not recovered at the beginning of the year ÷ Net cash flows of the year

Given the previous example of restaurant investment, the investment payback period of the restaurant is 2.33.

4.2.1 Selecting Criteria

The principle of using the payback period method to analyze the project capital budget is:

1. Single project(单一项目)

Accept the project if it pays back within the specified time.

2. Mutually exclusive projects(互斥项目)

Select alternative with the shortest payback period.

4.2.2 Why Use Payback Period?

The advantages and disadvantages of the payback period method mainly include:

1. Advantages

(1) Easy to understand.

(2) Biased toward liquidity.

2. Disadvantages

(1) Ignores the time value of money.

(2) Ignores cash flows after the payback period.

(3) Biased against long-term projects (R&D).

(4) Requires an arbitrary acceptance criteria.

(5) A project accepted based on the payback criteria may not have a positive NPV.

4.3 The Discounted Payback Period

This method aims to answer a question of how long it takes the project to "pay back" its initial investment, taking the time value of money into account. Apparently, for the restaurant example, the discounted payback period should be more than 2.33, as the net cash flows are less than the original taking the time value of money into account.

4.3.1 Selecting Criteria

The principle of using the discounted payback period method to analyze the project capital budget is:

1. Single project(单一项目)

Accept the project if it pays back within the specified time on a discounted basis.

2. Mutually exclusive projects(互斥项目)

Select alternative with the shortest discounted payback period.

4.3.2 Why Use Discounted Payback Period?

The advantages and disadvantages of the discounted payback period method mainly include:

1. Advantages

(1) Easy to understand.

(2) Biased toward liquidity.

2. Disadvantages

(1) Ignores cash flows after the payback period.

(2) Biased against long-term projects (R&D).

(3) Requires an arbitrary acceptance criteria.

(4) A project accepted based on the payback criteria may not have a positive NPV.

4.4 The Internal Rate of Return

Consider the cash flows for the restaurant example:（ $ ten thousands）

$$NPV = 0 = -200+\frac{\$50}{(1+IRR)}+\frac{\$100}{(1+IRR)^2}+\frac{\$150}{(1+IRR)^3}$$

If we graph NPV versus the discount rate, we can see the IRR as the x-axis intercept as shown in Figure 4-1.

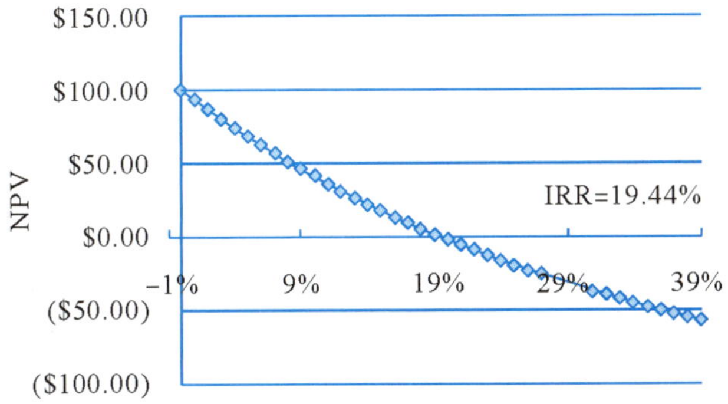

Figure 4-1 **NPV versus the discount rate for the project**

The Internal Rate of Return (IRR): the discount rate that sets NPV to zero, which dose not depend on the interest rate in the capital market (anything except the cash flows of the project). The higher the IRR, the better the value added of the investment project.

4.4.1 Selecting Criteria

1. Single Project(单一项目)

The principle of using the IRR method to analyze the project capital budget is:

Accept if the IRR exceeds the required return, suggesting that NPV is positive.

However, we may have some problems when using IRR for single project, for example:

(1) Multiple IRRs

【Example 4-2】

Suppose project A has the following cash flows. Figure 4-2 graphs the NPV curve versus the discount rate, and shows the two IRRs for this project:

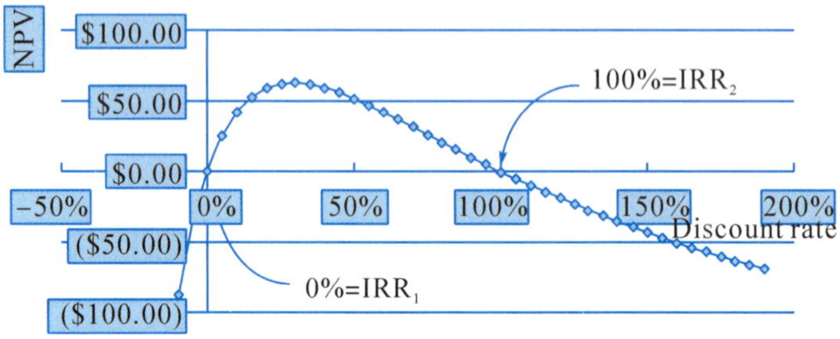

Figure 4-2 **NPV versus the discount rate for project A**

Since we have two IRRs for this project, which IRR should we use? Generally, the number of IRRs is equivalent to the number of sign changes in the cash flows. In this case, the selecting rule is to refer to NPV, that is, we should accept the project, when its NPV is positive.

(2) Are We Borrowing or Lending?

【Example 4-3】

Suppose Firm A is borrowing \$200 million from a bank, with the repayment for the next 3 periods as shown in Table 4-1.

Table 4-1 **Cash flows of Bank and Firm for each period**

Bank	N	0	1	2	3
	CF	-200	50.00	100.00	150.00
Firm	N	0	1	2	3
	CF	200	-50.00	-100.00	-150.00

Based on the above information, we can calculate the IRR for both the bank and firm is 19.44%. If we are borrowing money from the bank, IRR should be considered as the cost, which needs to be as low as possible. If we are lending money to the firm, IRR should be considered as the return, which needs to be as high as possible. Therefore, the former decision criteria which sets IRR is higher than the required return should be considered with the decision-making perspective.

2. Mutually Exclusive Projects(互斥项目)

We may also have some problems when using IRR for mutually exclusive projects, such as:

(1) The Scale Problem(规模问题)

Would you rather make 100% or 50% on your investments? What if the 100% return is on a \$1 investment, while the 50% return is on a \$1, 000 investment?

Obviously, the answer is to choose the project with 50% return as the absolute return is higher.

(2) The Timing Problem(时机问题)

【Example 4-4】

Suppose a firm is considering two projects A and B with the following cash flows for each period. The required return is 10%. The NPV curves for both two projects are graphed in Figure 4-3.

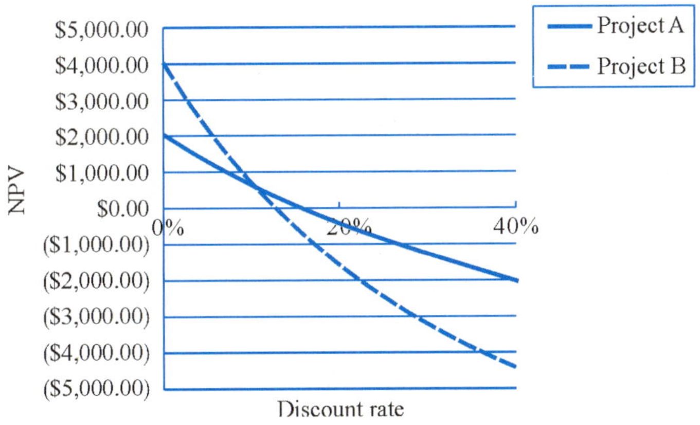

Figure 4-3 NPV versus the discount rate for project A and project B

Based on the above information, we can calculate that IRR for project A is 16. 04% and project B is 12. 94%. Should we choose project A whose IRR is higher? The answer is no. In fact, the choice decision depends on the cross over rate of the two projects. When the required return is smaller than the cross over rate, we should opt to project B, because in this case the dashed line is above the solid line (see Figure 4-3). By contrast, when the required return is larger than the cross over rate, project A is preferred, because Figure 4-3 shows that the solid line is now above the dashed line.

To compute the cross over rate, we make a new project "A-B" or "B-A" and present their cash flows in Table 4-2. Using the cash flows of the new projects, we can compute the IRR of either project "A-B" or "B-A". For example, IRR of project "A-B" can be given by the following formula:

$$0=0+\frac{9,000}{(1+IRR)}+\frac{0}{(1+IRR)^2}-\frac{11,000}{(1+IRR)^3}$$

Table 4-2 Cash flows of project "A-B" and project "B-A" for each period

	A	B	A-B	B-A
0	($ 10, 000)	($ 10, 000)	$ 0	$ 0
1	$ 10, 000	$ 10, 00	$ 9, 000	($ 9, 000, 00)
2	$ 10, 00	$ 10, 00	$ 0	$ 0
3	$ 10, 00	$ 12, 000	($ 11, 000, 00)	$ 11, 000

Using the cash flows of project "A-B", we can compute that IRR of project "A-B" is 10. 55% which is also the cross over rate. Similarly, we can compute that IRR of project "B-A" is 10. 55%. If we graph NPV versus the discount rate of both projects, we can see the IRR as the x-axis intercept as shown in Figure 4-4. Taken project "A-B" as an example, when the require return is smaller than IRR, the dashed line is below the x-axis suggesting that NPV of project "A-B" is negative. In this case, NPV of project A is smaller than project B, indicating project B is preferred. This is consistent with the result drawn in Figure 4-3.

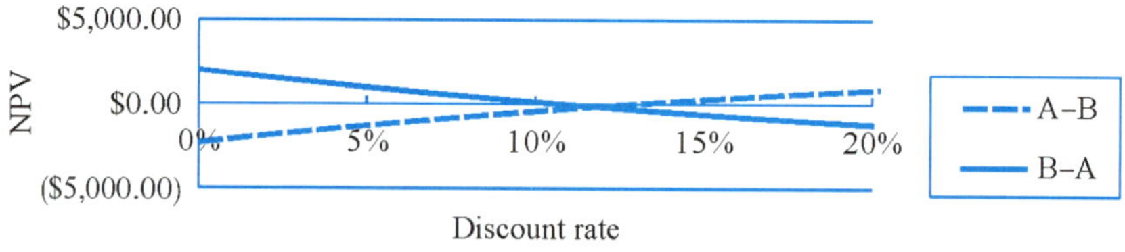

Figure 4-4 NPV versus the discount rate for project "A-B" and project "B-A"

4. 4. 2 NPV versus IRR

NPV and IRR will generally give the same decision, with some exceptions:

(1) Non-conventional cash flows: cash flow signs change more than once.

(2) Mutually exclusive projects.

- Initial investments are substantially different.
- Timing of cash flows is substantially different.

4.5 The Profitability Index

The profitability index measures the efficiency of using cash flows, and can be computed as follows:

$$PI = \frac{\text{Total PV of Future Cash Flows}}{\text{Initial Investment}}$$

4.5.1 Selecting Criteria

The principle of using the profitability index method to analyze the project capital budget is:

1. Single project(单一项目)

Accept if PI>1, suggesting that the present value of future cash flows generated by every 1 yuan of cost is greater than 1, and the project is thus profitable.

2. Mufually exclusive projects(互斥项目)

It is necessary to combine the NPV method to draw an effective conclusion.

For example, we have two options: for project A, the initial costs are \$400, 000, NPV is \$85, 000, PI is 1.21, and for project B, the initial costs are \$500, 000, NPV is \$89, 000, PI is 1.18, which one is better?

Referring to the NPV rule, we should choose project B, as it has higher NPV. However, when considering the efficiency of using cash flows, that is, to compare the value of cash flows generated from \$1 investment, project A outperforms, as it has higher PI.

4.5.2 Why Use Profitability Index?

The advantages and disadvantages of the profitability method mainly include:

1. Advantages

(1) Easy to understand and communicate.

(2) May be useful when available investment funds are limited.

(3) Correct decision when evaluating independent projects.

(5) Supplementary to NPV.

2. Disadvantages

(1) Problems with mutually exclusive investments.

(2) Cannot reflect the actual investment return that a project may achieve.

(3) Only represents the ability to obtain returns and does not represent the actual wealth that may be obtained.

4.6 The Practice of Capital Budgeting

So far, we have discussed five main investment decision-making methods. Unless there are limited funds, the NPV method usually has significant advantages over other decision-making indicators. Whether evaluating independent projects or choosing between projects with the same or different investment periods, making decisions based on NPVs is often in line with the goal of improving firm value. Therefore, the academia often regards the NPV method as the preferred method for capital budgeting. However, in practice, various capital budgeting methods can provide useful insights. For example, NPV is the best indicator for investment decisions, providing the most direct measure of the value created by the project for shareholders; IRR measures the rate of return of a project, while also providing information about the safety margin of the project; PI measures the profitability of each unit of initial investment and is particularly useful in situations of limited funds; The payback period provides a measure of project liquidity and risk.

Graham and Harvey(2001) have analyzed the commonly used capital budgeting methods of large corporations in practice based on a survey questionnaire sent to over 300 Fortune 500 companies in the United States. Figure 4-5 shows the result of the survey. It is found that the most frequently used technique for these corporations is either IRR or NPV. It is also worth noting that the payback period method has also been widely used in practice.

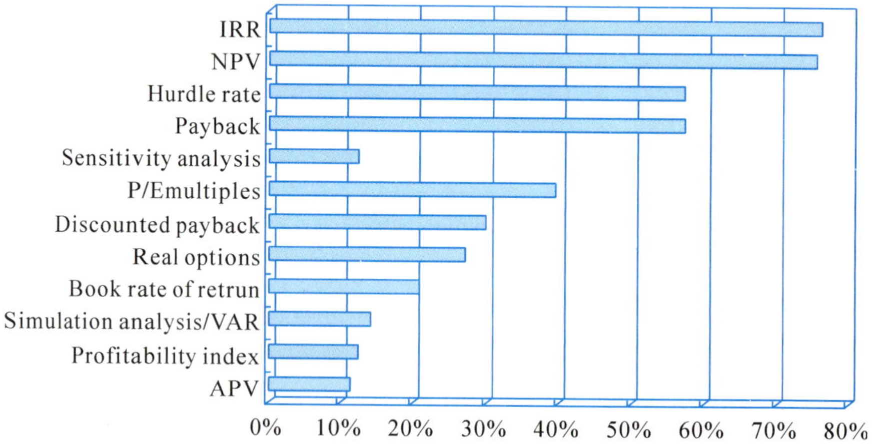

Figure 4-5 The using frequency of capital budgeting methods in large US corporations

Source: Graham, J.R., and C.R.Harvey. 2001. The theory and practice of corporate finance: Evidence from the field. Journal of Financial Economics, (60): 187-243.

案例分析 4-1 《论投资决策评价方法及性价比法在公立医院医疗设备政府采购中的应用(节选)》

某公立医院肾内科的血液透析业务量不断增加,现有的血滤机数量已无法满足临床需求,急需添置一台血滤机。经医院采购小组调研,血滤机市场价约为 34 万元,每年将诊治 120 人次,每人次 36 小时,人均收费 200 元/小时,设备使用年限为 10 年,耗材使用量为 10 万元/年,维修费 10 万元/年,人员工资 3.12 万元/年(血透室年税前工资平均 15.6 万元/人,每台血滤机占用工作人员 0.2 人),水电费 30 万元/年。折现率暂估为8%。由此可知,该血透机预计年收入 = 120×36×0.02 = 86.4 万元。预计年均成本 = 10+10+3.12+30 = 53.12 万元, 每年盈余 = 86.4−53.12 = 33.28 万元。分别按回收期法、折线回收期法、净现值法、内部收益率法及盈利指数法 5 种投资决策评价方法分析如下。

1. 回收期法

回收期 = 34/33.28 = 1.02 年,回收期短于设备使用年限(10 年),故该血滤机采购项目可行。

2. 折现回收期法

第 1 年现金流量现值 = 33.28×0.925,9 = 30.81(万元),

第 2 年现金流量现值 = 33.28×0.857,3 = 28.53(万元),

回收期 = 1+(34−30.81)/28.53 = 1.11 年,回收期短于设备使用年限(10 年),故该血滤机采购项目可行。

3. 净现值法

10 年期的年金现值系数 = 6.71,净现值 = 33.28×6.71−34 = 189.31 万元,净现值>0,故该血滤机采购项目可行。

4. 内部收益率法

净现值 NPV = −34+33.28×(P/A,i,10) = 0,经预估,内部收益率 IRR 远大于资本成本率(8%),故该血滤机采购项目可行。

5. 盈利指数法

盈利指数 PI = 33.28×6.71/34 = 6.57, 大于 1,故该血滤机采购项目可行。

按以上 5 种投资决策评价方法分析结果,该血滤机采购项目在经济可行性方面可行。

资料来源:徐力.论投资决策评价方法及性价比法在公医院医疗设备政府采购中的应用[J].中国总会计师,2023(4):172-174.

Key Concepts and Skills

1. Definition and application of NPV, IRR, payback period, and profitability index, as well as the advantages and disadvantages of the various methods.

2. Selection of mutually exclusive projects with the same or different lifespans using NPV.

3. Selection of mutually exclusive projects using IRR.

4. Selection of projects under the limited capital condition using the profitability index method.

本章重点与难点

1. 净现值法、内部收益率法、回收期法、盈利指数法的含义和运用，以及各种方法的优缺点。

2. 用净现值选择寿命相同或者不同的互斥项目。

3. 用内部收益率法对互斥项目进行选择。

4. 用盈利指数法在资本限量下进行选择。

Self-Test Questions

Ⅰ. Single Choice Questions

1. Which of the following is not an advantage of the NPV method? (　　)

A. Time value of money is taken into account.

B. All net cash flows over the investment period of the project are taken into account.

C. Investment risk is taken into account.

D. The actual rate of return on investment can be reflected in a dynamical way.

2. The decision-making method that cannot be used in the decision-making of multiple mutually exclusive projects with unequal initial investments is (　　)

A. NPV method

B. Profitability index method

C. IRR method

D. None of them can be used

3. Factor that does not have an impact on the size of the internal rate of return

(IRR) of an investment project is ( )

A. Initial investment of the project

B. Cash flows from the project

C. Investment duration of the project

D. Cost of capital of the project

4. The most accurate expression of the internal rate of return (IRR) is ( )

A. The calculation of IRR does not take into account the time value of money.

B. Comparison of IRR with the cost of capital can determine project trade-offs.

C. IRR is the actual rate of return on the project, which varies with the risk of the project.

D. IRR method is superior to NPV method.

5. Which of the following is not calculated on a discounted basis? ( )

A. net present value (NPV)

B. profitability index

C. payback period

D. internal rate of return (IRR)

6. NPV value greater than 0 means that ( )

A. IRR is greater than the predetermined discount rate.

B. IRR is less than the predetermined discount rate.

C. IRR is equal to the predetermined discount rate.

D. Discounted value of cash inflows is less than discounted value of cash outflows.

7. A project with a NPV of $4.5 million and a discount rate of 12% indicates that IRR ( )

A. >12%

B. =12%

C. <12%

D. indeterminate

8. The advantage of the profitability index method over the NPV method is ( )

A. To facilitate comparison of programs with the same scale of investment.

B. To facilitate comparison of profitability of independent projects.

C. To consider the timing of cash flows.

D. To consider the risk of investments.

9. The mutual disadvantage of the NPV and profitability index methods is ( )

A. Not to reflect the relationship between inputs and outputs.

B. To fail to consider the time value of money.

C. Not to utilize full net cash flow information.

D. Not to directly reflect the real rate of return-on-investment projects.

10. Which of the following is not a disadvantage of the payback period method? ( )

A. Ignoring the time value of money

B. Need a subjective payback period as judgment criterion

C. Does not reflect all the level of risk of the project

D. Does not consider cash flows after payback period

Ⅱ. Calculation Questions

1. Company A is considering a capital budgeting project. The payback cutoff is 3 years. The expected return of the project is 10%. Net cash flows of each year are generated as follows:

	0	1	2	3	4	5
Net cash flows	−1,000	500	300	300	300	200

Questions:

(1) What is the payback period, NPV, IRR and profitability index.

(2) If you are the financial manager of the company, how would you report to your senior?

2. Company A is considering two potential projects. The expected return of the projects is 12%. The payback cutoff is 4 years. The cash flows of each year are generated as follows:

	0	1	2	3	4	5
Project A	−100	32	32	32	32	32
Project B	−100	60	35	20	20	10

Questions:

(1) What is payback period, NPV, IRR and profitability index of Project A and Project B?

(2) If they are independent projects, which one would be selected? Why?

(3) If they are mutually exclusive projects, how would you make your

decision based on the NPV and IRR rules?

3. Consider the following cash flows of two mutually exclusive projects. Assume the discount rate is 10%.

Year	Project A	Project B
0	-1,500	-800
1	700	400
2	800	500
3	700	400

Questions:

(1) Based on the payback period rule, which project should be taken?

(2) Based on the NPV rule, which project should be taken?

(3) Based on the incremental IRR rule, which project should be taken? (The incremental IRR is between 13% to 14%.)

(4) Explain the results by using different investment methods, and conclude the optimal selecting rule.

4. Consider the following independent projects:

Project	Cash flows ($)					
	C_0	C_1	C_2	C_3	C_4	C_5
A	-1,000	1,000	0	0	0	0
B	-2,000	1,000	1,000	4,000	1,000	1,000
C	-3,000	1,000	1,000	0	1,000	1,000

Questions:

(1) If the discount rate for the projects is 10 %, based on the NPV rule, which projects can be taken?

(2) Calculate the payback period for each project.

(3) Which project(s) would a firm accept using the payback period rule accept if the cutoff period is three years?

(4) Calculate the discounted payback period for each project.

(5) Which project(s) would a firm accept using the discounted payback period rule accept if the cutoff period is three years?

5. Consider the following two mutually exclusive projects:

Project	Cash flows ($)			
	C_0	C_1	C_2	C_3
A	-100	60	60	0
B	-110	0	0	140

Questions:

(1) Based on the payback period rule, which project should be taken?

(2) Calculate the NPV of each project for discount rates of 0, 10%, and 20%. Plot these on a graph with NPV on the vertical axis and discount rate on the horizontal axis.

(3) What is the approximate IRR for each project? In what circumstances should the company accept project A?

(4) Based on the incremental IRR rule, which project should be taken?

6. Consider the following cash flows of two projects. Assume the discount rate is 12%.

Year	Project A	Project B
0	-100,000	-100,000
1	65,000	35,000
2	30,000	35,000
3	30,000	35,000
4	10,000	35,000

Questions:

(1) Based on the above information, calculate the payback period, NPV, and IRR for the two projects. (IRR for project A is between 17% to 19%; IRR for project B is between 14% to 16%.)

(2) If the two projects are independent, which project(s) should be taken? Why?

(3) If the two projects are mutually exclusive, based on the NPV rule, which project should be taken?

(4) If the two projects are mutually exclusive, based on the IRR rule, which project should be taken? (IRR for project with incremental cash flows is between 5% to 7%.)

本章习题答案

Chapter 5 Capital Budgeting （资本预算）

Learning Objectives

●Learn to determine the relevant cash flows for various types of capital investments.

●Understand the effect of inflation on capital budgeting.

●Learn to compute the incremental cash flows of capital investments.

●Understand the various methods for computing operating cash flows.

●Understand special cases of discounted cash flow valuation.

Capital refers to the operational assets used in production, and budget refers to the detailed planning of cash flows to occur in the future. Capital budget is a summary of the operational asset investment plan. It refers to the whole process of describing the future cash inflows and outflows of investment projects in detail and deciding which cash flows should be included in investment decisions. Estimating the cash flows of an investment project is an important step in capital budgeting. To estimate the cash flows of an investment project, you need to know what the cash flows relevant to the investment project are, and then know how to calculate the relevant cash flows for investment decisions.

5.1 Cash Flows

In the capital budgeting process, the most important and difficult step is to estimate the cash flows of the project. For this complex work, analysts need to follow two principles in the estimation process: Actual cash flow principle（实际现金流原则）and With/without principle（相关/不相关原则）.

5.1.1 Actual Cash Flow Principle（实际现金流原则）

The actual cash flow principle has two meanings: first, any cash flows of investment projects must be measured according to their actual occurrence time; Second, the value of all future cash flows of the project must be calculated according to the expected future price and cost. This principle highlights the importance of cash flows instead of accounting earnings, which are on the accrual basis. For example, you never write a check to pay the "depreciation", suggesting the occurrence of depreciation does not affect the current cash flows. The accounting earnings do not represent REAL money, so we need to make some adjustment to convert the earnings from income statements into cash flows to be used in capital budgeting decision.

Also, inflation is an important factor of economic life and must be considered in capital budgeting. In this case, the future cash flows will increase due to inflation, and therefore generating two kinds of cash flows:

(1) Nominal cash flows which refer to the actual dollars to be received (or paid out).

(2) Real cash flows which refer to the cash flows' purchasing power.

Consider the relationship between interest rate and inflation, it is often referred to as the Fisher equation:

$$(1 + \text{Nominal Rate}) = (1 + \text{Real Rate}) \times (1 + \text{Inflation Rate})$$

For low rates of inflation, this is often approximated:

$$\text{Real Rate} = \text{Nominal Rate} - \text{Inflation Rate}$$

In capital budgeting, which interest rate should be used to discount cash flows? The principle is to keep consistency. That is, one must compare real cash flows discounted at real rate or nominal cash flows discounted at nominal rate.

5.1.2 With/Without Principle(相关/不相关原则)

This principle is to highlight the importance of incremental (relevant) cash flows (增量现金流) which should be considered in capital budgeting. The incremental (relevant) cash flows refer to the changes in the firm's cash flows that occur as a direct consequence of accepting the project (The difference between the cash flows with and without the project). To identify if the cash flows are relevant or not, we need to discuss the following cash flows that commonly occur in company's operation.

1. Sunk Costs(沉没成本)

The sunk cost refers to the cash outflows that have occurred in the investment decision. As these cash flows cannot be changed by the decision to accept or reject the project, according to the with/without principle, sunk cost need not to be included in the relevant cash flows of project. For example, the MYK company is currently evaluating the NPV of establishing a line of new product. As part of the evaluation, the company paid a consulting firm $100,000 last year for a test marketing analysis. Is this cost relevant for the capital budgeting decision? Obviously, this cost has already occurred, and it has no impact on the capital budgeting. Therefore, this cost DOES NOT matter.

2. Opportunity Costs(机会成本)

Opportunity cost refers to the maximum value of giving up an option in order to get others. When calculating the cash flows of investment projects, it is necessary to consider not only the direct cash inflows and outflows, but also the possible gains from other investment opportunities abandoned due to the implementation of a certain investment scheme. Since this abandonment will reduce the cash flows of the project, according to the with/without principle, the opportunity cost is the relevant cash flow. For example, the HWT company has an empty warehouse in Kuiming that can be used to store a new line of shoes machines. The company hopes to sell these machines to southwestern consumers. Should the sales price of the warehouse be considered a cost in the decision to sell the machines? The potential revenues from the warehouse being used elsewhere should be viewed as a cost to accept the project of selling shoes machines. It is because by taking the project, the company forgoes the sales revenues of the warehouse. The sales price of the wharehouse is a cost in the decision to accept the project of selling shoes machines.

3. Side Effects (Erosion Costs)(侵蚀成本)

Erosion occurs when a new product reduces the sales and hence the cash flows of existing products. It is also called as side effects, and hence a relevant cash flow. For example, the MC company is determining the NPV of a new version of smart phone. Some of the would-be purchasers are owners of MC's old smart phone. All the sales and profits from the new version smart phone cannot be considered incremental as the sale of new phone reduces the cash flows of old smart phone.

4. Allocated Costs(已分配成本)

In capital budgeting, the inconsistency between investment analysts and accountants is also reflected in the allocation of indirect expenses. Indirect expenses include managers' salaries, rents, utilities. For accountants, these expenses will be allocated to each new investment of the company and deducted from profits. However, when analyzing the cash flows of investment, it is necessary to further identify these costs, because these costs may not be related to the project being evaluated. For the indirect costs arising from the appraised project should be included in the relevant cash flows of the project, while the indirect costs unrelated to the project should not be allocated in the relevant cash flows of the project. For example, the YWC company wants to start a new project. If the salary of the project manager is \$10,000 per month, should this \$10,000 be considered as the relevant cash flows to the new project? The answer is NO. Because \$10,000 is the indirect cost allocated by the existing projects. However, if the project manager needs to work overtime because of the new project, and he will get an extra \$2,000 of overtime salary every month, this \$2,000 should be considered as the relevant cash flows of the new project. Hence, the allocated cost should be viewed as a cash outflow of a project only if it is an incremental cost of this project.

5. Interest Expense (Financing Costs)(融资成本)

Interest expense is related to financing not investment. In capital budgeting, the consideration of financing costs is not reflected in the cash flows, but in the discount rate used to calculate the present value of the project's cash flows. Later chapters will deal with the impact of the amount of debt in its capital structure on firm value (cost of capital). For now, it is enough to assume that the firm's level of debt (and hence, interest expense) is independent of the project at hand, that is, to assume the project is financed only with equity.

5.2 Estimating Cash Flows

The general formula to calculate cash flows from assets is given as follows:

Cash flows from assets (CFFA)

= Operating cash flows (OCFs) − Net capital spending(NCS) − Changes in NWC (NNWC)

= Cash flows to creditors + Cash flows to shareholders

(1) Estimating OCFs(估计经营现金流)

OCFs = EBIT − Taxes + Depreciation

= (Sales−Costs)(1−T)+depreciation(Top−Down Approach)

= NI + depreciation (NO interest expenses, Bottom−Up Approach)

= (Sales − Cash Costs − depreciation) (1 − T) +Depreciation

= (Sales−Cash Costs) (1−T) +Depreciation * T (Tax Shield Approach)

(2) Estimating Net Capital Spending(估计净资本支出)

Net Capital Spending = Closing balance − opening balance + depreciation

Capital budgeting: do not forget salvage value (after tax, of course).

(3) Estimating Changes in Net Working Capital(估计净营运资本变化)

Changes in Net Working Capital = Ending NWC − beginning NWC

Capital budgeting: when the project winds down, we enjoy a return of net working capital.

【Example 5-1】

The financial cash flows of company HWT in 2023 are as follows. By using the above formula in Table 5-1, we can compute cash flows from assets and find that cash flows from assets equal to cash flows to creditors and shareholders. The calculations of OCFs, net capital spending, as well as cash flows to creditors and shareholders are presented from Table 5-2 to Table 5-5. NWC grew to $392 million in 2023 from $344 million in 2022. This increase of $48 million is the addition to NWC.

Table 5-1 Calculation of cash flows from assets and cash flows to creditors and shareholders

Cash flows from assets (CFFA)	
Operating cash flows (OCFs) (Earnings before interest and taxes plus depreciation minus taxes)	$ 412
Net capital spending (Acquisitions of fixed assets minus sales of fixed assets)	−215
Additions to net working capital	−48
Total	$ 149
Cash flows to creditors and shareholders	
Debt (Interests plus retirement of debt minus long-term debt financing)	$ 110
Equity (Dividends plus repurchase of equity minus new equity financing)	39
Total	$ 149

Table 5-2 Calculation of operating cash flows (OCFs)

Operating Cash Flows (OCFs)	
EBIT	\$ 356
Depreciation	\$ 150
Current Taxes	- \$ 94(not real)
OCF	\$ 412

Table 5-3 Calculation of net capital spending

Net Capital Spending	
Purchase of fixed assets	\$ 278
Sales of fixed assets	- \$ 63
Net Capital Spending	\$ 215

Table 5-4 Calculation of cash flows to creditors

Cash Flows to Creditors	
Interests	\$ 94
Retirement of debt	42
Debt service	55
Proceeds from new debt sales	-81
Total	\$ 110

Table 5-5 Calculation of cash flow to creditors

Cash Flows to Stockholders	
Dividends	\$ 75
Repurchase of stock	20
Cash to Stockholders	52
Proceeds from new stock issue	-108
Total	\$ 39

5.3 The HWT Company: An Example

The HWT company is considering to launch a new product, and has following information:

(1) Costs of test marketing (already spent): $200, 000.

(2) Current market value of a proposed factory site (which the company owns): $200, 000 (after taxes).

(3) Costs of new production line: $150, 000 (straightly depreciated to 0 within 5 years, and with a market value of $40, 000 at the end of year 5).

(4) Production (in units) by year during 5-year life of the machine: 8, 000, 9, 000, 13, 000, 12, 000, 8, 000.

(5) Price during the first year is $30; price increases by 2% per year thereafter.

(6) Production costs during the first year are $20 per unit and increase by 10% per year thereafter.

(7) Net Working Capital: initial $10, 000, equals to 10% of sales for that year at the end of each year (to purchase raw materials and against unforeseen expenditures, credit sales and payment).

(8) The expected return of rate is 10%, and tax rate is 40%. All cash flows occur at the end of the year.

●Cash flows of investments ($ thousands)

Investments:		Year 0	Year 1	Year 2	Year 3	Year 4	Year 5
(1)	New production line	-150. 00					24. 00
(2)	Depreciation		30. 00	30. 00	30. 00	30. 00	30. 00
(3)	Accumulated depreciation		30. 00	60. 00	90. 00	120. 00	150. 00
(4)	Adjusted basis of machine after depreciation (end of year)		120. 00	90. 00	60. 00	30. 00	0. 00
(5)	Opportunity cost (warehouse)	-200. 00					200. 00
(6)	Net working capital (end of year)	10. 00	24. 00	27. 54	40. 58	38. 20	0
(7)	Changes in net working capital	-10. 00	-14. 00	-3. 54	-13. 04	2. 38	38. 2
(8)	Total cash flows of investments [(1) + (5) + (7)]	-360. 00	-14. 00	-3. 54	-13. 04	2. 38	262. 2

Note: The salvage value of the machine in year 5 is calculated by 40-(40-0) * 0. 4 = 24.

● Incremental cash flows ($ thousands)

		Year 0	Year 1	Year 2	Year 3	Year 4	Year 5
(9)	Sales Revenues		240. 00	275. 4	405. 76	382. 03	259. 78
(10)	Operating costs		-160. 00	-198. 00	-314. 60	-319. 44	-234. 26
(11)	Tax shield of depreciation		12. 00	12. 00	12. 00	12. 00	12. 00
(12)	OCFs=[(9)-(10)] * (1-T)+(11)		60	58. 44	66. 69	49. 56	27. 32
(13)	Total cash flows of investments	-360. 00	-14. 00	-3. 54	-13. 04	2. 38	262. 2
(14)	IATCFs=(12) + (13)	-360.	46. 00	54. 90	53. 65	51. 94	289. 52

Note: Sales revenues for year 1 are calculated by ($ 30 * 8, 000), while operating costs for year 1 are calculated by ($ 20 * 8, 000). Similarly, for year 2 to year 4, sales revenues and operating costs are calculated following the same logic note that price and costs increase accordingly each year. Operating cash flows are calculated by the tax shield approach.

The NPV of this new project can be calculated as follows:

$$NPV = -\$360 + \frac{\$46.00}{(1.10)} + \frac{\$54.90}{(1.10)^2} + \frac{\$53.65}{(1.10)^3} + \frac{\$51.94}{(1.10)^4} + \frac{\$289.52}{(1.10)^5}$$

$$= -\$17.26$$

As NPV is negative, HWT company should not accept the project for launching the new production line.

5.4 Special Cases of Discounted Cash Flow Valuation

5.4.1 Cost-Cutting Proposals(成本节约计划)

【Example 5-2】

Suppose Firm A is considering to purchase a new equipment in order to replace a current equipment. Information is given as follows:

($ 1 dollar)

Old equipment	New equipment
Original value = 100, 000	Original value = 150, 000
Depreciation = 9, 000	Expected to be used for 5 years

Table(continue)

Purchased 5 years ago	Salvage value in year 5 = 0
Book value = 55, 000	Cost savings for each year = 50, 000
Current salvage value = 65, 000	Depreciation based on MACRS for 3 years
Salvage value in year 5 = 10, 000	

The expected return of rate is 10%, and tax rate is 40%. Should we change the equipment?

Answer:

If we decide to replace the equipment, the relevant cash flows are as follows:

- Purchase cost of new equipment.
- Salvage value of old equipment in year 0.
- Depreciation of new equipment.
- Loss in depreciation of old equipment.
- Annual cost savings of new equipment.
- Loss in salvage value of old equipment in year 5.

Then, we can adopt the general formula to calculate CFFA of the replacement for each year. The cash flows for the project period are presented in Table 5-6.

Table 5-6 Cash flows for the project period

Year	0	1	2	3	4	5
Net capital investment	-89, 000					-10, 000
Cost savings		50, 000	50, 000	50, 000	50, 000	50, 000
Depreciation						
New equipment		49, 500	67, 500	22, 500	10, 500	0
Old equipment		-9, 000	-9, 000	-9, 000	-9, 000	-9, 000
Increase in depreciation		40, 500	58, 500	13, 500	1, 500	-9, 000
OCF		46, 200	53, 400	35, 400	30, 600	26, 400
CFFA	-89, 000	46, 200	53, 400	35, 400	30, 600	16, 400

Note:

Net capital investment in year 0 = -150, 000+[65, 000-(65, 000-55, 000) * 40%] = -89, 000

Net capital investment in year 5 = -[10, 000-(10, 000-10, 000) * 40%] = -10, 000

$$NPV = -89,000 + \frac{46,200}{1+0.1} + \frac{53,400}{(1+0.1)^2} + \frac{35,400}{(1+0.1)^3} + \frac{30,600}{(1+0.1)^4} + \frac{16,400}{(1+0.1)^5} = 232,812.10$$

As the NPV is positive, we should change the equipment.

5.4.2 Setting the Bid Price(确定报价)

【Example 5-3】

Firm A is considering to upgrate its digitalization and thus quote for multi-functionaldigital equipments to a specialized company. In the next three years, 4 sets can be sold every year. It is estimated that the labor and material cost of each equipment is \$10,000, and the annual rent of the production site is \$12,000. The investment on required fixed assets is \$50,000, and is expected to straightly depreciated to \$10,000 in three years, with a market value of \$10,000 at the end of year 3. The NWC required at the beginning of the project is \$10,000. The expected return of rate is 15%, and tax rate is 40%. What's the price per set of equipment?

Answer:

$$\text{Annual depreciation} = \frac{(50,000 - 10,000)}{3} = 13,333.33$$

$$\text{Annual OCF} = (4 * (P - 10,000) - 12,000 - 13,333.33) * (1 - 40\%) + 13,333.33$$

$CFFA_0 = -50,000 - 10,000 = -60,000$

$CFFA_{1,2} = \text{Annual OCF}$

$CFFA_3 = \text{Annual OCF} + 10,000 + 10,000$

$$NPV = -60,000 + \text{Annual OCF} * (P/A, 15\%, 3) + \frac{(10,000 + 10,000)}{(1 + 15\%)^3} = 0$$

$$\text{Annual OCF} = \frac{60,000 - 11,435.06}{2.283,2} = 20,519.30$$

$$(4 * (P - 10,000) - 12,000 - 13,333.33) * (1 - 40\%) + 13,333.33 = 20,519.30$$

$P = 19,327.49$

5.4.3 Investments of Unequal Lives(不同生命周期的项目)

There are times when application of the NPV rule can lead to the wrong decision.

【Example 5-4】

Consider a factory that must have an air cleaner. There are two choices:

● The "A Cleaner" costs \$4,000 today, has annual operating costs of \$100, and lasts 10 years.

● The "B Cleaner" costs \$1,000 today, has annual operating costs of \$500, and lasts 5 years.

Assuming a 10% discount rate, which one should we choose?

Answer:

	A Cleaner	B Cleaner
CF_0	-4,000	-1,000
PMT	-100	-500
N	10	5
I	10	10
NPV	-4,614.46	-2,895.39

At first glance, B Cleaner has a higher NPV (lower present costs), but this overlooks the fact that A Cleaner lasts twice as long. Here, we should opt to **Equivalent Annual Cost (EAC，约当年均成本)** as the criteria. The EAC is the value of the level payment annuity that has the same PV as our original set of cash flows. It can be calculated by the following formula:

$$EAC = \frac{\text{PV of furture cash flows}}{(P/A, i, n)}$$

Therefore, when we incorporate the difference in lives, the cost of A Cleaner per year is actually cheaper. In effect, the EAC for A Cleaner is $\frac{\$4,614.46}{(P/A, 10\%, 10)} = \$750.98$, and the EAC for B cleaner is $\frac{\$2,895.39}{(P/A, 10\%, 5)} = \$763.79$. Thus, we should choose A Cleaner.

延伸阅读 5-1 《新经济时代企业价值的内涵及其综合评估体系（节选）》

利润和企业价值(或股东财富)都是投资人利益回报的衡量与体现。尽管长期以来其占据了财务管理的主导地位,但"利润最大化"目标本身存在着容易被企业管理人员操纵、经营行为短期化等致命缺陷。因此,自20世纪60年代以来"利润最大化"的企业财务管理目标逐步被"企业价值最大化"目标取代。现在"企业价值最大化"目标不仅在理论上已被越来越多的学者所接受,最终成为现代企业财务管理的主流观点,而且在实践上也被越来越多的企业用来作为激励的基础。另外,随着以计算机技术为代表的科技革命的来临,随着经济国际化、全球化的来临，企业面对的需求挑战、竞争环境、商机的获得和盈利模式都发生了重大变化，企业价值的内涵及其决定因素也发生了变化。因此，准确评价企业价值，设计一套适合于新经济时代竞争优势的形成和可持续发展需要的企业价值综合指标评估体系，是摆在我们面前的一项重要的任务。

前瞻性、综合性概念的扩大不仅充分说明了新经济时代企业价值新的内涵，而且事实上也指明了新经济时代企业价值衡量应当遵循的最基本的原则。也就是说，在新经济时代衡量企业价值应该从前瞻性和综合性两方面着手：前瞻性就是要强调企业的可持续发展，就是要从企业未来的角度来认识企业价值，就是要着眼于未来时期的财富的增长；综合性就是要考虑现金流量、风险、可持续发展、企业核心能力等或涉及企业价值时必须考虑的所有重要因素。

折现现金流量法、相对估价法、期权估价法、经济增加价值（EVA Economic Value Added）法等现行企业价值评估方法具有简单、数据易得、使用方便、理解直观等优点，在资产评估、资产重组、企业并购等方面都起到了很大的作用，在一定程度上满足了相关利益者的要求。特别是在众多国际性大公司中，EVA 正取代传统会计业绩评价指标成为衡量企业经营业绩的主要标准。但总的说来，现行的企业价值评估方法存在主观性较大、误差大、较粗糙等缺点。更重要的是，上述现行评估方法难以反映新经济时代企业价值已经扩大的内涵，难以反映上述前瞻性和综合性的概念及其衡量原则。因此，在企业价值评估中它们只能是一种有益补充。这就要求我们建立一套适应新经济时代要求的企业价值综合指标评估体系。企业价值直接反映了企业存在的意义，反映了企业对整个社会的贡献，也反映了企业各利益相关者（投资人、债权人、企业职工、政府机构、消费者和社会公众）的相关利益。因此，根据对新经济时代企业价值内涵的理解，根据新经济时代衡量企业价值应该遵循的前瞻性和综合性原则，综合考虑传统企业价值评估方法，我们对企业价值的衡量应从财务、客户、内部业务流程及学习与成长四个方面进行衡量。

（1）财务衡量指标。即使在新经济时代，财务指标在企业竞争战略及经营业绩评价中仍然居支配地位，是企业经营业绩评价的主要工具。其优点在于：①财务指标的可计量性为企业的各利益相关者评价企业的经营活动提供了客观依据。②财务指标本身也不断发展，使得其所蕴含的信息能更真实地反映企业的业绩。③企业价值本身就是一个长期性的财务指标。因此，企业价值的衡量将财务目标作为所有目标衡量的焦点。

财务衡量指标主要包括四个方面的内容，即财务效益状况、资产营运状况、偿债能力状况、发展能力状况。净资产的收益率、总资产报酬率、资本保值增值率、销售（营业）利润率、成本费用利润率等指标用来反映财务效益状况；总资产周转率、流动资产周转率、应收账款周转率、不良资产比率等指标用来反映企业的资产营运状况；资产负债率、已获利息倍数、流动比率、现金流量、现金流动负债比率指标用来反映企业的偿债能力状况；销售（营业）增长率是指企业本年销售（营业）收入增长额同上年销售（营业）收入总额的比率是评价企业成长状况和发展能力的重要指标；另外，资本积累率（指企业本年所有者权益增长额同年初所有者权益的比率，表示企业当年资本的积累能力，是企业当年所有者权益总的增长率）也反映了企业所有者权益在当年的变动比率，是评价企业发展潜力的重要指标；人力（智力）资本比率指标通过智力资本在总资本中所占的比重反映了企业是否重视智力资本以及人力资本对该企业生产经营活动的作用，揭示了企业对未来成长的预先准备情况。

与此同时，我们对财务指标的局限性也必须有清醒的认识，因为以会计数据为基础的财务指标不能真实地、客观地反映经济活动的现实。大多数财务指标是面向过去的，而企业价值却要求反映现有经营行为对未来价值的影响，环境的不确定性以及经营活动的复杂性，使得单纯的财务指标评价难以涵盖企业经营的方方面面。

（2）客户衡量指标。①客户满意度。顾客满意是现代企业活动的基本准则，它以构成顾客满意度的各个要素作为评价基础。企业的顾客满意水平主要有三项影响因素，即顾客经历的产品或服务质量、顾客感知价值和顾客预期的产品或服务质量[3]。②产品市场占有率。它指企业某种主导产品的产销量占整个行业中该产品产销量的比例，是企业该种产品在整个市场中的份额，反映企业在当下及未来一段时间的竞争力。③客户保持率。它指企业争取到的客户继续保持交易关系的部分所占的比重，从侧面反映了客户的满意程度，是企业保持现有市场占有率的关键。④新客户获得率。它指企业在争取新客户时获得成功的部分的比例，反映了企业挖掘潜在市场、扩大市场占有率的能力。⑤从客户处获得利润。它指企业为客户提供产品和劳务后所取得的净利润水平，能否长期获利成为决定保留或排除客户的关键点。上述五个指标应该成为从客户角度对企业价值进行衡量的核心指标。

（3）内部业务流程衡量指标。企业财务业绩的实现、客户各种需求的满足，以及股东价值的追求，都需要靠其内部的良好经营来支持。这一过程又可细分为创新、生产经营和售后服务三个具体过程。①创新过程。企业发展的过程是企业财富积累的过程，是企业利润增加的过程，是创新的过程。企业不同的经营要素之间的组合形式是多种多样的，生产要素新的组合就是创新。企业经营要素新组合的创新主要包括以下几个方面：产品（服务）创新、工艺创新、市场创新。②生产经营过程。它指从接受客户订单开始到把现有产品和服务生产出来并提供给客户的过程，应以生产能力利用率、机器完好率、设备利用率、安全生产率、产品退货率、产品返修率、产品维修期限、成本降低率等指标进行衡量。③售后服务过程。它指在售出产品和服务之后给客户提供的服务活动过程，衡量售后服务的指标大致有公司对产品故障的反应和处理时间、售后服务一次成功率、客户付款的时间等。

（4）学习与成长衡量指标。企业的学习和成长主要来自三个方面的资源：人员、信息系统和企业的程序。其中提高员工能力、激发员工士气尤为重要。反映员工方面的指标主要有员工满意度、员工流动率、员工保持率、员工知识水平、员工培训次数、管理水平、技术开发人员的比重、信息系统的效果（共享性、自动化程度）、经理人员素质等。上述财务、客户、企业内部业务流程和学习与成长等各项指标在企业价值构成中的作用各不相同。各种指标的组合构成了企业价值综合指标评估体系。在企业价值综合评估体系中，对选择好的衡量指标需做进一步的实证分析，各指标权重也有待进一步探讨。有了各指标的权重，就可以加权合成一个基于财务指标和非财务指标相结合的企业价值衡量的综合指标。总之，基于财务与非财务相结合的企业价值衡量方法，为企业价值最大化财务管理目标提供了新思路。

参考文献：

[1] Kaplan R, Norton D. The Balance Scorecard: Translating Strategy Into Action[M]. Harvard Business School Press, 1996.

[2] 胡奕明. 非财务指标的选择——价值相关分析[J]. 财经研究, 2001(5).

[3] 曹礼和, 田志龙. 试论企业的顾客满意战略[J]. 经济师, 2001(4).

资料来源：姚益龙，高筠燕. 新经济时代企业价值的内涵及其综合评估体系. 中山大学学报（社会科学版），2003(6).

延伸阅读 5-2 《和谐社会背景下政府公共投资项目社会影响评价研究（节选）》

公共投资项目从广义上说，是指政府为了推动国民经济或区域经济发展、满足社会公共需要，以政府为实际投资主体，以财政性资金为资金来源的固定资产投资项目。与一般性的商业投资项目相比，政府公共投资项目不仅具有投资规模大、风险高、影响面广等经济性特征，而且还具有公益性、非竞争性及非盈利性等社会性特征。对当前我国政府公共投资项目进行社会影响评价，不仅能够满足社会公共需求，实现项目的社会价值，规避项目潜在的社会风险，还有助于和谐社会的建设。

政府公共投资项目社会影响评价主要关注的是项目对人们就业、收入、消费等经济环境产生的影响，对人们健康、生活方式、价值文化等社会环境产生的影响，对社区治理、村民自治、民主决策等政治环境产生的影响等。我国在对政府公共投资项目进行社会影响评价时，至少应包括四个方面的内容：其一，重点评价项目对提高当地社会效益的影响，即运用成本—绩效分析方法，识别那些无法用货币表达的社会绩效和社会价值。例如，项目对促进当地人力资本的提升和就业的效用，对帮助落后地区脱贫的效用，对推动当地现代化进程、加快城乡一体化的效用，对实现地区间均衡发展的效用。其二，评价项目对当地居民生活的影响。即评价在项目规划和建设过程中，当地居民参与的状况，当地居民对项目的感觉和看法，当地政府对项目所持的态度，项目对当地居民风俗习惯的影响、对居民生活质量和生活方式的影响、对当地社区环境与治安产生的影响，尤其是项目对当地“利益相关群体”（如非自愿搬迁的群体）的影响。其三，评价项目对当地自然环境的影响。评价项目在选址、规划、实施过程中是否有效保护当地的自然生态，尽可能减少对植被的破坏；是否注意避免可能诱发的地震或水土流失，保护珍贵的自然景观，尽可能减少对自然环境的污染；是否能有效地利用资源和能源，注意保护和节约自然资源，合理开发和利用土地等。其四，评价项目对当地特殊群体的影响。即项目是否关注贫困群体的需求和利益，积极吸收贫困群体参与项目的决策和建设，倾听他们的声音，赋予他们更多自我发展的权利和机会等。

针对我国政府公共投资项目所开展的社会影响评价，我们应该采取的具体方法大致包括：①确定评价范围，即项目的直接影响区（与项目建设直接关联的地区）、间接影响区（与直接影响区接壤的地区）。②确定评价对象，即项目可能影响到的相关群体、组织和社区等，考察项目使谁受益或受损，项目是否考虑并妥善处置某些需要予以特别关注的人群（如少数民族、贫困人口、妇女儿童）等。③确定评价内容，即关注项目的公众参与情况，项目是否适应项目区人口的需求，项目与当地文化、社区的互适性等。④构建指标体系，即项目的经济效益指标、社会发展指标、项目对居民生活影响指标、项目对自然环境影响指标等。⑤探索评价模式，即通过每次的评估实践，总结出一套适用于政府发展项目全过程的社会影响评价模式，并不断促进项目社会影响评价的本土化。

对我国政府公共投资项目进行社会影响评价，既是实现我国经济发展方式从出口导向型向内需主导型转变的一个重要举措，也是促进我国经济系统、社会系统与生态环境系统协调发展的必然要求。目前，对政府公共投资项目进行社会影响评价的重要性已经越来越多地引起了人们的关注。但是，总的来说，由于项目社会影响评价理论在我国的发展历程较短，其未来的发展道路仍然面临着诸多不利因素，具体表现在几个方面：①一些地方政府对开展投资项目社会影响评价的重视程度不够。在许多政府投资项目中，决策者更多地关注项目的经济效益，关注如何提高项目的经济价值、减少项目的财务风险，而相对忽略项目的社会价值。一些地方政府在项目的可行性研究中，出于审批的需要，在项目论证中加入社会影响评价的内容，但在项目的准备、实施、监控、运营各个阶段，却很少展开科学严谨的社会影响评价工作。②社会影响评价理论、方法、操作规范体系研究的滞后，影响和制约了项目社会影响评价的发展。我国的项目社会影响评价的理论和方法主要借鉴美国等发达国家的研究成果，尚未形成适合中国国情的本土化评估理论和方法体系。同时，在投资项目的社会调查、社会监测、评估报告编制、社会评估管理等方面也缺乏系统化、规范化的操作标准，因此，常常导致在对项目进行社会影响评价时缺乏统一的理论、方法、规范和标准。③针对社会影响评价的法律制度和规范机制的不健全，使项目社会影响评价的开展缺乏强有力的推动。目前，除少数世界银行、亚洲开发银行贷款项目外，国内还未有对投资项目进行社会评估的强制性法律制度或行业规范，社会评估在大多数项目中居于边缘地位。法律制度和规范的缺失使得投资项目的社会影响评价尚未有硬性实施机制，也使得针对投资项目进行的社会影响评价不被重视。

虽然目前我国的项目社会影响评价领域仍处在起步阶段，面临诸多理论和现实问题，但是社会影响评价在不断发展前进。事实上，近年来社会影响评价方法已逐渐应用于一些大型政府投资项目中，并且取得了不错的效果。从事项目管理和评估的政策制定者和研究者，应积极努力改变社会影响评价在项目评估中较为边缘的地位。以当前我国政府公共投资项目的社会影响评价为契机，努力提高项目的经济价值与社会价值，突出政府项目的"公益性"，增进国民对政府项目的信任与好感，促进项目建设的顺利进行。

资料来源：刘军伟，李华燊．和谐社会背景下政府公共投资项目社会影响评价研究［J］．广西社会科学，2012(1)．

Key Concepts and Skills

1. Principles of estimating cash flows.
2. Distinguish between relevant cash flows in capital budgeting.
3. Three approaches to calculating incremental cash flows.
4. Three special cases in capital budgeting.
5. Concepts and calculation of EAC.

本章重点与难点

1. 现金流量估计的基本原则。
2. 区分资本预算中的相关现金流。
3. 计算增量现金流的三种不同方法。
4. 资本预算中的三种特殊案例。
5. 约当年均成本的概念和计算。

Self-Test Questions

Ⅰ. Single Choice Questions

1. The most basic principle to determine the cash flows associated with an investment project is ( )

A. Only incremental cash flows are project-related cash flows.

B. Only stock cash flows are project-related cash flows.

C. Cash outflows are related cash flows as they result from the adoption of a project.

D. Cash inflows are related cash flows as they result from the adoption of a project.

2. Which of the following should be included in capital budgeting? ( )

A. Research costs for last year

B. R&D costs already invested

C. Interest costs on debt for project financing

D. Tax savings arising from depreciation of fixed assets

3. The formula for calculating the tax shield due to depreciation is ( )

A. Depreciation * tax rate

B. Depreciation * (1 - tax rate)

C. (cash cost + depreciation) * tax rate

D. (cash cost + depreciation) * (1 - tax rate)

4. Which of the following is irrelevant to the decision-making of an investment project? ( )

A. Sunk costs

B. Relevant costs

C. Opportunity cost

D. Replacement costs

5. Which of the following is not included in the cash outflows of an investment project? ( )

A. Fixed-asset investment

B. Depreciation and amortization

C. Intangible-asset investment

D. Incremental operation costs

6. The opportunity costs of building a new parking lot underneath a major shopping mall are ( )

A. Determined by the sum of all parking costs incurred in the future.

B. Determined by maximum value generated for other uses.

C. Determined by the depreciation cost of machinery and equipment used for the construction of the parking lot.

D. Determined by the service cost for parking in a parking lot.

7. In capital budgeting, we focus only on the related after-tax incremental cash flows. Since depreciation is a non-cash cost, the treatment of depreciation in estimating cash flows is ( )

A. To be ignored.

B. To be counted as a cash outflow.

C. To be counted as cash inflows, due to tax shield.

D. To be counted or not.

8. A company is considering whether to go into production with a new product. The cash flows should not be included in the investment decision for this project are ( )

A. Working capital of \$0. 8million required for new product start-up.

B. Occupation of existing equipment that could be leased out for \$2 million.

C. The sale of the new product will reduce the revenue of the company's existing similar product by \$1 million.

D. Market research costs of \$30, 000 for new products incurred in the past year.

Ⅱ. Calculation Questions

1. XYZ is evaluating a new equipment which costs \$160, 000 and an initial fixed expense of \$40, 000. It has a three-year life; the depreciation rate is 40% (year 1), 32% (year 2) and 28% (year 3). The equipment has salvage value of \$20, 000 at the end of the project's life. It also requires an initial investment in net working capital of \$6, 500. The project is estimated to save \$81, 000 in annual costs. The tax rate is 25%. The relevant discount rate 10%.

Questions:

(1) Calculate the project's initial time 0 cash flows, taking into account all side effects.

(2) Calculate the project's year 1-3 incremental cash flows.

(3) What is the project's net present value (NPV)? Should the company make the investment?

2. You are evaluating two different machines (Machine A and Machine Project B) to fit same need. Machine A costs \$261, 000, has a three-year life,

and has pretax operating costs of \$42,000 per year. Machine B costs \$368,000, has a five-year life, and has pretax operating costs of \$45,000 per year. For both machines, use straight-line depreciation to zero over the project's life and assume a salvage value of \$20,000. If your tax rate is 35% and discount rate is 12%, Which machine do you prefer and why?

3. Firm X is evaluating an equipment and has two options:

(1) Option A costs \$60,000 with a 5-year life. The salvage value is 0. The project is expected to generate \$68,000 in annual sales, with cash costs of \$50,000.

(2) Option B costs \$80,000 with a 5-year life. The after-tax salvage value is \$1,000. The project is expected to generate \$80,000 in annual sales. Cash costs are \$54,000 for each year. It requires a maintenance fee of \$1,000 from year 2 and also requires an initial investment in net working capital of \$6,000.

Assume the fixed asset will be depreciated straight-line to zero over its 5-year tax life. The tax rate is 25%. The relevant discount rate 8%.

Questions:

(1) Calculate cashflows of Option A and its NPV.

(2) Calculate cashflows of Option B and its NPV

(3) What is your choice?

4. Firm B is evaluating a new product lasting for 5 years. This project requires an initial investment for purchasing equipment of \$105,000 and net working capital of \$50,000. It is expected to generate \$80,000 in annual sales with \$50,000 in cash costs. For the first 4 years, it also requires an annual maintenance fee of \$2,000. Assume the fixed asset will be depreciated straight-line to 5,000 over its 5-year tax life, and its salvage value is \$10,000. The tax rate is 15%. The relevant discount rate 10%.

Questions:

(1) Calculate the project's net cashflows for each year.

(2) Calculate the project's internal rate of return (IRR).

(3) Make your decision by referring to IRR rule.

5. Firm B has spent \$200,000 for market testing, and now is evaluating a new equipment which costs \$2,000,000. This equipment aims to significantly increase the productivity. To purchase this equipment, firm B needs to spend \$20,000 for shipping and \$35,000 for installation. It will be depreciated straight-line to 0 over its 5-year tax life. It has salvage value of \$20,000 at the end of the project's life. The project is estimated to generate \$1,000,000 in annual

sales, with \$200,000 in annual cash costs. As the estimating sales increase, average inventory is expected to rise by \$200,000, and accounts payable by \$50,000. The tax rate is 15%. The relevant discount rate 12%.

Questions:

(1) Calculate the project's net cashflows for each year.

(2) Calculate the project's NPV, and make the decision.

本章习题答案

Chapter 6 Bond Valuation （债券估值）

Learning Objectives

●Know the bond features and bond types.

●Understand bond values and why they fluctuate, and be able to compute the present value of bonds.

●Understand bond ratings.

●Understand government bonds and corporate bonds.

●Understand the impact of inflation on interest rates.

A bond refers to a long-term debt, which is normally an interest-only loan that the borrower will pay the interest every period, but none of the principal will be repaid until the end of the loan. In this chapter, we should fully understand the concept of bond features, bond markets, bond values and bond ratings. The emphasis is to determine the value of a bond using the discounted cash flow procedure. Then, we discuss the impact of inflation on interest rates and estimate the real and nominal rates of interest, and examine how bond prices vary with interest rates.

6.1 Bond and Bond Market: Basic Concepts

A bond is a legally binding agreement between a borrower and a lender that specifies the following terms:

●Par (face) value

●Coupon rate

●Coupon payment

●Maturity Date

6.1.1 Par (face) Value（面值）

Par value of a bond refers to the stated face value that is set by the issuer. It is unrelated to the market value of the bond. It represents the amount of money repaid on the maturity date. Government bonds frequently have much larger par values.

6.1.2 Coupon Rate（息票率）

The coupon rate is the yield to maturity that the bond pays on its issue date. The yield to maturity is the required market interest rate on the bond. The coupon rate is normally calculated by adding the total amount of coupons paid per year and dividing by the bond's face value.

6.1.3 Coupon Payments（息票支付）

Coupon payment is normally described as a periodic interest payment that is required to be paid for the bondholders. For example, if a bond has a face value of $1,000 and a coupon rate of 10%, then it pays total coupons of $100 per year.

6.1.4 Maturity Date（到期日）

The number of years until the face value is paid is called the bond's time to maturity. A corporate bond normally has a maturity of 30 years, but this varies. The original maturities of most bonds ranging from 10 to 40 years. Once the bond has been issued, the number of years to maturity declines as time passes. For example, company A issued bonds on March 15, 2015, the maturity date is March 15, 2025. Thus, company A's bonds have a 10-year maturity at the time they were issued. Then, in 2016, they have a 9-year maturity, and in 2017, they have a 8-year maturity, and so on.

6.1.5 Bond Market（债券市场）

Bond market can be referred to as the debt market, fixed-income market, or credit market. It is the place where bonds are traded in enormous quantities every day that can be considered as an important part of the multi-level capital market.

Before 2002, there is a lack of transparency in the bond market, most transactions are privately negotiated between parties. Because most bond trading is primarily over the counter (OTC), it has little or no market transparency in many cases. As a result, information of bond price and volume can be quite hard to find for some types. It can be difficult to get the up-to-date individual bond prices, especially for the smaller-sized corporations. Since 2002, newly published regulations require corporate bond dealers to report trade information through trade reporting and compliance engine (TRACE), which has improved the transparency in corporate bond market dramatically.

Chinese Bond Market

In China, the exchange market for bond is part of the two Stock Exchanges located in Shanghai and Shenzhen, which were established since 1990. The regulator of the exchange bond market is the China Securities Regulatory Commission (CSRC) that performs the regulations and rules about the exchange market. The Chinese bond markets are supervised by the People's Bank of China, the China Banking and Insurance Regulatory Commission as well as the China Securities Regulatory Commission.

The equity and bond markets have grown dramatically with the rapid development of Chinese economy in recent years, from an average of approximately 11 percent of the financial system in 1990-1994 to an average of about 32.4 percent in 2022. Now China has become the world's second largest bond market with approximately 142.3 trillion RMB in total amount outstanding by the end of August 2022 (Bank of China, 2022).Recently, China announced to further facilitate foreign institutional investments in the bond market and deepen the opening-up of the interbank and exchange bond markets. Chinese bond market has become a key instrument of serving the real economy and forestalling risks.

6.2 Bond Values and Yields

To determine the value of a bond at a particular point in time, we need to know the number of periods remaining until maturity, the face value, the coupon, and the market interest rate for bonds with similar features. The interest rate required in the market on a bond is called the bond's yield to maturity (YTM). Given all these information, we can calculate the present value of the cash flows as an estimate of the bond's current market value.

6.2.1 Bond Pricing Equation

If a bond has ① a face value of F paid at maturity, ② a coupon of C paid per period, ③ T periods to maturity, ④ a yield of r per period, as the coupon is constant and paid annually, the general expression for the value of a bond is expressed as follows.

$$\text{Bond value} = C \times [1-1/(1+r)^{T}]/r + F/(1+r)^{T} \qquad (6.1)$$

Bond value = Present value of the coupons + Present value of the face amount.

Therefore, bond value is determined by the present value of the coupon payments and the present value of its par value.

【Example 6-1】

Suppose you purchase 100 dollars of bonds in United States in June 2023, and the coupon rate is 5%. If the bond matures in 2029 and the yield to maturity is 3.8%, what is the value of the bond?

Answer this question, you need to calculate the present value of the coupon payments and the present value of the bond's face value.

Bond value = (\$100 * 5%) * [1 − 1/ (1 + 3.8%)^6] /3.8% + \$100/ (1 + 3.8%)^6 = \$106.33

6.2.2 Bond Price and Yields

Yield to maturity is the rate implied by the current bond price. We need to use the method of trial and error to find the yield to maturity if we do not have a financial calculator. It is similar to the process for finding interest rate with an annuity.

Example:

A bond is issued on January 1, 2016. The par value of the bond is \$1,000. Coupon payments are made semiannually and the coupon rate is 6.375%, maturity date is December 2020. If the YTM is 5%, what is the present value of the bond. What if the required yield is 11%? How does this change the bond's price?

As shown in Figure 6.1, we compute and plot bond prices under different discount rates for 6.375% coupon bond. We can see that the bond value is linearly related to bond yield. Bond prices and market interest rates move in opposite directions.

If the YTM is 5%, the present value of the bond can be calculated from the equation below:

$$PV = \frac{\$31.875}{0.05}\left[1-\frac{1}{(1.025)^{10}}\right]+\frac{\$1,000}{(1.025)^{10}} = \$1,060.17$$

If YTM is equal to 6.375%, we get the bond present value is equal to \$1,000.

If the YTM is 11%, we get the present value of the bond is equal to:

$$PV=\frac{\$31.875}{0.11}\left[1-\frac{1}{(1.055)^{10}}\right]+\frac{\$1,000}{(1.055)^{10}}=\$825.69$$

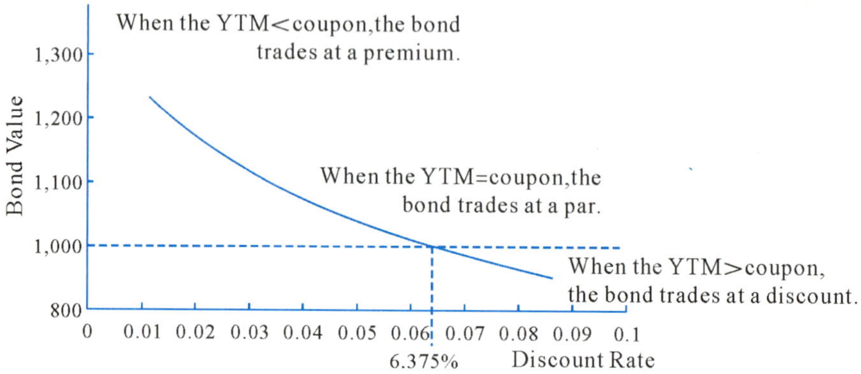

Figure 6-1 Bond price and yield to maturity

According to the results above, we get the following conclusions:

(1) When coupon rate = YTM, price = par value

(2) When coupon rate > YTM, price > par value (premium bond)

(3) When coupon rate < YTM, price < par value (discount bond)

6.3 Bond Types

6.3.1 Zero Coupon Bonds (零息债券)

Zero coupon bonds refer to the bonds that pay no coupons at all and must be offered at a price much lower than their face value. The coupon rate of zero coupon bonds is equal to zero, there are no coupon payments before the maturity date. Treasury Bills and principal-only Treasury strips are examples of zero coupon bonds.

【Example 6-2】

Company A issues a \$1,000 face value, eight-year zero coupon bond. What is the yield to maturity on the bond if the bond is offered at \$627? Assume annual compounding. The yield to maturity, y, can be calculated from the equation:

$$\frac{\$1,000}{(1+y)^{8}}=\$627$$

Solving the equation, we find that y equals 6 percent. Thus, the yield to maturity is 6 percent.

6.3.2 Pure Discount Bonds (纯贴现债券)

Pure discount bonds means that the bonds have "pure" interest rates because they contain no risk of default and pay no coupons, only a single sum of payment at the maturity date is involved. The main difference between zero coupon bonds and pure discount bonds is the length of time to maturity. There is no strict distinction between the concepts of zero coupon bonds and pure discount bonds because the difference between the two is relatively small.

【Example 6-3】

What is the value of a 15-year zero coupon bond with a \$1,000 par value and a YTM of 12% that paid semiannually? The bond value can be calculated from the equation below:

$$\text{PV}=\frac{F}{(1+r)^{T}}=\frac{\$1,000}{(1.06)^{30}}=\$174.11$$

Thus, we get the bond value is \$174.11.

6.3.3 Government Bonds (政府债券)

Governments bonds refer to the bonds issued by the government to raise capital to fund infrastructural improvements or pay debts. Government bonds are quite attractive to conservative investors because they are considered to have no risk of default. In the United States, government issues Treasury-Bills (T-bills), Treasury notes (T-notes) and Treasury bonds (T-bonds) in electronic form to the public to borrow money. T-bills are pure discount bonds with original maturity less than one year; T-notes are coupon debt with original maturity between one and ten years; T-bonds are coupon debt with original maturity greater than ten years. Treasuries are issued on the primary market and can be traded on the secondary market. Investors can buy or sell existing debt through a broker or a third party.

State and local governments in the US also issue bonds to raise capital, such issues are called municipal bonds. In comparison with Treasury bonds, municipal bonds have varying degree of default risk, and the yields on municipal bonds are generally much lower than the yields on Treasury bonds because municipal bonds' coupons are exempt from federal income taxes.

In China, Treasury bonds are issued by the Ministry of Finance, including two types of Treasury bonds which are book-entry Treasury bonds and certificate Treasury bonds. Book-entry Treasury bonds can be traded freely in the markets, while certificate Treasury bonds cannot be traded or transferred and hence can be only used as a saving vehicle. The liquidity of certificate Treasury bonds is restricted for the purpose of protecting investors' interests and preventing market risk. In contrast, the U.S. Treasury bonds are freely traded in the markets with higher flexibility and liquidity. Such differences reflect the different characteristics of the two countries' financial markets such as variations in investor base, market depth, market liquidity, macroeconomic conditions, etc.

6.3.4 Corporate Bonds (公司债券)

Corporate bonds are issued by the corporations to finance for their operations and development. As corporate bonds have greater default risk relative to government bonds. They cannot borrow at the same low interest rates as governments. The interest rates on government bonds can be regarded as benchmarks for all interest rates. Furthermore, corporate bonds offer greater varieties than government bonds. For instance, some corporate bonds are convertible, which means that if you buy a convertible bond, you can choose to exchange it for a specified number of common stock shares. If you would like to know more about convertible bonds, please read the further reading material 6—Convertible bonds: the case of Wanke.

延伸阅读 6-1 《可转换债券融资—以万科为例》

可转换债券(convertible bond)是一种可以在特定时间、按特定条件转换为普通股票的特殊企业债券,又简称可转债。可转换债券兼具债权和股权的双重特性。1996 年中国政府决定选择有条件的公司进行可转换债券的试点,1997 年颁布了《可转换公司债券管理暂行办法》,2001 年 4 月中国证监会发布了《上市公司发行可转换公司债券实施办法》,极大地规范、促进了可转换债券的发展。近年来,使用可转换债券进行融资的企业数量迅速增加,可转换债券已成为当前我国资本市场上的一种重要融资方式。

公司发行可转换债券的主要原因是增强证券对投资者的吸引力,能以较低的成本筹集到所需要的资金。接下来我们以万科公司发行可转换债券为例,对其进行分析。万科的现金流曾出现 7.25 亿元的负值,为了弥补资金缺口,万科董事会通过了发行可转换债券的决议。万科公司于 2002 年 6 月 13 日向社会公开发行 1 500 万张可转换公司债券(简称"万科转债"),每张面值人民币 100 元,发行总额 15 亿元,期限 5 年,票面利率 1.5%。原万科 A 股股东按照每股配售 2.94 元的比例可优先配售 150 000 万元。原 A 股股东有效申购数量为 444 748 000 元,占此次发行总量的 29.65%,全部获得优先配售。

万科转债网上发行量 519 908 手，合计 519 908 000 元，占此次发行数量的 34.66%。网上有效申购数量为 1 361 283 000 元，中签率为 38.192%。网下发行数量为 535 344 手，合计 535 344 000 元，占此次发行数量的 35.69%。网下申购合计 140 750 000 元，获售比例为 38.191%。

万科公司利用万科转债募集资金进行投资，在 2002 年末万科公司已完成的初始项目投资金额占承诺投资金额的 84%，已结算部分的投资收益与预测的投资收益率相差不大，表明万科转债募集资金的使用情况呈现良好态势。万科可转换债券发行降低了资产负债率，全部债券转股权后，资产负债率明显下降，可转债的发行规模 15 亿元，充分考虑了债券发行对公司偿债能力的影响，以及未来转股后股本扩张对公司业绩摊薄的压力等综合因素，使万科筹集了巨额资金，充分利用财务杠杆减缓了财务压力，带来了较好的理财收益。

资料来源：吴维海.企业融资 170 种模式及操作案例[M].中国金融出版社，2014.

6.3.5 Bond Ratings（债券评级）

Unlike Treasury bonds, corporate bonds have varying degree of default risk. Thus, a company needs to carry a rating from a credit rating agency before issuing bonds, and the bonds are rated based on their default risk. Bond rating indicates a company's capacity to pay interest and principal; in other words, it represents the likelihood of default.

In China, corporate bonds broadly cover all fixed-income securities issued by non-financial firms. The issuance of corporate bonds has been regulated by National Development and Reform Commission (NDRC). The Chinese credit rating agencies (CRAs) are a direct product of Chinese regulators' mandate (Livingston et al., 2018)[1]. Table 6-1 lists the major Chinese credit rating agencies. There are eight major CRAs in China including three global-partnered CRAs and five domestic CRAs.

[1] Livingston, M. P., Winnie, P. H. and Zhou, L. (2018). Are Chinese Credit Ratings Relevant? A Study of the Chinese Bond Market and Credit Rating Industry. Journal of Banking and Finance, Vol. 87, pp: 216-232.

Table 6-1 List of major Chinese credit rating agencies (CRAs)

	Company Name	Global Partner	Website
Global-partnered CRAs	Chengxin _ Moody (CCXI) China	Moody's	www.ccxi.com.cn
	Lianhe Credit Rating Co., Ltd.	Fitch	www.lhratings.com
	Shanghai Brilliance Credit Rating &Investors Service Co., Ltd.	S&P	www.shxsj.com
Domestic CRAs	Chengxin Credit Rating Group (CCXR)	None	www.ccxr.com.cn
	Dagong Global Credit Rating Co., Ltd	None	www.dagongcredit.com
	Dongfang Jincheng Credit Rating Co., Ltd	None	www.dfratings.com
	Lianhe Credit Rating Co., Ltd.	None	www. lianhecreditrating. com.cn
	CSCI Pengyuan Credit Rating Co., Ltd.	None	www.pyrating.cn

Sources: www.chinabond.com.cn; CSRC

The CRAs will give a credit rating of the company based on its asset value, profitability, reputation, loan repayment capacity and growth characteristics, etc. Table 6-2 shows the main scale used by the credit rating agencies in China. The highest bond rating a company can have is AAA. Such corporate bond is considered to be the best quality and to have the lowest degree of risk. The bond ratings classes of investment grade signify high-quality with relatively low risk of default, are considered to be worth investing in. Debt rated below BB+ while above CC is more likely a speculative or junk bond. Even though such bond might have some quality, it is regarded as predominantly speculative with large uncertainties and higher risks. The rating classes of C and D are typically in default; debt rated in these categories are considered to have little capacity to pay interest and principal.

Table 6-2 Agency rating scales

Category	Scale
Investment grade	AAA, AA+, AA, AA-, A+, A, A-, BBB+, BBB, BBB
Speculative or "junk"	BB+, BB, BB-, B+, B, B-, CCC+, CCC, CCC-, CC
Nonperforming	C, D

Sources: www.chinabond.com.cn

案例分析 6-2 《永煤控股债券违约风波》

一、案例正文

（一）永煤债券违约事件

2020 年 11 月 10 日，中国河南永煤控股（以下简称“永煤控股”）一纸无法按期兑付本息的公告，将国企债券违约的话题推向了风口浪尖。永煤控股公告称，因流动资金紧张，其发行的 10 亿元人民币 270 天期的超短融“20 永煤 SCP003”不能按期足额偿付本息，同时，该公司作为发行人的 20 笔债券触发了交叉违约。

作为一家拥有“AAA”主体信用评级的国有企业，永煤控股毫无征兆地打破了投资者对高信用评级国有企业债券刚性兑付的信仰，整个市场对信用债的恐慌情绪迅速扩散。这次违约事件也使得信用债的一级、二级，基金以及利率债市场受到了不同程度的影响。首先在一级市场方面，自事情发生起的 10 天之内，就有超过 50 只计划公开发行的债券取消或者推迟发行。主要受影响的企业为地方性国有企业，原因是“近期市场波动大，为了降低发行风险”，整体受影响的债券发行规模超过了 390 亿元[1]。二级市场上，具有相似企业背景的多只河南煤炭企业主体发行债券的价格持续暴跌。债券基金市场也遭受了冲击。自永煤控股违约以来至 11 月 19 日，华泰证券资管、博时基金、融通基金、金信基金等多家基金公司旗下债券基金跌幅超过 6%[2]。信用债市场“地震波”也传导至利率债市场，利率持续上行，截至 11 月 19 日，10 年期国债收益率已经上行到 3.34%，突破了 3.3%这一关键点位。

（二）债券市场受冲击，投资逻辑重塑

一直以来投资者都对国有资产拥有“大而不倒”的信心，认为国有企业有国有资产兜底，不论其经营状况如何，其信用都是被国家担保的。所以当投资者看到发债企业的国有企业标签时，大多会毫不犹疑地相信其偿付能力。不仅仅是投资者，评级机构也会对国有企业另眼相待，在评级时增加企业预期获得外部支持的可能性。原本企业根据自身水平获得的评级是 AA，而如果该企业拥有国有企业背景，评级机构可能会将该评级提高至 AA+，甚至 AAA。

“近期的债券市场的风风雨雨还在发酵当中，沸沸扬扬，没过去。表现突出的，更多的是对所谓国企信仰的惊诧。”[3]在这场风波中，我们也看到政府的角色正在发生转变。此次永煤控股违约事件，河南省国资委并没有直接出

---

[1] 永煤违约链式反应：殃及国企债城池，逃废债恐慌蔓延，监管重拳打向金融机构，经济观察报，2020-11-20。

[2] WIND 资讯。

[3] 中国人民大学财政金融学院教授、博士生导师、信用管理研究中心执行主任关伟。

手救助，而是希望永煤控股通过市场化方式化解债务。这为信用债市场传递了市场化违约正在到来的信号，并预示了投资逻辑正在经历转变。在市场化环境下，投资者自身应当增强对风险的识别和判断意识，在投资前应当对宏观形势、产业状况、企业经营状况及前景等有深入的了解，不应当以国有企业标签作为企业信用的"背书"[1]。对于债券的发行企业来说，在更加市场化的环境下，它们应当注重自身风险的控制以及竞争能力的提升，如此才能获取投资者的信任，以低成本进行融资，这才是发展的良性循环。

（三）多家金融中介机构被查

知名信用评级机构以及各大券商、银行在内的多家金融中介机构是这次事件的另一个风暴中心。信用评级机构是金融市场中一个特殊的中介服务机构，旨在为投资者提示信用风险，提供决策参考；而券商、银行作为债券的承销商，应做好"看门人"的工作，履行尽职调查的义务并承担核查把关责任。如果金融中介发生违规行为，市场环境的公平性、公正性、有效性就得不到保障。

我国采用的是国际通用的"四等十级制"评级标准来评价企业的信用等级[2]，具体的等级符号及含义见表1。在本次事件发生前，永煤控股拥有我国最高一类的信用评级——"AAA"级。"AAA"级的企业意味着其信用程度高、债务风险小，拥有优秀的信用记录和经营状况，盈利能力强，发展前景广阔，且不确定性因素对其经营与发展的影响极小。而在债券违约发生后，评级机构中诚信国际迅速将永煤控股的主体信用评级直降四档至BB级，即信用欠佳，偿还能力不足。这样前后差异巨大的评级结果，以及错误的信用评级引发的后果，让公众对评级机构的专业性产生质疑。

表1　企业信用等级符号及其含义

企业信用等级符号	含义
AAA级	信用极好。企业的信用程度高、债务风险小。该类企业具有优秀的信用记录，经营状况佳，盈利能力强，发展前景广阔，不确定性因素对其经营与发展的影响极小。
AA级	信用优良。企业的信用程度较高，债务风险较小。该类企业具有优良的信用记录，经营状况较佳，盈利水平较高，发展前景较为广阔，不确定性因素对其经营与发展的影响很小。

[1] 银行、保险、学者、评级机构齐论信用债违约：不能简单依靠财政信仰，每日经济新闻，2020-11-19。

[2] 信用中国，https://www.creditchina.gov.cn/home/xinyongyanjiu/201807/t20180720_121177.html。

表1(续)

企业信用等级符号	含义
A 级	信用较好。企业的信用程度良好,在正常情况下偿还债务没有问题。该类企业具有良好的信用记录,经营处于良性循环状态,但是可能存在一些影响其未来经营与发展的不确定因素,进而削弱其盈利能力和偿债能力。
BBB 级	信用一般。企业的信用程度一般,偿还债务的能力一般。该类企业的信用记录正常,但其经营状况、盈利水平及未来发展易受不确定因素的影响,偿债能力不稳定。
BB 级	信用欠佳。企业信用程度较差,偿债能力不足。该类企业有较多不良信用记录,未来前景不明朗,含有投机性因素。
B 级	信用较差。企业的信用程度差,偿债能力较弱。
CCC 级	信用很差。企业信用很差,几乎没有偿债能力。
CC 级	信用极差。企业信用极差,没有偿债能力。
C 级	没有信用。企业无信用。
D 级	没有信用。企业已濒临破产。

来源:信用中国。

此外,承销商在本次事件中也有着不可推卸的责任。据报道,“20 永煤 SCP003”违约三周前,永煤控股发行了一只 10 亿元的中期票据“20 永煤 MTN006”,海通证券就是“20 永煤 MTN006”的承销商团成员之一。承销商为何没有承担其应有的责任,在永煤债爆雷前还为其发行新债,其中必然少不了违规的操作。11 月 18 日,银行间市场交易商协会(以下简称“交易商协会”)发布通告称,近日,协会对永煤控股开展了自律调查,调查获取的线索及相关市场交易信息证明,海通证券及其相关子公司涉嫌为发行人违规发行债券提供帮助,并涉嫌操纵市场。11 月 19 日,交易商协会再次对相关中介机构启动自律调查。其表示,在对永煤控股开展自律调查和对多家中介机构进行约谈过程中,发现兴业银行股份有限公司、中国光大银行股份有限公司和中原银行股份有限公司等主承销商,以及中诚信国际信用评级有限责任公司、希格玛会计师事务所(特殊普通合伙)均存在涉嫌违反银行间债券市场自律管理规则的行为。

(四)监管措施出台

11 月 21 日,在永煤债违约发生仅仅 10 天后,国务院金融稳定发展委员会主任刘鹤就针对规范债券市场发展、维护债券市场稳定召开了会议[1],足见党中央对此次事件的重视。会议主要从监管的角度出发,为债券市场的健

[1] 中国政府网 2020 年 11 月 22 日发表的《刘鹤主持召开国务院金融稳定发展委员会第四十三次会议》。

康发展提出了五点要求：一是要求金融监管部门和地方政府切实履行监督市场的责任；二是秉持“零容忍”态度，严肃查处危害投资者合法权益的行为，维护市场公平和秩序；三是要求发债企业及各类中介机构加强自律和监督，强化市场约束机制；四是要求建立健全风险预防、发现、预警、处置机制，确保不发生系统性金融风险；五是要求债券逐步完善市场化改革。

除了官方出台的监管措施，中国银行间市场交易商协会也对可能引发此次风波的导火索——中介机构“结构化”发债及违规承销，进行了调查。所谓“结构化”发债，是指私募机构、承销商通过发行人自购、分级资管产品等设计，实现债权发行的方式，其本质是债券募资自融。11 月 18 日，交易商协会发布《关于进一步加强债务融资工具发行业务规范有关事项的通知》（以下简称《通知》）[1]，严禁发行人自融，即发行人不得直接认购，或者实际由发行人出资，但通过关联机构、资管产品等方式间接认购自己发行的债务融资工具，认购资产支持票据及其他符合法律法规、自律规则规定的情况除外。“结构化”发债动力来源于交易双方的互利，首先，对于资管产品的管理人而言，此种交易模式有助于其管理规模的扩大，也有助于增加管理费和业绩提成收入。对于债券发行人而言，一方面可以保证债券募满，增加表观发行量，不浪费批文额度；另一方面也降低了发行人的表观票面利率。事实上，表观发行量的增加以及表观票面利率的降低有利于引导市场恢复对该发行人（甚至是该类发行人）的信心。但是，“结构化”发行存在潜在风险，例如，交易结构可能会干扰资金供给方的判断，使其低估该交易内含的风险。早在 2019 年 12 月 13 日，上海证券交易所和深圳证券交易所同期发布了《关于规范公司债券发行有关事项的通知》，对公司债券发行进行规范，指出发行人不得在发行环节直接或者间接认购自己发行的债券，禁止“结构化”发行债券。此次交易商协会发布《通知》进一步增强了监管的力度，在一定程度上对债务违约风险的管控起到了作用。

二、案例讨论

1. 本案例中，信用评级机构体现出哪些问题，背后原因是什么？

2. 结合案例，思考打破刚性兑付对中国未来金融市场发展的影响。

3. 结合案例，分析高评级国企信用债违约的责任划分与承担（地方政府、发债主体、承销机构、评级公司等）并提出防范后续风险的政策建议。

---

[1] 中国银行间市场交易协会 http://www.nafmii.org.cn/。

6.4 Inflation and Interest Rates

6.4.1 Real and Nominal Rates of Interest（实际和名义收益率）

Suppose the one-year interest rate is 15.5 percent, so that anyone depositing \$100 in a bank today will end up with \$115.50 next year. Further imagine a burger's price is \$5 today, implying that \$100 can buy 20 burgers. Finally, assume that the inflation rate is 5 percent, leading to the price of burger being \$5.25 next year. How many burgers can you buy next year if you deposit \$100 today? Clearly, you can buy \$115.50/\$5.25 = 22 burgers. This is up from 20 burgers, implying a 10 percent increase in purchasing power. Economists say that, while the nominal rate of interest is 15.5 percent, the real rate of interest is only 10 percent.

The difference between nominal and real rates is important and bears repeating: The nominal rate on an investment is the percentage change in the number of dollars you have. The real rate on an investment is the percentage change in how much you can buy with your dollars. In other words, the real rate is the percentage change in your buying power.

We can generalize the relation between nominal rates, real rates, and inflation as:

$$1 + R = (1 + r) \times (1 + h) \tag{6.2}$$

where R is the nominal rate, r is the real rate, and h is the inflation rate. In the preceding example, the nominal rate was 15.50 percent and the inflation rate was 5 percent. What was the real rate? We can determine it by plugging in these numbers:

$$1 + 0.155 = (1 + r) \times (1 + 0.05)$$
$$1 + r = (1.550/1.05) = 1.10$$
$$r = 10\%$$

This real rate is the same as we had before. We can rearrange things a little as follows:

$$1 + R = (1 + r) \times (1 + h)$$
$$R = r + h + r \times h \tag{6.3}$$

What this tells us is that the nominal rate has three components. First, there is the real rate on the investment, r. Next, there is the compensation for the decrease in the value of the money originally invested because of inflation, h. The third component represents compensation for the fact that the dollars earned on the investment are also worth less because of inflation.

This third component is usually small, so it is often dropped. The nominal rate is then approximately equal to the real rate plus the inflation rate:

$$R \approx r + h \tag{6.4}$$

It is important to note that financial rates, such as interest rates, discount rates, and rates of return, are almost always quoted in nominal terms. To remind you of this, we will henceforth use the symbol R instead of r in most of our discussions about such rates.

6.4.2 The Fisher Effect（费雪效应）

If the nominal interest rate is 2 percent and the inflation rate is 5 percent, a bank deposit of \$100 today will still turn into \$102 at the end of the year. However, because of inflation, a sandwich priced at \$1 today will cost \$1.05 next year, the \$102 will only buy about 97 (=102/1.05) sandwiches next year. Since the initial \$100 allows one to buy 100 sandwiches today, there is a reduction in purchasing power.

Irving Fisher conjectured many decades ago that the nominal interest rate should rise just enough to keep the real interest rate constant. That is, the real rate should stay at 2 percent in our example. We can use Equation 6.4 to determine that the new nominal rate will be (approximately):

$$2\% + 5\% \cong 7.0\%$$

Fisher's thinking is that investors are not foolish. They know that inflation reduces purchasing power, therefore they will demand an increase in the nominal rate before lending money. Fisher's hypothesis, typically called the Fisher effect, can be stated as:

A rise in the rate of inflation causes the nominal rate to rise just enough so that the real rate of interest is unaffected. In other words, the real rate is invariant to the rate of inflation.

While Fisher's reasoning makes sense, it's important to point out that the claim that the nominal rate will rise to 7.0 percent is only a hypothesis. It may be true and it may be false in any real-world situation. For example, if investors are foolish after all, the nominal rate could stay at 2 percent, even in the presence of inflation. Alternatively, even if investors understand the impact of inflation, the nominal rate may not rise all the way to 7.0 percent. That is, there may be some unknown force preventing a full rise.

6.4.3 Real versus Nominal Rates

The formula for converting nominal cash flows in a future period t to real cash flows today is

$$\text{Real cash flow at date } t = \frac{\text{Nominal cash flow at date } t}{(1+\text{inflation rate})^t} \qquad (6.5)$$

For example, suppose you invest in a 20-year Treasury strip, but inflation over the 20 years averages 6% per year. The strip pays \$1,000 in year 20, but the real value of that payoff is only 1,000/1.06 20 = \$311.80. In this example, the purchasing power of \$1 today declines to just over \$0.31 after 20 years.

The journey from nominal to real interest rates is similar. When a bond dealer says that your bond yields 10%, she is quoting a nominal interest rate. That rate tells you how rapidly your money will grow over one year, as shown in the table below:

Invest Current Dollars	Receive Dollars in Year 1	Result
\$1,000→	\$1,100	10% nominal rate of return

However, with an expected inflation rate of 6%, you are only 3.774% better off at the end of the year than at the start:

Invest Current Dollars	Expected Real Value of Dollars in Year 1	Result
\$1,000→	\$1,037.74 (=1,100/1.06)	3.774% expected real rate of return

Thus, we could say, "The bond offers a 10% nominal rate of return," or "It offers a 3.774% expected real rate of return."

The formula for calculating the real rate of return is:

$$1+r_{\text{real}} = (1+r_{\text{nominal}})/(1+\text{inflation rate}) \qquad (6.6)$$

In our example, $1 + r_{real} = 1.10/1.06 = 1.037,74$.

Key Concepts and Skills

1. Important features of bond.
2. Concepts of bond market.
3. Composition of bond values and the reasons for their fluctuation.

4. Calculation of bond present value.
5. Government and corporate bonds.
6. Bond ratings.
7. The impact of inflation on interest rates.

本章重点与难点

1. 债券的重要特点。
2. 了解债券市场。
3. 债券价值的构成及债券价值波动的原因。
4. 如何计算债券的现值。
5. 了解政府债券和公司债券。
6. 了解债券评级。
7. 通货膨胀对利率的影响。

Self-Test Questions

Ⅰ. Multiple Choice Questions

1. A bond is a legally binding agreement between a borrower and a lender that specifies which of the following terms? (　　)

A. Par value

B. Coupon rate

C. Coupon payment

D. Maturity Date

2. Which of the following statements about the Fisher Effect is true? (　　)

A. It assumed that investors are foolish.

B. It is proposed by Irving Fisher.

C. A rise in the rate of inflation causes the nominal rate to rise just enough so that the real rate of interest is unaffected.

D. The real rate is invariant to the rate of inflation.

3. Which of the following statements about bond value is true? (　　)

A. Bond value is determined by the present value of the coupon payments and par value.

B. It is an estimate of the bond's current market value.

C. The interest rate required in the market on a bond is called the bond's yield to maturity.

D. It is determined by the face value only.

Ⅱ. True (T) or False (F) Questions

1. Zero coupon bond refers to a bond that pays no coupons at all must be offered at a price much lower than its face value. ( )

2. Face value of a bond is unrelated to the market value of the bond. ( )

3. Government bonds frequently have much smaller par values. ( )

4. The yield to maturity is the required market interest rate on the bond. ( )

5. The real rate on an investment is the percentage change in your buying power. ( )

6. The debt ratings refer to an assessment of the creditworthiness of the corporate issuer. ( )

Ⅲ. Calculation Questions

1. A 10-year government bond has a face of £ 100 and an annual coupon rate of 5%. Assume that the interest rate is equal to 6% per year.

(1) What is the bond's PV

(2) If the interest is paid semi-annually, what is the PV?

2. A 10-year treasury bond with a value of $ 10,000 pays a coupon of 5.5% (2.75%) of face value every six months). The semi-annually compounded interest rate is 5.2% (a six-month discount rate of 5.2/2 = 2.6%).

(1) What is the present value of the bond?

(2) Generate a graph or table showing how the bond's present value changes for semi-annually compounded interest rates between 1% and 15%

3. There is a zero-coupon bond with a par value of $ 10,000 and 17 years to maturity. If the yield to maturity on this bond is 4.9 percent, what is the dollar price of the bond? Assume semiannual compounding periods.

4. If the nominal rate of an investment is 12 percent over the coming year, the real return on this investment will be 8percent. What does the inflation rate will be over the next year?

本章习题答案

Chapter 7 Stock Valuation（股票估值）

Learning Objectives

● Understand the concepts of stock and stock market.

● Understand how stock prices depend on future dividends and dividend growth.

● Learn to compute stock price using the dividend growth model.

In this chapter, we concentrate on the other major source of external financing for corporations, common stock. We first introduce the basic concepts of stock and stock markets. We then describe the cash flows associated with common stock and talk about the dividend growth model and the discounted cash flow approach. This chapter has covered the basics of stock and stock valuation.

7.1 Stock and Stock Market: Basic Concepts

The stock market includes the primary market and the secondary market. The primary market, also known as the issuance market, is the market that firms sell new securities to the public for the first time. An initial public offering (IPO) is an example of a primary market. The secondary market is where investors buy and sell securities that have been issued. For example, the Shanghai Stock Exchange and Shenzhen Stock Exchange, the New York Stock Exchange, the Nasdaq are the secondary markets.

A stock can be valued by discounting its dividends. Dividend refers to the distribution of a company's earnings to its shareholders, either in cash or in stock. The dividend yield is the dividend per share and is expressed as a percentage of a company's share price. Dividends payments are determined by the company's board of directors, they can choose to issue dividends over various time frames and with different payout rates. Dividends can be distributed at a scheduled frequency, such as monthly, quarterly, or annually.

7.2 Valuation of Stocks

We have mentioned in the previous chapters, the value of an asset is determined by the present value of its future cash flows. Thus, to determine the value of a share of stock, we need to identify all expected future cash flows of it. As stock ownership produces cash flows from dividends and capital gains, the dividend discount model (DDM) is expressed as follows:

$$P_0 = \frac{\text{Div}_1}{(1+r)^1} + \frac{\text{Div}_2}{(1+r)^2} + \cdots + \frac{\text{Div}_t}{(1+r)^t}$$

where Div_t is the dividend on the stock at the end of year t . P_0 is the present value of the common stock. r is the required rate of return, refers to the appropriate discount rate for the stock.

7.2.1 One-Year Holding Period

$$P_0 = \frac{\text{dividend to received}}{1+r} + \frac{\text{year end price}}{1+r}$$

【Example 7-1】

An investor bought a stock and hold it for one year that paid a \$1.05 dividend at the end of the first year. The stock will sell for \$12.80 at year end. And the required rate of return on equity is 13.2%. Calculate the value of the stock.

Answer:

The investor has a one-year holding period. We can compute the present value of the expected future cash flows as follows:

$$P_0 = \frac{\$1.05 + \$12.80}{1 + 13.2\%} = \$12.23$$

Therefore, the value of the stock is \$12.23.

7.2.2 Valuation of Different Types of Stocks

For the valuation of different types of stocks, there are three types of situations: 1) the case of zero growth of dividends; 2) the case of constant growth dividends; 3) the case of differential growth. We then introduce the three cases step by step in the following paragraphs.

1. Zero Growth(零增长)

It is assumed that $Div_1 = Div_2 = \cdots = Div$. Dividends are expected to be constant which means that the growth rate of dividends is zero. The price of the stock is expressed as:

$$P_0 = \frac{Div_1}{1+r} + \frac{Div_2}{(1+r)^2} + \cdots = \frac{Div}{r}$$

This formula is useful in valuing preferred stocks where the dividends paid out are constant.

【Example 7-2】

A company's bonds are currently yielding 8.5%, and its preferred shares are selling to yield 50 basis points (0.5%) below the firm's bond yield. Calculated the value of the company's 5%, \$100 par value preferred stock.

Answer:

Determine the discount rate: $r = 8.5\% - 0.5\% = 8.0\%$

$Div = 5\% \times \$100 = \$5$

Value the preferred stock:

$$P_0 = \frac{Div}{r} = \frac{\$5}{0.08} = \$62.5$$

2. Constant Growth(固定增长)

Assume that the growth rate in dividends from year to year is constant. If Div is the dividend at the end of the first period, next period's dividend is equal to Div $(1+g)$, the third year's dividend is Div $(1+g)^2$, and so on, where g is a constant growth rate. The extended equation using this assumption is as follows:

$$P_0 = \frac{Div}{1+r} + \frac{Div(1+g)}{(1+r)^1} + \frac{Div(1+g)^2}{(1+r)^2} + \ldots + \frac{Div(1+g)^t}{(1+r)^t}$$

This equation simplifies to:

$$P_0 = \frac{Div}{r-g}$$

This is the formula for the present value of a growing perpetuity.

【Example 7-3】

Calculate the value of a stock that paid a \$2 dividend at the end of the first year, if dividends are expected to grow at 5% forever. The required rate of return is 12%.

Answer:

$$\text{The stock's value} = \frac{\text{Div}}{r-g} = \frac{\$2}{0.12-0.05} = \$30$$

3. Differential Growth(不同增长)

It is assumed that dividends will grow at different rates in the foreseeable future and then will grow at a constant rate thereafter. To value a differential growth stock, we need to:①estimate future dividends in the foreseeable future;②estimate the future stock price when the stock becomes a constant growth stock;③compute the total present value of the estimated future dividends and future stock price at the appropriate discount rate.

4. The Determines of Stock Prices

The discounted-cash-flow (DCF) formula for the present value of a stock is just the same as it is for the present value of any other asset. We just discount the cash flows by the return that can be earned in the capital market on securities of comparable risk. Shareholders receive cash from the company in the form of a stream of dividends. So

$$\text{PV(stock)} = \text{PV(expected future dividends)}$$

7.3 Estimating the Cost of Equity Capital

Suppose we forecast a constant growth rate for a company's dividends, which does not preclude year-to-year deviations from the trend, only that *expected* dividends grow at a constant rate. We divide the first year's cash payment by the difference between the discount rate and the growth rate to find its present value:

$$P_0 = \frac{\text{DIV}_1}{r-g}$$

This formula can be used only when g, the growth rate, is less than r, the discount rate. Obviously, r must be greater than g if growth is perpetual.

The growing perpetuity formula explains P_0 in terms of next year's expected dividend DIV_1, the projected growth trend g, and the expected rate of return on other securities of comparable risk r. Alternatively, the formula can be turned around to obtain an estimate of r from DIV_1, P_0, and g:

$$r = \frac{\text{DIV}_1}{P_0} + g$$

The expected return equals the **dividend yield** (DIV_1/P_0, **股利收益率**)

plus the expected rate of growth in dividends（g）.

案例分析 7-1 《海尔的股权分置改革对股权融资的影响分析》

一、股权分置改革背景介绍

股权分置，是指A股市场的上市公司的股份分为流通股与非流通股。股东所持向社会公开发行的股份，且能在证券交易所上市交易的，称为流通股；而公开发行前股份暂不上市交易的，称为非流通股。这种同一上市公司股份分为流通股和非流通股的股权分置状况，为证券市场所独有。2005年4月，经国务院批准，中国证监会发布《关于上市公司股权分置改革试点有关问题的通知》，启动了股权分置改革的试点工作。2005年8月，中国证监会、国务院国资委、财政部、中国人民银行、商务部联合发布《关于上市公司股权分置改革的指导意见》；9月4日，中国证监会发布《上市公司股权分置改革管理办法》，我国的股权分置改革进入全面展开阶段。股权分置改革是为了解决A股市场相关股东之间的利益平衡问题而采取的举措。这一改革在中国改革开放进程中具有重要的意义和作用。

二、青岛海尔的股权分置改革情况

以青岛海尔为例，股改前由于股权分割导致流通股和非流通股的获利机制不同，通过股权融资获取超额收益和套取现金成了非流通大股东的重要获利方式，因此上市公司的再融资决策基本是随股权融资政策的变化而变化的，债务融资和内源融资成了股权融资的附属和补充。股改后，大股东和中小股东利益趋同，以前的股权融资超额收益也在逐步消失，大股东利益格局的变化以及证券市场的规范化逐步促使上市企业的融资决策理性化和多样化。

1. 青岛海尔(600690)公司背景简介

青岛海尔股份有限公司的前身是成立于1984年的青岛电冰箱总厂，1989年3月24日在对其改组的基础上，以定向募集资金1.5亿元人民币的方式设立股份有限公司。1993年3月和9月由定向募集公司转为社会募集公司，并增发社会公众股5 000万股，于1993年11月在上交所上市交易。公司名称是青岛海尔电冰箱股份有限公司，简称青岛海尔(600690)。主营业务为电冰箱和冰柜。2001年1月21日，青岛海尔用公募和自筹资金共计2亿元人民币收购青岛海尔空调器有限总公司74.45%股权，收购后拥有该公司99.9%的股权。至此青岛海尔拥有电冰箱和空调两大主营业务，于2001年5月31日公司名称变更为青岛海尔股份有限公司，简称仍为青岛海尔(600690)。2006年5月17日，青岛海尔完成股权分置改革，表1为其控股股东持股变化情况。

表 1　青岛海尔控股股东持股变化

控股股东	1993-11-19	1997-6-30	1997-12-26	1999-9-15	1999-12-31	2001-1-12	2001-9-30	2006-6-13	2007-5-22
海尔集团	61. 75%	54. 74%	35. 08%	31. 44%	31. 44%	26. 71%	12%	10. 54%	20. 03%
青岛海尔洗衣机	-	-	20. 01%	17. 93%	-	-	-	-	-
青岛海尔电器国际	-	-	-	-	17. 93%	15. 24%	29. 95%	26. 3%	23. 51%

注：青岛海尔洗衣机的股权结构是：海尔集团公司占 93. 09%，青岛海尔经济咨询公司占 6. 67%，内部职工股占 0. 24%；青岛海尔电器国际股份有限公司成立于 1996 年 12 月 23 日，海尔集团持股 88. 17%，2001 年 9 月变更后海尔集团持有电器国际股权 93. 44%。

资料来源：青岛海尔的公司公告。

2. 青岛海尔的股权融资历史

青岛海尔是我国家电行业的标杆，历年来的优良业绩使海尔获得了尽可能多的股权融资机会。从 1996 年到 2001 年，青岛海尔的股权融资频率非常高，几乎每年都有股权融资，而且金额巨大。特别是 2001 年，在净资产仅为 28. 9 亿元的情况下，海尔通过一次增发就筹得 17. 48 亿元，占融资前股东权益的 60%；时隔半年后，海尔的董事会又提出发行可转换债券 25. 8 亿元的申请。可惜这次发行不仅没有成功，还为海尔多年来的股权融资画上了一个句点——在此后长达六年的时间里，海尔再也没有进行过股权融资，直到股改后为了解决遗留问题，海尔才再次进行股权融资。

海尔股权融资进程中断是否和中国的股权分置改革有关？在海尔中断股权融资的几年里，我国股市因为股改问题而长期处于低迷状态，证券发行也大幅减少。从 2002 年到 2004 年，年平均证券发行总额比 2001 年下降了 30%，比 2002 年下降了 46. 8%。

3. 青岛海尔的融资决策与我国股票市场融资政策变动的关系

经过分析发现，青岛海尔的每次融资经历都和政策变迁紧密相关，青岛海尔的股权融资历史基本代表了我国股权融资政策的发展史（见表 2）。

表 2　我国股市融资政策变更情况表

我国股票市场的融资政策要求			青岛海尔		
融资政策	相关政策发布日期	主要财务指标	涵盖的会计期间	公告日期	融资政策
第一次配股政策	1993-12-17	连续两年实现盈利，并且税后利润连续增长	1993-1994		上市增发
第二次配股政策	1994-9-28	净资产税后利润率三年平均在 10%以上	1994-1995	1996-6-5	第一次配股
第三次配股政策	1996-1-24	最近三年净资产税后利润率每年都在 10%以上	1996-1998	1997-11-28	第二次配股
第四次配股政策	1999-3-27	最近三个完整会计年度的净资产收益率平均在 10%以上，任何一年的净资产收益率不得低于 6%	1999-2000	1999-9-15	第三次配股

表2(续)

我国股票市场的融资政策要求			青岛海尔		
融资政策	相关政策发布日期	主要财务指标	涵盖的会计期间	公告日期	融资政策
第一次增发政策	2000-4-30	无具体财务指标,要求连续三年盈利,最近三个会计年度加权平均净资产收益率平均不低于6%	2000-2001	2001-2-6	公募增发
第二次增发政策	2001-3-15	无具体财务指标,要求连续三年盈利,最近三个会计年度加权平均净资产收益率平均不低于6%	2001-2002		
第一次可转换债券政策	1997-3-25	连续三年盈利,最近三年净资产利润率平均在10%以上	1997-2006	2001-10-31	拟发行可转换债券
可转换债券发行补充政策	2001-4-26	增加主承销商应重点核查发行人的事项:如现金分红、是否有足够的现金等	2001-2006		
上市公司证券发行管理办法	2006-5-8	增发和可转换债券:最近三个会计年度加权平均净资产收益率平均不低于6%;配股和非公开发行没有具体财务指标要求	2006至今	2007-5-24	定向增发

资料来源:配股政策根据证监会发布的文件整理;青岛海尔的资料根据其发布的公司公告整理。所有数据来源于Wind数据库。

从1994年到2000年,我国股市再融资的手段主要是配股,配股资格又主要围绕着10%的净资产收益率。在这期间,青岛海尔的净资产收益率均高于10%,所以它的融资首选就是配股。从1998年起我国增加了新的股权融资方式——增发,但直到2000年4月才有正式文件出台,且增发要求比配股要求低得多。青岛海尔闻风而动,于2000年9月29日通过临时股东大会作出增发的决议,但是此次增发远远超过前三次配股的融资金额的总和。这一年,我国上市公司股权融资出现重大转折:配股急剧减少,增发迅速上升。增发过滥引起股市恐慌,再加上国有股减持预期等因素导致我国股市进入了熊市阶段。在此期间,上市公司的股权融资水平整体处于下滑状态。由于股市低迷,投资者信心普遍下降,企业从股市获取资金的难度加大,因此纯粹的股权融资在2001—2003年呈下降趋势;但可转换债券由于有固定利率作保证,反而呈现了上升趋势。

于是2001年后期,青岛海尔的董事会又提出发行25.8亿元的可转换债券,申请募集资金的项目多达12个,其中关联交易项目有7个(见表3),关联交易金额占筹资总额的56%。

表 3　青岛海尔拟施行的关联交易收购

序号	被收购方	母公司	收购比例	股权收购金额/万元	增资金额/万元	出资和/万元
1	贵州海尔电器	海尔集团	59%	4 438.48	5 985	10 423.48
2	武汉海尔电器	海尔集团	60%	6 945.74	3 000	9 945.74
3	青岛海尔空调器电子	青岛海尔投资	75%	48 365.64	20 512	67 877.64
4	合肥海尔空调器	青岛海尔投资	78%	7 487	7 380	14 867
5	收购海尔电器国际的洗衣机业务	青岛海尔投资		24 661.97	800	25 461.97
6	顺德海尔电器	海尔集团	60%	4 617.92	1 000	5 617.92
7	合肥海尔洗衣机	青岛海尔投资	80%	3 680.67	3 000	6 680.67

注：海尔集团及其子公司海尔电器国际共持有青岛海尔 41.95%的股份，是前两大控股股东；青岛海尔投资发展有限公司的出资人为海尔集团公司、青岛海尔集体资产内部持股会。

资料来源：根据《青岛海尔股份有限公司第三届董事会第三次会议决议暨召开 2001 年度第一次临时股东大会公告》整理。

从海尔历次证券发行的公告数量来看，这次可转换债券的发行最隆重：关联交易事项说明、关联董事公告、独立董事意见函、各个被收购方公司的审计报告、资产评估报告、独立财务、顾问报告以及审计、评估结果说明等，所有报告都意图说明海尔的关联交易是公允的，没有对流通股股东造成伤害。这次发行尽管通过一次临时股东大会和两次股东大会的审议，还有多家银行的担保，历时两年多，但最后还是没能执行。这可能是青岛海尔唯一的一次股权融资失败。

既然融资失败，那么原定 25.8 亿元的融资项目怎么办？根据后来可查的公司公告和财务报告，直到 2006 年股改之前，前七项关联交易没有再被提及；后五个项目中有两个也没能在公开资料中找到说明；总共十一个融资项目只有三个通过短期借款的方式施行，涉及金额占融资计划的 36%。

直到 2001 年以前，青岛海尔较少采用债务融资方式，即便需要借款，也多以短期借款为主。2002 年短期借款急剧增加，原因可以参考青岛海尔 2002 年第二次董事会会议决议公告：公司将 2 亿元贷款用于提前建设大连出口加工区投资建设的出口电冰箱、出口空调器生产基地项目，公司将在本次可转换债券发行完成后，以募集资金偿还上述 2 亿元贷款。另外青岛海尔在 2002 年还通过短期借款投资原融资方案中的特种冰箱项目。后来可转债融资没有成功，海尔也没有就可转债发行方案中的项目继续借款。于是，海尔的短期借款开始急剧下降，直到 2004 年降为零。由此可见，如果不是可转债发行失败，如果不是股市持续低迷导致海尔难以从股市中融资，海尔的债务将一直保持在较低的水平。

随着股改进程的推进，海尔在 2006 年 5 月发布了股改实施公告。为了解决股改后与子公司的同业竞争问题，青岛海尔于同年9月提出了定向增发申请以收购上述公司。巧的是，这次收购的标的公司正是上次可转债发行准备收购的前四家公司，虽然前次收购失败，但这次则收购成功。总的看来，海尔的融资决策基本就是在各个股权融资品种中进行选择，债务融资和内源融资被当成了股权融资不足或失败后的补充。

青岛海尔从1996年开始至今共进行了六次股权融资，涉及配股、公募增发、可转换债券和定向增发四个融资品种。海尔每次融资方法的改变基本都源于融资政策的改变和股票市场的改革。股改后，青岛海尔一改通过流通股获利的融资方法，通过向大股东定向增发完成融资收购，提升了上市公司的每股净资产，为上市公司的发展注入更多血液，而该行为导致的股价上升也为大股东带来了收益。比起股改前，大股东明显更重视市场反应，更受市价和监管的制约，融资决策更加谨慎，这相比起以前随心所欲地侵害中小股东利益的行为有了很大进步，说明至少从短期来看股权分置改革起到了一定的作用。

资料来源：王克明，余洋.股权分置改革对公司股权融资偏好的影响：以青岛海尔为例.管理案例研究与评论，2010(12).Vol.3. No.6. pp:449-459.

Key Concepts and Skills

1. The basic concepts of stock market.
2. The determinants of stock price.
3. Calculation of stock price using the dividend growth model.

本章重点与难点

1. 股票市场，知道股票市场是如何运作的.
2. 股票价格的影响因素.
3. 熟练运用模型计算股票价值.

Self-Test Questions

Ⅰ. Multiple Choice Questions

1. Which of the following statements about stock price is true? (　　)

A. It reflects the relationship between capital and profit.

B. It is affected by the expected earnings per share.

C. It can be valued by discounting its dividends.

D. It reflects the risk of earnings per share.

2. Which of the following approaches can be used to value stocks? ( )

A. The price-to-earnings multiple

B. Monte Carlo simulation

C. Discounted cash flow approach

D. Revenue multiplier method

3. Which of the following terms is related to a stock exchange? ( )

A. Knowledge Process Outsourcing

B. Net Asset Value

C. Initial Public Offering (IPO)

D. National Stock Exchange

Ⅱ. True (T) or False (F) Questions

1. A stock's value is the present value of its future expected cash flows. ( )

2. The New York Stock Exchange and the Nasdaq are the secondary markets. ( )

3. The stock market includes the primary market and the issuance market. ( )

4. Dividends can be distributed at a scheduled frequency, such as monthly, quarterly, or annually. ( )

5. Dividends payments are determined by the company's suppliers. ( )

6. All stocks in an equivalent-risk class are priced to offer the same expected rate of return. ( )

Ⅲ. Calculation Questions

1. Company A's dividends per share are expected to grow indefinitely by 6% a year. If the dividend of next year is \$12, the market capitalization rate is 9%, what is the current stock price?

2. Common stock dividends of Company B have been growing at an annual rate of 7 percent over the past years. Last annual dividends were \$3.6 per share. What is the fair (intrinsic) value of a share of this stock to an investor who requires an 11% rate of return if the following conditions exist:

(1) The company's future dividends grow at constant annual rate 6 percent?

(2) The company's future dividends are constant \$3.6?

3. Company C currently has earnings per share of \$8.5, the company has no growth and pays out all earnings as dividends. It has a new project which will require an investment of \$1.80 per share at the end of first year. The project is only a two-year project, and it will increase earnings in the two years following the in-

vestment by \$2.50 and 3.50 respectively. Investors require a 12 percent return on the stock.

(1) What is the value per share of the company's stock assuming the firm does not undertake the investment?

(2) If the company does undertake the investment, what is the value per share now?

(3) If the company does undertake the investment, and the investment will not generate earnings in the first 2-years, but the dividend will maintain a constant 5% growth rate from the end of the third year, please draw the structure of cash flows and calculate the value per share.

本章习题答案

Part Three
Financing Decision
(融资决策)

Chapter 8 Cost of Capital（资本成本）

Learning Objectives

- Learn to determine a firm's cost of equity capital.
- Know the estimation of beta and understand the impact of beta in determining a firm's cost of equity capital.
- Learn to determine the firm's overall cost of capital.
- Learn to determine the weighted average cost of capital.

The learning objective of this chapter is to understand how the investors choose the best combination or portfolio of securities to hold and to learn how to compute a company's cost of capital. We first describe the sources of capital, and then discuss the estimation of the cost of each source. The analysis of cost of capital is built on beta and the capital asset pricing model (CAPM). Then we introduce how to value the firms or projects by using the weighted average cost of capital (WACC).

8.1 Cost of Capital: Basic Concepts

The cost of capital is defined as the expected return on a portfolio of all the company's outstanding debt and equity securities. It is the opportunity cost of capital for investment in all of the firm's assets, and therefore the appropriate discount rate for the firm's average-risk projects. If the firm has no debt outstanding, then the cost of capital is just the expected rate of return on the firm's stock.

The cost of capital is not the correct discount rate if the new projects are more or less risky than the firm's existing business. Each project should in principle be evaluated at its own opportunity cost of capital. For a firm composed of assets A and B, the firm value is:

$$\text{Firm value} = PV(AB) = PV(A) + PV(B)$$
$$= \text{sum of separate asset values}$$

As the cost of capital is defined as "the expected return on a portfolio of all the company's existing securities." That portfolio usually includes debt as well as equity. Thus, the cost of capital is estimated as a blend of the cost of debt and the cost of equity.

The values of debt and equity add up to overall firm value ($D+E=V$) and firm value V equals asset value. It should be noted that these figures are all market values, not book (accounting) values. The market value of equity is normally much larger than the book value, so the market debt ratio D/V is often much lower than a debt ratio computed from the book balance sheet.

$$\text{Company cost of capital} = (r_D \times \frac{D}{V}) + (r_E \times \frac{E}{V})$$

8.1.1 Cost of Debt(债务资本成本)

The cost of debt is the return that a company provides to its debtholders and creditors. These capital providers need to be compensated for any risk exposure that comes with lending to a company.

Since observable interest rates play an important role in quantifying the cost of debt, it is relatively more straightforward to calculate the cost of debt than the cost of equity. Not only does the cost of debt reflect the default risk of a company, but it also reflects the level of interest rates in the market. In addition, it is an integral part of calculating a company's Weighted Average Cost of Capital or WACC.

Debt is one part of a company's capital structure, which also includes equity. Capital structure deals with how a firm finances its overall operations and growth through different sources of funds, which may include debt such as bonds or loans. The cost of debt measure is helpful in understanding the overall rate being paid by a company to use these types of debt financing. The measure can also give investors an idea of the company's risk level compared to others because riskier companies generally have a higher cost of debt.

So far, we have ignored taxes. In the real world, interest payments are tax deductible under most countries' tax laws. Therefore, we should tax-adjust the cost of debt. The after-tax cost of debt can be written as:

$$\text{After-tax cost of debt} = (1 - \text{tax rate}) \times \text{borrowing rate}$$

8.1.2 Cost of Equity(权益资本成本)

The cost of equity is the return that a company requires to decide if an investment meets capital return requirements. Firms often use it as a capital budgeting threshold for the required rate of return. A firm's cost of equity represents the compensation that the market demands in exchange for owning the asset and bearing the risk of ownership. The traditional formula for the cost of equity is the dividend capitalization model and the capital asset pricing model (CAPM,资本资产定价模型).

Using the dividend capitalization model, the cost of equity is:

$$\text{Cost of Equity} = \frac{\text{DPS}}{V} + G$$

where:

DPS = dividends per share, for next year

V = current market value of stock

G = growth rate of dividends

The CAPM Formula is:

$$\text{Cost of Equity} = \text{expected return} = R_f + \beta \times (R_m - R_f)$$

In this equation, the risk-free rate (无风险收益率) is the rate of return paid on risk-free investments such as Treasuries. *Beta* (贝塔系数) is a measure of risk calculated as a regression on the company's stock price. The higher the volatility, the higher the beta and relative risk compared to the general market. The market rate of return (市场收益率) is the average market rate. In general, a company with a high beta—that is, a company with a high degree of risk—will have a higher cost of equity.

The cost of equity refers to two separate concepts, depending on the party involved. If you are the investor, the cost of equity is the rate of return required on an investment in equity. If you are the company, the cost of equity determines the required rate of return on a particular project or investment.

There are two ways that a company can raise capital: debt or equity. Debt is cheaper, but the company must pay it back. Equity does not need to be repaid, but it generally costs more than debt capital due to the tax advantages of interest payments. Since the cost of equity is higher than debt, it generally provides a higher rate of return.

8.1.3 Weighted Average Cost of Capital(加权平均资本成本)

The weighted average cost of capital (WACC) represents a firm's average cost of capital from all sources, including common stock, preferred stock, bonds, and other forms of debt.

The weighted average cost of capital is a common way to determine required rate of return because it expresses, in a single number, the return that both bondholders and shareholders demand in order to provide the company with capital. A firm's WACC is likely to be higher if its stock is relatively volatile or if its debt is seen as risky because investors will demand greater returns.

In most cases, a lower WACC indicates a healthy business that's able to attract investors at a lower cost. By contrast, a higher WACC usually coincides with businesses that are seen as riskier and need to compensate investors with higher returns.

In order to express the cost of capital in a single figure, one has to weigh its cost of debt and cost of equity proportionally based on how much financing is acquired through each source. WACC formula and calculation is:

$$\text{WACC} = (R_E \times \frac{E}{V}) + [R_D \times \frac{D}{V} \times (1 - T_c)]$$

where:

E = Market value of the firm's equity

D = Market value of the firm's debt

V = E+D

R_E = Cost of equity

R_D = Cost of debt

T_c = Corporate tax rate

WACC is calculated by multiplying the cost of each capital source (debt and equity) by its relevant weight and then adding the products together. In the above formula, E/V represents the proportion of equity-based financing, while D/V represents the proportion of debt-based financing. The WACC formula thus involves the summation of two terms:

$$R_E \times \frac{E}{V} \text{ and } R_D \times \frac{D}{V} \times (1 - T_c)$$

The former represents the weighted value of equity capital, while the latter represents the weighted value of debt capital.

8.1.4 Beta(贝塔系数)

Beta (β) is a measure of the volatility—or systematic risk—of a security or portfolio compared to the market as a whole (usually the S&P 500). Stocks with betas higher than 1.0 can be interpreted as more volatile than the S&P 500.

Beta is used in the capital asset pricing model (CAPM), which describes the relationship between systematic risk and expected return for assets (usually stocks). CAPM is widely used as a method for pricing risky securities and for generating estimates of the expected returns of assets, considering both the risk of those assets and the cost of capital.

Beta effectively describes the activity of a security's returns as it responds to swings in the market. A security's beta is calculated by dividing the product of the covariance of the security's returns and the market's returns by the variance of the market's returns over a specified period. The calculation for beta is as follows:

$$\beta_i = \frac{\mathrm{Cov}(R_i, R_M)}{\sigma^2(R_M)}$$

where $Cov(R_i, R_M)$ is the covariance between the return on Asset i and the return on the market portfolio, and $\sigma^2(R_M)$ is the variance of the market.

One useful property is that the average beta across all securities, when weighted by the proportion of each security's market value to that of the market portfolio, is 1. That is:

$$\sum_{i=1}^{N} X_i \beta_i = 1$$

where Xi is the proportion of Security i's market value to that of the entire market and N is the number of securities in the market. This equation is intuitive, once you think about it. If you weight all securities by their market values, the resulting portfolio is the market. By definition, the beta of the market portfolio is 1. That is, for every 1 percent movement in the market, the market must move 1 percent—by definition.

8.1.5 Asset Beta

The after-tax WACC depends on the average risk of the company's assets, but it also depends on taxes and financing. It's easier to think about project risk if you measure it directly. The direct measure is called the asset beta. We calculate the asset beta as a blend of the separate betas of debt (β_D) and equity (β_E):

$$\text{Asset Beta} = \beta_A = \beta_D(D/V) + \beta_E(E/V)$$

Calculating an asset beta is similar to calculating a weighted-average cost of capital. The debt and equity weights D/V and E/V are the same. The logic is also the same: Suppose you purchased a portfolio consisting of 100% of the firm's debt and 100% of its equity. Then you would own 100% of its assets lock, stock, and barrel, and the beta of your portfolio would equal the beta of the assets. The portfolio beta is of course just a weighted average of the betas of debt and equity.

8.2 Return and Risk: The Capital Asset Pricing Model (CAPM)

The Capital Asset Pricing Model (CAPM) describes the relationship between systematic risk and expected return for assets, particularly stocks. CAPM is widely used throughout finance for pricing risky securities and generating expected returns for assets given the risk of those assets and cost of capital.

The formula for calculating the expected return of an asset given its risk is as follows:

$$R_i = R_f + \beta_i(R_m - R_f)$$

where:

R_i = expected return of investment

R_f = risk-free rate

β_i = beta of the investment

$(R_m - R_f)$ = market risk premium

where R_f is the risk-free rate, and $R_m - R_f$ is the difference between the expected return on the market portfolio and the riskless rate. This difference is often called the expected excess market return or market risk premium.

Investors expect to be compensated for risk and the time value of money. The risk-free rate in the CAPM formula accounts for the time value of money. The other components of the CAPM formula account for the investor taking on additional risk.

The beta of a potential investment is a measure of how much risk the investment will add to a portfolio that looks like the market. If a stock is riskier than the market, it will have a beta greater than one. If a stock has a beta of less than one, the formula assumes it will reduce the risk of a portfolio. A stock's beta is then multiplied by the market risk premium, which is the return expected from the market above the risk-free rate. The risk-free rate is then added to the product of the stock's beta and the market risk premium. The result should give an investor the required return or discount rate they can use to find the value of an asset.

8.2.1 Expected Return(期望收益率)

This is the return that an individual expects a stock to earn over the next period. An individual's expectation may simply be the average return per period a security has earned in the past. Alternatively, the expectation may be based on a detailed analysis of a firm's prospects, on some computer-based model, or on special (or inside) information.

It is calculated by multiplying potential outcomes by the chances of them occurring and then totaling these results. For example, if an investment has a 50% chance of gaining 20% and a 50% chance of losing 10%, the expected return would be 5% = (50% x 20% + 50% x −10% = 5%).

8.2.2 Variance and Standard Deviation(方差和标准差)

There are many ways to assess the volatility of a security's return. One of the most common is variance, which is a measure of the squared deviations of a security's return from its expected return. In statistics, variance measures variability from the average or mean. It is calculated by taking the differences between each number in the data set and the mean, then squaring the differences to make them positive, and finally dividing the sum of the squares by the number of values in the data set. Algebraically, the formula for variance can be expressed as:

$$\mathrm{Var}(R) = \text{Expected value of } (R - \bar{R})^2$$

where $\bar{R}$ is the security's expected return and R is the actual return.

Standard deviation is simply the square root of the variance. The general formula for the standard deviation is:

$$\mathrm{SD}(R) = \sqrt{\mathrm{Var}(R)}$$

8.2.3 Covariance and Correlation(协方差和相关性)

Returns on individual securities are related to one another. Covariance is a statistic measuring the interrelationship between two securities. Alternatively, this relationship can be restated in terms of the correlation between the two securities. Covariance and correlation are building blocks to an understanding of the beta coefficient.

Covariance measures the directional relationship between the returns on two assets. A positive covariance means that asset returns move together while a negative covariance means they move inversely. Covariance is calculated by analyzing at-return surprises (standard deviations from the expected return) or by multiplying the correlation between the two random variables by the standard deviation of each variable.

The formula for covariance can be written algebraically as:

$$\sigma_{AB} = \mathrm{Cov}(R_A, R_B) = \text{Expected value of } [(R_A - \bar{R}_A) \times (R_B - \bar{R}_B)]$$

where $\bar{R}_A$ and $\bar{R}_B$ are the expected returns on the two securities and R_A and R_B are the actual returns. The ordering of the two variables is unimportant. That is, the covariance of A with B is equal to the covariance of B with A. This can be stated more formally as $\mathrm{Cov}(R_A, R_B) = \mathrm{Cov}(R_B, R_A)$ or $\sigma_{AB} = \sigma_{BA}$.

To calculate the correlation, divide the covariance by the product of the standard deviations of both of the two securities:

$$\rho_{AB} = \mathrm{Corr}(R_A, R_B) = \frac{\mathrm{Cov}(R_A, R_B)}{\sigma_A \times \sigma_B}$$

As with covariance, the ordering of the two variables is unimportant. That is, the correlation of A with B is equal to the correlation of B with A. More formally, $\mathrm{Corr}(R_A, R_B) = \mathrm{Corr}(R_B, R_A)$, or $\sigma_{AB} = \sigma_{BA}$.

Because the standard deviation is always positive, the sign of the correlation between two variables must be the same as that of the covariance between the two variables. If the correlation is positive, we say that the variables are positively correlated; if it is negative, we say that they are negatively correlated; and if it is zero, we say that they are uncorrelated. Furthermore, it can be proved that the correlation is always between +1 and −1. This is due to the standardizing procedure of dividing by the product of the two standard deviations.

Suppose an investor has estimates of the expected returns and standard deviations on individual securities and the correlations between securities. How does the investor choose the best combination or portfolio of securities to hold? The investor would like a portfolio with a high expected return and a low standard deviation of return. Thus, it is worthwhile to consider:

1. The relationship between the expected returns on individual securities and the expected return on a portfolio made up of these securities.

2. The relationship between the standard deviations of individual securities, the correlations between these securities, and the standard deviation of a portfolio made up of these securities.

8.2.4 The Expected Return on a Portfolio

The expected return on a portfolio is a weighted average of the expected returns on the individual securities. Algebraically, we can write:

$$\text{Expected return on portfolio} = X_A \bar{R}_A + X_B \bar{R}_B = \bar{R}_p$$

Where X_A and X_B are the proportions of the total portfolio in the assets A and B, respectively. (Because our investor can invest in only two securities, $X_A + X_B$ must equal 1 or 100 percent.) $\overline{R}_A$ and $\overline{R}_B$ are the expected returns on the two securities.

8.2.5 Risk: Systematic and Unsystematic

Risk is defined in financial terms as the chance that an outcome or investment's actual gains will differ from an expected outcome or return. Risk includes the possibility of losing some or all of an original investment. In general, financial theory classifies investment risks affecting asset values into two categories: systematic risk and unsystematic risk. Investors are exposed to both systematic and unsystematic risks. The following definitions describe the difference:

- A systematic risk is any risk that affects a large number of assets, each to a greater or lesser degree.
- An unsystematic risk is a risk that specifically affects a single asset or a small group of assets.

Uncertainty about general economic conditions, such as GNP, interest rates, or inflation, are examples of systematic risk. These conditions affect nearly all stocks to some degree. An unanticipated or surprise increase in inflation affects wages and the costs of the supplies that companies buy, the value of the assets that companies own, and the prices at which companies sell their products. These forces to which all companies are susceptible are the essence of systematic risk.

In contrast, the announcement of a small oil strike by a company may affect that company alone or a few other companies. Certainly, it is unlikely to have an effect on the world oil market. To stress that such information is unsystematic and affects only some specific companies, we sometimes call it an idiosyncratic risk.

8.2.6 Relationship between Risk and Expected Return (CAPM)

It is commonplace to argue that the expected return on an asset should be positively related to its risk. That is, individuals will hold a risky asset only if its expected return compensates for its risk. In Figure 8-1, we can see that the firm's expected return is linearly related to its beta. The diagonal line is a depiction of CAPM and represents the relationship between the cost of capital and the firm's risk.

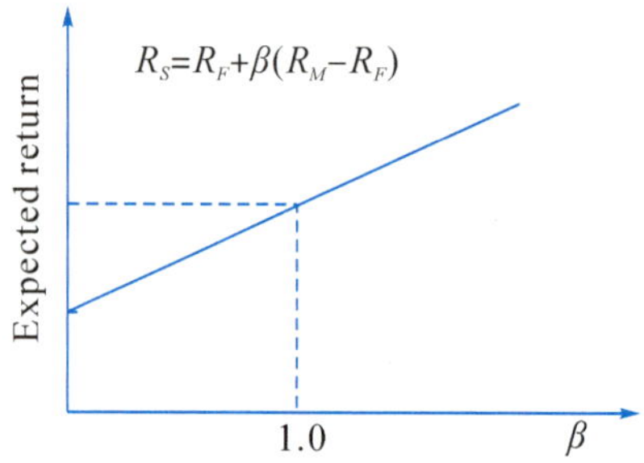

Figure 8-1 Relationship between risk and expected return

1. Expected return on market

Economists frequently argue that the expected return on the market can be represented as:

$$\bar{R}_m = R_f + \text{Market risk premium}$$

$$\text{Market risk premium} = \beta \times (\bar{R}_m - R_f)$$

In words, the expected return on the market is the sum of the risk-free rate plus some compensation for the risk inherent in the market portfolio. Note that the equation refers to the expected return on the market, not the actual return in a particular month or year. Because stocks have risk, the actual return on the market over a particular period can be below R_f or can even be negative. Because investors want compensation for risk, the risk premium is presumably positive.

2. Expected return on individual security

Now that we have estimated the expected return on the market as a whole, what is the expected return on an individual security? We have argued that the beta of a security is the appropriate measure of its risk in a large, diversified portfolio. Because most investors are diversified, the expected return on a security should be positively related to its beta.

Actually, economists can be more precise about the relationship between expected return and beta. They posit that under plausible conditions the relationship between expected return and beta can be represented by the following equation:

$$\bar{R} = R_f + \beta \times (\bar{R}_m - R_f)$$

This formula, which is called the capital asset pricing model (CAPM), implies that the expected return on a security is linearly related to its beta. Alternatively, we could say that this expected return is the required return on the stock, based on the stock's risk. Similarly, this expected return can be viewed as the firm's cost of equity capital. Because the average return on the market has been higher than the average risk-free rate over long periods of time, $\bar{R}_m - R_f$ is presumably positive. Thus, the formula implies that the expected return on a security is positively related to its beta.

SUMMARY

1. A company's cost of capital is the rate of return that investors require on a portfolio of all of the company's outstanding debt and equity. It is usually calculated as an after-tax weighted-average cost of capital (after-tax WACC), that is, as the weighted average of the after-tax cost of debt and the cost of equity. The weights are the relative market values of debt and equity. The cost of debt is calculated after tax because interest is a tax-deductible expense.

$$\text{Company cost of capital} = (r_D \times \frac{D}{V}) + (r_E \times \frac{E}{V})$$

2. The hardest part of calculating the after-tax WACC is estimation of the cost of equity. Most large, public corporations use the capital asset pricing model (CAPM) to do this. They generally estimate the firm's equity beta from past rates of return for the firm's common stock and for the market, and they check their estimate against the average beta of similar firms.

$$\text{Cost of Equity} = \text{expected return} = R_F + \beta \times (R_M - R_F)$$

3. The after-tax WACC is the correct discount rate for projects that have the same market risk as the company's existing business.

$$\text{After-tax WACC} = (\frac{E}{V} \times R_E) + [\frac{D}{V} \times R_D \times (1 - T_c)]$$

4. Beta measures the responsiveness of a security to movements in the market portfolio. The actual definition of beta is:

$$\beta_i = \frac{\text{Cov}(R_i, R_M)}{\sigma^2(R_M)}$$

5. Asset beta is a blend of the separate betas of debt (β_D) and equity (β_E). That is:

$$\text{Asset Beta} = \beta_A = \beta_D(D/V) + \beta_E(E/V)$$

6. The CAPM states that:

$$\bar{R} = R_F + \beta \times (\bar{R}_M - R_F)$$

The expected return on a security is positively and linearly related to the security's beta.

延伸阅读 8-1 《党纪在公司财务治理中的作用》

2021 年是全国国有企业党的建设工作会议召开五周年。这五年，广大国有企业深入贯彻落实习近平总书记重要讲话精神，对加强党的领导和完善公司治理进行了深入探索和有效实践，红色引擎作用更为强劲。立足新发展阶段，贯彻新发展理念，构建新发展格局，国有企业更要牢记“国之大者”，源源不断地从习近平新时代中国特色社会主义思想中感悟真理力量和实践伟力，始终坚持“两个一以贯之”，坚决做到“两个维护”，在不断完善公司治理中进一步加强党的领导，以高质量党建引领高质量发展。

一、系统总结经验做法，始终坚持“两个一以贯之”，准确把握在完善公司治理中加强党的领导的实践认识

习近平总书记在 2016 年全国国有企业党的建设工作会议上指出：“坚持

党对国有企业的领导是重大政治原则，必须一以贯之；建立现代企业制度是国有企业改革的方向，也必须一以贯之。”五年来的实践证明，必须坚持“两个一以贯之”，确保国有企业党委(党组)把方向、管大局、保落实，董事会定战略、作决策、防风险，经理层谋经营、抓落实、强管理，各治理主体不缺位、不越位，不相互替代、不各自为政。

第一，深刻认识顶层设计体制机制的重要作用。近年来，中央制定出台了《中国共产党国有企业基层组织工作条例(试行)》《关于中央企业在完善公司治理中加强党的领导的意见》等法规，从制度层面明确了党的领导和公司治理的权责边界，为党的领导的制度优势迅速转化为公司的治理效能奠定了基础。在执行层面，推动“制度融合”，把党建工作要求写入公司章程，进一步明确党组织在公司法人治理结构中的法定地位。目前，全部中央企业以及97%以上的省属国有企业的党建工作要求已写入公司章程。推动“人的融合”，坚持和完善“双向进入、交叉任职”领导体制。截至2020年年底，设董事会的国有企业中党委(党组)书记、董事长“一肩挑”的超过80%。推动“事的融合”，明确党组织研究讨论是董事会、经理层决策重大问题的前置程序。目前，国有企业集团层面及96%的重要子企业已完成清单制定，基本厘清了各治理主体权责边界。

第二，深刻认识国有企业党组织发挥领导作用的本质内涵。党对国有企业的领导是政治领导、思想领导、组织领导的有机统一，把方向、管大局、保落实是发挥党组织领导核心和政治核心作用的本质和内涵。把方向，就是要牢牢把握国企改革发展的正确方向。管大局，就是要坚持总揽全局、协调各方原则，议大事、抓重点。促落实，就是要发挥党组织的凝聚力、战斗力，管干部、建班子、带队伍，抓基层、打基础，形成齐心协力抓落实的工作局面。

第三，深刻认识党组织在各治理主体中的核心地位。进一步完善“双向进入、交叉任职”领导体制，通过落实研究重大事项前置程序，保证企业党组织行使“三项权利”(对保障落实党中央重大方针政策、内部重要人事任免行使决定权，对企业发展战略等重大经营管理事项行使把关权，对企业遵守国家法律法规等具有监督权)，做好“四个协调”(协调好与董事会、经理层和监督力量的关系，协调好党管干部和市场化选人用人关系)，确保国有企业“做正确的事”“选合适的人”“正确地做事”。

二、巩固扩大落实成果，坚决做到“两个维护”，全面推进在完善公司治理中加强党的领导的各项工作

第一，坚持党的全面领导，牢牢把握国企发展道路和方向。一是坚持把做到“两个维护”作为首要任务，全面建立学习贯彻习近平总书记重要指示批示精神“首要责任”“第一议题”制度，按照“有没有学习研讨、有没有贯彻措施、有没有督导推动、有没有跟踪问效”四项标准督促跟踪落实情况，确保总书记重要指示批示精神落地生根。二是坚决贯彻党中央决策部署。引导广大党员干部切实提高政治判断力、政治领悟力、政治执行力，服务人民需要，执行国家战略，确保国有企业把党中央决策部署和习近平总书记重要指示批示精神落到实处。

第二，坚持建立和完善中国特色现代国有企业制度，把加强党的领导和完善公司治理统一起来。一是在完善公司治理中加强党的领导。建立和完善中国特色现代国有企业制度，就是要把党的领导融入公司治理各环节，将党建工作和中心工作一起谋划、一起部署、一起考核，切实解决"两张皮"痼疾。二是在健全机制中更好促进各治理主体发挥作用。完善董事会、经理层评价办法，健全市场化经营机制，深化企业内部人事、劳动、分配三项制度改革，加快形成权责法定、权责透明、协调运转、有效制衡的公司治理机制。

第三，坚持把党管干部党管人才原则与市场化选人用人机制结合起来，建设高素质国企干部人才队伍。一是精准科学选人用人。坚持党管干部党管人才原则，发挥"揭榜挂帅""赛场选马"等市场机制作用，实施经理层任期制和契约化管理，"一企一策"建强配优领导班子，选拔基层经验丰富、实干实绩突出的优秀年轻干部，培养、引进、用活、用好各类人才。二是加大培养锻炼力度。按照"政治家+企业家"培养方向，积极开展专业化培训和轮岗交流，让干部到吃劲负重岗位经受摔打，在开拓市场、推进改革等一线经受磨练，加快成长为善于治企兴企、管党治党的复合型干部。三是激励干部担当作为。坚持严管与厚爱相结合、激励与约束并重，落实"三个区分开来"，建立容错机制，完善激励政策，激发调动干事创业积极性。

第四，坚持强基固本，把国企基层党组织建设成坚强的战斗堡垒。一是立起做好基层党建的标尺，围绕提升组织力、突出政治功能、建强战斗堡垒这个根本要求，细化完善"三会一课"、组织生活会等组织生活制度的标准程序，加强党支部标准化规范化建设。二是树起做实基层党建的标杆，推进基层党建与经营发展深度融合，建立党组织和党员发挥作用载体和平台，用好党内表彰评选，形成巩固先进、推动一般、整顿后进的良好机制。三是扛起做强基层党建的责任，围绕责任设计制度，依据制度考核责任，探索党建工作责任制和生产经营责任制有效联动、同向发力的方式方法，建立健全"明责履责、考责问责"基层党建责任体系，确保管党治党责任抓实抓好抓到位。

第五，坚持加强和改进思想政治工作，为做强做优做大国企汇聚团结奋进的正能量。一是创新宣传思想工作。强化正面宣传和舆论引导，落实好"三必访四必问五必谈"，引导干部员工听党话、跟党走。树立先进典型，弘扬劳模精神、劳动精神、工匠精神，为国企改革发展汇聚强大合力。二是加强党对群团工作的领导。坚持和完善企务公开等制度，支持工会组织充分发挥桥梁纽带作用，鼓励职工代表有序参与公司治理。深化"爱企业、献良策、做贡献"

活动，加强新时代统战工作。深化党建带团建，团结凝聚广大团员青年为国企发展建功立业。

第六，坚持深化全面从严治党，营造风清气正的政治生态。一是切实加强政治监督。贯彻落实习近平总书记重要指示批示精神和党中央决策部署，聚焦高质量发展、科技创新等重点任务，制定督查办法，建立工作台账，加大政治监督力度。二是把党风廉政建设摆在突出位置，融入生产经营管理。层层压实主体责任，健全完善责任清单，主要负责人要切实履行第一责任人的责任，做到重要工作亲自部署、重大问题亲自过问、重要环节亲自协调、重要案件亲自督办，坚决防止主体责任虚化空转。三是严抓党规党纪教育，增强各级干部员工纪律意识、规矩意识，做到知敬畏、存戒惧、守底线，持续巩固落实中央八项规定精神成果，驰而不息纠正“四风”。四是强化监督执纪问责，健全党委全面监督、纪委专责监督、党的工作部门职能监督、党的基层组织日常监督、党员民主监督的党内监督体系。始终保持反腐败高压态势，持续加大问责力度，让有错必究、失责必问、问责必严成为常态。发挥巡视利剑作用，一体推进“不敢腐、不能腐、不想腐”体制机制建设，促进治理腐败效能不断增强。

资料来源：贾志强.在完善公司治理中加强党的领导[J].中国党政干部论坛，2021(12)：79-82.

延伸阅读 8-2 《纪委监督在国有企业公司治理中的重要角色》

现代企业一个显著特征是所有权和经营权的分离，它造就了新兴的职业管理者阶层。职业管理者取代业主控制企业的经营，对企业持续健康发展是有利的，但同时又产生了“委托人”与“代理人 ”问题。如果管理者的权力不受制约就会侵害所有者的权益，两者的契约关系需要制度上的相应安排，因此体现了全新理念的公司治理结构理论成为现代企业普遍遵循的治理方式。公司治理结构虽有不同的模式，但总体而言，其基本构成是股东大会、董事会、监事会以及经理层，即通常所说的“新三会 ”或四结构的治理模式。公司治理的实质就是强调企业所有权和企业所有者在公司治理中的主导作用，强调公司治理结构的相互制衡，公司治理的要旨就在于划分股东、董事会、经理和监督机构之间的权力、责任和利益，形成相互制约的关系，保证公司的有效运行。随着经济全球化的发展和世界经济环境的变化，各国的公司治理实践也在发生着深刻变革，越来越多的投资者和公司的决策者认识到，良好的公司治理是企业增强竞争力和提高经营绩效的必要条件，是保护所有者及其他利益相关者、保证现代市场体系有序和高效运行的微观基础。在我国，健全法人治理结构已成为建立现代企业制度的核心，完善公司治理结构是国有企业经营体制改革、公司化改造过程中的一个重要目标。

作为基层党组织的企业纪委，要履行党章赋予的职责，其使命也就与企业的发展利益结合起来了。《中共中央关于加强党的执政能力建设的决定》中提出："国有企业党组织要适应建立现代企业制度的要求，完善工作机制，充分发挥政治核心作用。"所以，国有企业纪委一方面要充分发挥政治核心作用，另一方面要积极地为企业健全完善公司治理结构提供保障。多年来，中央纪委始终把国有企业的反腐倡廉工作作为党风廉政建设的重要部分来抓，从制定《国有企业领导人员廉洁从业若干规定（试行）》，到提出加强对企业经营投资决策的监督检查，加强对国有企业改制过程中产权、股权交易行为的监督检查和建立健全企业内控机制，中央纪委由对企业领导人员个人行为的监督发展到对企业经营管理法人行为的监管，表现出纪委监督在国有企业内部的深化，已与国有企业的改革发展紧密结合在一起。

中央在《建立健全教育、制度、监督并重的惩治和预防腐败体系实施纲要》中提出："加强国有资产和金融的监管。健全国有资本投资决策和项目法人约束机制，实行重大投资项目论证制和重大投资决策失误追究制。完善国有企业法人治理结构，规范公司股东会、董事会、监事会和经营管理者的权责。加强对资本运营各个环节的监管，防止国有资产流失，维护职工合法权益。"在《建立健全惩治和预防腐败体系 2008—2012 年工作规划》中，又进一步提出"健全现代企业制度，完善公司法人治理结构。加强大型国有企业董事会建设，未设立董事会的企业逐步实行党委（党组）书记和总经理分设。推进国有企业监管体制改革。健全国有资本经营预算、企业经营业绩考核和企业重大决策失误追究等制度。建立健全国有企业及国有资本占控股地位、主导地位企业领导人员的经济责任审计制度。健全国有企业经营管理者薪酬制度和国有企业管理层投资持股制度，规范收入分配秩序。完善国有金融资产、行政事业性资产和自然资源资产监管制度，建立具有中国特色的国有企业监管体制"。这些内容已深入到完善公司治理结构中，也为企业纪委的工作制定了明确规划。

在十余年建立现代企业制度的努力中，国有企业取得了很大的进步，但不可否认的是，多数国有企业的公司治理结构还存在诸多问题，如股权过于集中，国有股持股比例过高；董事会独立性不强，独立董事作用不明显；监事会的作用有限；没有建立起有效的激励机制；监管力度不够等。公司治理是一个复杂的体系，涉及该国的制度环境、市场结构、文化资源等因素，几乎没有明确的做法和方案可以确保产生有效的公司治理结构。因此，致力于解决所有权与控制权相分离而产生的代理成本问题的传统的公司治理研究，其结果也充满了多样性，这种研究范围的不确定性，在经济转轨和制度转型的背景下，被大大强化了。当前国有企业公司治理中暴露的问题，一方面需要进一步深化国有企业经营体制改革，健全完善公司治理结构；另一方面也需要深入研究国有企业所处制度环境的特点，认真分析国外公司治理结构在国有企业内部的适应性，确立适应国有企业能行之有效的公司治理结构。而从另一个渠道来看，加强国有企业纪委监督职能的发挥，也是对完善国有企业公司治理结构的一种有效补充。虽然纪委的监督属于公司治理结构外的范畴，但只要在体制外科学定位，找到切入点，再通过创新工作机制，开拓监督领域，必然能走出一条有助于公司治理的监督新路。

资料来源：张响贤.论纪委在国有企业公司治理中的三重角色——对中国人寿保险(集团)公司纪检监察工作实践的思考[J].保险研究，2008(11)：61-65.

Key Concepts and Skills

1. Calculation of a firm's cost of debt and cost of equity capital.
2. Calculation of the weighted average cost of capital and estimation of weights.
3. Application of the weighted average cost of capital in capital budgeting.
4. Estimation of beta and its impact in determining a firm's cost of equity capital.
5. The difference between project beta and asset beta.

本章重点与难点

1. 债务资本成本、权益资本成本的计算方法。
2. 加权平均资本成本的计算方法和权重的确定方法。
3. 加权平均资本成本在资本预算中的运用。
4. 贝塔系数的估计及其对公司权益资本成本的影响。
5. 项目贝塔系数和资产贝塔系数的区别。

Self-Test Questions

Ⅰ. Single Choice Questions

1. If the weighting of equity in total capital is 1/4, that of debt is 3/4, the return on equity is 15% that of debt is 10% and the corporate tax rate is 30%, what is the Weighted Average Cost of Capital (WACC)? (　　)

A. 10.5%

B. 7.5%

C. 9%

D. 11%

2. Which of the following risk will be decreased by owning more stocks in a portfolio? ( )

A. Systematic risk

B. Unsystematic risk

C. Exchange rate risk

D. Economic risk

3. Which of the following event is systematic risk? ( )

A. A dramatic increase in furniture price

B. A decrease in consumption of fast food

C. Airline pilots strike

D. The People's Bank of China raised benchmark interest rates

4. Suppose a firm is 100 percent equity financed, and it has a stock beta of 1.2. The firm is considering a new project whose average beta is equal to the firm's existing project. The risk-free rate is 5 percent. If the market risk premium is 8percent, what is the appropriate discount rate for the new project? ( )

A. 15.6%

B. 16%

C. 14.6%

D. 13%

Ⅱ. True (T) or False (F) Questions

1. If the firm has no debt outstanding, then the cost of capital is just the expected rate of return on the firm's stock. ( )

2. The cost of debt only reflects the default risk of a firm. It does not reflect the level of interest rates in the market. ( )

3. The expected return on a security is linearly related to the security's beta. ( )

4. The expected return on a security is positively related to the security's beta. ( )

5. The value of the firm is the present value of expected future cash flow discounted at the WACC. ( )

6. A company's capital structure only includes stocks and preferred stocks. ( )

Ⅲ. Calculation Questions

1. A Company's common stock has a beta of 1.15. If the risk-free rate is 3.

8percent and the expected return on the market is 11 percent, what is company's cost of equity capital?

2. Suppose a firm has a debt issue outstanding with 13 years to maturity that is quoted at 95 percent of face value. The issue makes semiannual payments and has a coupon rate of 7 percent. What is the company's pretax cost of debt? If the corporate tax rate is 30 percent, what is the after-tax cost of debt?

3. Consider a company whose debt has a market value of $30 million and it holds 2 million outstanding shares of stock, each selling for $25 per share. The company pays a 5 percent rate of interest on its new debt and has a beta of 1.3. The corporate tax rate is 32 percent. If the risk premium on the market is 9.5 percent, and that the current Treasury bill rate is 1 percent. What is the company's weighted average cost capital?

本章习题答案

Chapter 9 Capital Structure (资本结构)

Learning Objectives

- Understand the concepts of capital structure.
- Understand the effect of capital structure on firm value.
- Understand capital structure theories with and without taxes.
- Learn to compute the value of the unlevered and levered firm.

A company's decision about how to choose its capital structure is always a significant and controversial issue in academia. In this chapter, we first introduce the important concepts of capital structure. Then we examine the effect of capital structure on firm value; discussing how capital structure can contribute to maximizing the value of the firm. We also introduce capital structure theories including MM theory with and without taxes, trade-off theory, pecking order theory, etc. This chapter can help you develop skills required to compute the value of the unlevered and levered firm and to understand the implications of capital structure.

9.1 Capital Structure: Basic Concepts

A company's capital structure refers to the composition of its liabilities. In other words, it is the way a company finances its assets through some combination of equity, debt or hybrid securities. In the real world, capital structure may be highly complex and contain many different sources of capital. The optimal capital structure is the structure of liabilities that can maximize the value of the company. Financial leverage ratios represent the proportion of capital that is obtained through debt. A company's decision about whether to sell debt or equity is known as capital structure decision.

9.1.1 Capital Structure and Firm Value

First, we define the value of the firm is the sum of the firm's financial claims, which are debt and equity. The value of the firm is presented as below:

$$V = B + S \tag{9.1}$$

where V is the value of the firm, B is the market value of the debt, S is the market value of the equity.

Then, we discuss two important questions:

1. How should a firm choose its debt-equity ratio?

2. Why should the shareholders in the firm care about maximizing the value of the entire firm?

The following case is a typical example illustrating that financial managers should choose the capital structure that can maximize the firm value for the shareholders.

【Example 9-1】

The market value of Company A is \$1,000. The company currently has no debt, and each of Company A's 100 shares of stock sells for \$10. (Company A with no debt is called an unlevered company at this stage). Company A plans to borrow \$500, and pay the \$500 proceeds to shareholders as an extra cash dividend of \$5 per share. After the issuance of debt, the firm becomes levered. What will the value of the firm be after the proposed restructuring?

Answer:

Management recognizes that only one of three outcomes can occur from restructuring. Firm value after restructuring can be ① greater than the original firm value of \$1,000, ② equal to \$1,000, or ③ less than \$1,000. After consulting with investment bankers, management believes that restructuring will not change firm value more than \$250 in either direction. Thus, it views firm values of \$1,250, \$1,000, and \$750 as the relevant range. The original capital structure and these three possibilities under the new capital structure are presented in Table 9-1:

Table 9-1 The original capital structure and three possibilities under new capital structure

No Debt (Original Capital Structure)		Value of Debt plus Equity after Payment of Dividend (Three Possibilities)		
		I	II	III
Debt	\$0	\$500	\$500	\$500
Equity	1,000	750	500	250
Firm value	\$1,000	\$1,250	\$1,000	\$750

These three possibilities are only to be viewed as representative outcomes. Then we determine the payoff to stockholders under the three possibilities in Table 9-2:

Table 9-2 Payoff to stockholders under the three possibilities

	Payoff to Shareholders after Restructuring		
	I	II	III
Capital gains	-\$250	-\$500	-\$750
Dividends	500	500	500
Net gain or loss to stockholders	250	\$0	-\$250

1. Imagine the first possibility that managers believe that Outcome I is most likely. They should definitely restructure the firm because the stockholders would gain \$250. That is, although the price of the stock declines by \$250 to \$750, they receive \$500 in dividends. Their net gain is \$250 = -\$250 + \$500. Also, notice that the value of the firm would rise by \$250 = \$1,250 - \$1,000.

2. Imagine that managers believe that Outcome III is most likely. In this case they should not restructure the firm because the stockholders would expect a \$250 loss. That is, the stock falls by \$750 to \$250 and they receive \$500 in dividends. Their net loss is -\$250 = -\$750 + \$500. Also, notice that the value of the firm would change by -\$250 = \$750 - \$1,000.

3. Imagine that the managers believe that Outcome II is most likely. Restructuring would not affect the stockholders' interest because the net gain to stockholders in this case is zero. Also notice that the value of the firm is unchanged if Outcome II occurs.

This example explains why managers should attempt to maximize the value of the firm.

9.2 Capital Structure Theories

Capital structure theory is characterized by a board set of theories. The Miller and Modigliani (MM or M&M) theory, agency cost theory, signaling theory, trade-off theory and pecking order theory laid the ground for research into capital structure. This section mainly illustrates MM theory, trade-off theory and pecking order theory.

9.2.1 Modigliani and Miller Proposition I(MM 理论:定理 I)

MM Proposition I (no taxes) states that in a world of no taxes, the value of the firm is unaffected by capital structure. In other words, the value of the firm is always the same under different capital structures. This is the famous MM proposition I:

$$V_L = V_U \tag{9.2}$$

where V_L represents the value of the levered firm, V_U represents the value of the unlevered firm, the value of the levered firm is equal to the value of the unlevered firm.

This is one of the most important results in corporate finance. Before MM, the effect of leverage on the value of a firm was considered complex and convoluted. Modigliani and Miller showed a blindingly simple result. If levered firms are priced too high, rational investors will simply borrow on their personal accounts to buy shares in unlevered firms. This substitution is often called homemade leverage. As long as individuals borrow (and lend) on the same terms as the firms, they can duplicate the effects of corporate leverage on their own.

The theorem is valid under very strict assumptions: ① at any given level of risk, individuals and companies can all borrow at that same rate of interest, which remains constant regardless of the gearing; ② there are no costs attached to market transactions, the supply of information or the process of bankruptcy; ③ there is no difference between corporate borrowing and personal borrowing in terms of risk; ④ there is no taxation.

9.2.2 Modigliani and Miller Proposition II(MM 理论:定理 II)

1. MM Proposition II (No Taxes)

In a world of no taxes, MM Proposition II states that leverage increases the risk and return to stockholders. There is a positive relationship between return on equity and firm leverage because the risk to equity-holders increases with leverage. Recall weighted average cost of capital (WACC) that we have learned in the previous chapter, R_{WACC} can be written as:

$$R_{WACC} = \frac{B}{B+S} \times R_B + \frac{S}{B+S} \times R_S \tag{9.3}$$

Where R_{WACC} is the firm's weighted average cost of capital. R_B is the cost of debt. R_S is the expected return on equity, also called the cost of equity. B is the value of debt. S is the value of the firm's equity.

Then we set $R_{WACC} = R_0$, and R_0 is the cost of capital for an all-equity firm. If we multiply both sides by $(B+S)/S$ and then rearranging Equation 9.3, we will get

$$R_S = R_0 + \frac{B}{S}(R_0 - R_B) \tag{9.4}$$

Equation 9.4 implies that the return on equity is a linear function of the firm's debt-to-equity ratio.

2. MM Proposition II (With Taxes)

Modigliani and Miller (1963)[1] revisited their work in 1963 and included tax effects into their model, suggesting that firms should finance completely by debt to maximize company value. They argue that the tax advantage of debt financing is greater than originally suggested, because issuing debt can provide the firms with tax shields in the form of interest deductibility.

In a world of taxes, MM Proposition II states that leverage increases the risk and return to stockholders, but some of the increase in equity risk and return is offset by the interest tax shield. The equation can be written as:

$$R_S = R_0 + \frac{B}{S}(1 - T_C) \times (R_0 - R_B) \tag{9.5}$$

where R_S is the cost of equity. R_B is the cost of debt. R_0 is the cost of capital for an all-equity firm. B is the value of debt. S is the value of the firm's equity. T_C represents the corporate taxes.

---

[1] Modigliani, F. and Miller, M.H. (1963). Corporate Income Taxes and the Cost of Capital: A Correction. The American Economic Review, Vol. 53 (3), pp: 433-443.

However, the MM theory with tax effects is challenged because of the possibility of discontinuity caused by bankruptcy and the distortions due to asymmetric information. Since then, the trade-off theory and pecking order theory of capital structure have been emerging.

9.2.3 Trade-Off Theory(权衡理论)

The traditional trade-off theory of capital structure implies a significant tax incentive for corporate borrowing (Modigliani and Miller, 1963)[1]. Due to the effects of agency costs and bankruptcy costs, there exists an optimal capital structure for companies that requires them to trade-off between the tax benefits of increasing leverage and the costs of financial distress that is caused by high debt ratios (Myers, 1984)[2]. This is illustrated in Figure 9-1 below:

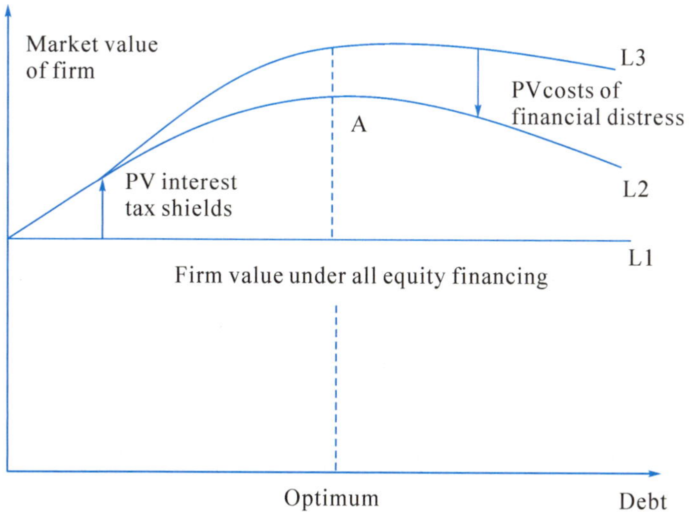

Figure 9-1 The static trade-off theory of capital structure

Source: Myers, S.C. (1984) The Capital Structure Puzzle. The Journal of Finance, Vol. 39 (3), pp: 575-592.

Figure 9-1 shows that a firm's optimal debt ratio is determined by the trade-off of benefits and costs of debt financing. The straight line L1 indicates the market value of an all-equity firm under the Modigliani and Miller (1958)[3] regime, in

[1] Modigliani, F. and Miller, M.H. (1963). Corporate Income Taxes and the Cost of Capital: A Correction. The American Economic Review, Vol. 53 (3), pp: 433-443.

[2] Myers, S.C. (1984). The Capital Structure Puzzle. The Journal of Finance, Vol. 39 (3), pp: 575-592.

[3] Modigliani, F. and Miller, M.H. (1958). The Cost of Capital, Corporation Finance and the Theory of Investment. The American Economic Review, Vol. 4 8(3), pp: 261- 297.

which firm value is irrelevant to its capital structure. Curve L3 shows how the costs of financial distress increase with the increasing leverage in this firm. Here, the costs of financial distress include legal and administrative costs of bankruptcy, moral hazard, monitoring and contracting costs (Myers, 1984)[1]. Curve L2 illustrates that the market value of the firm rises with the increase of debt level, then after financing a certain proportion of debt (the optimum debt ratio), the value of the firm begins to decline (point A), because the costs of financial distress outweigh the benefits of tax shields. If there is no cost of adjusting to the optimum, each firm's observed debt level should be equal to its optimal debt ratio. However, the adjustment costs cannot be avoided in practice, therefore wide variations observed in firms' actual debt ratios.

9.2.4 Pecking-Order Theory(有序融资理论)

The pecking-order theory is based on information asymmetry that explains how companies prioritize financing sources for an optimal capital structure choice (Myers and Majluf, 1984)[2]. Asymmetric information has significant effects on the choices between internal and external financing and on the choices between the new issues of debt and equity; it implies that external financing is costly and therefore avoided by companies. Hence, the pecking order theory suggests that firms prefer funding internal equity first, and then issue debt, with the last being external equity financing (Myers, 2001)[3].

案例分析 9-1 《江苏苏州小微企业"债权+股权"综合融资案例》

近年来，江苏苏州通过实施《金融支持企业自主创新行动计划》，依托"三平台一中心"（综合金融服务平台、股权融资服务平台、地方企业征信平台、企业自主创新金融支持中心），为小微企业提供了"债权+股权"综合融资方案，逐渐形成"政府+市场"双轮驱动的发展模式。

江苏苏州创新征信工作机制、政银信息共享、征信平台开发，形成"企业授权+机构征信+政府增信"的框架。为了保障征信信息的安全性以及采集的合法性，平台采用信息收集与查询双授权模式。征信平台通过金融机构活动

[1] Myers, S.C. (1984). The Capital Structure Puzzle. The Journal of Finance, Vol. 39 (3), pp: 575-592.

[2] Myers, S.C. and Majluf, N. (1984). Corporate Financing Decisions When Firms Have Investment Information that Investors Do Not. Journal of Financial Economics, Vol. 13 (2), pp: 187-220.

[3] Myers, S.C. (2001). Capital Structure. Journal of Economic Perspectives, Vol. 15, pp: 81-102.

小微企业的信息采集授权，通过代为管理的辖内金融综合服务平台以及各接入的政府部门获得小微企业的查询授权后，可从征信平台处查询企业信用资质，为企业提供相关融资服务。

苏州综合金融服务平台帮助企业通过平台在线发布融资需求，实现金融机构在线受理企业融资申请。双方之间双向选择、自主对接，让企业在融资过程中"多走网络，少跑马路"。苏州综合金融服务平台已累计帮助 6 万多家企业解决融资 1 万多亿元。苏州综合金融服务平台提供的"债权融资"服务与苏州股权融资服务平台提供的"股权融资"服务相互补充，为小微企业提供了"债权+股权"的一揽子综合融资方案。通过平台的搭建、政策的配套，充分地调动各类金融资源服务实体经济发展，重点解决企业和金融机构之间信息不对称的问题，帮助广大的创新创业型中小微企业成长发展。

资料来源：

[1]雷曜.小微企业融资的全球经验[M].机械工业出版社，2020.4.185－194.

[2]苏州综合金融服务平台.苏州市 2 0 1 9 年 6 月金融运行情况及《行动计划》实施情况［EB/OL］.（2019－08－05）［2019－08－06］. http://www.szjr.suzhou.gov.cn.

9.3 Financial Leverage and Firm Value: MM with Taxes

In a world of taxes, but no bankruptcy costs, the value of the firm increases with leverage. This is M&M Proposition I (with taxes):

$$V_L = V_U + T_C B \tag{9.6}$$

where V_L is the value of levered firm, V_U is the value of the unlevered firm, B is the value of debt, T_C is the corporate taxes. Equation 9.6 implies that the value of the levered firm is equal to the value of an all-equity firm plus the tax rate times the firm's debt value. $T_C B$ represents the present value of the tax shield in the case of perpetual cash flows.

The value of an unlevered firm is the present value of EBIT×$(1 - T_C)$:

$$V_U = \frac{\text{EBIT} \times (1 - T_C)}{R_0} \tag{9.7}$$

where EBIT is earnings before interest and taxes, R_0 is the cost of capital for an all-equity firm. We combine Equation 9.6 and 9.7, and then we get

$$V_L = \frac{\text{EBIT} \times (1 - T_C)}{R_0} + T_C B \tag{9.8}$$

【Example 9-2】

Company ABC is currently an unlevered firm which expects EBIT to be $145,000 annually forever. This company can borrow at 8%, and its expected return on equity is 14%. If the tax rate is 35%, what is the company's value? If the company borrows $135,000 and uses the proceeds to repurchase shares, what is the value of the company?

Answer:

The unlevered value of Company ABC is:

$$V_U = \frac{\text{EBIT} \times (1 - T_C)}{R_0} = \frac{145,000 \times (1-0.35)}{0.14} = \$673,214.29$$

The value of the levered Company ABC is equal to:

$$V_L = V_U + T_C B = \$673,214.29 + 35\% \times 135,000 = \$720,464.29$$

Key Concepts and Skills

1. The concepts of capital structure.
2. The effect of capital structure on firm value.
3. Maximization of firm value versus maximization of shareholders' interests.
4. The capital structure theories.
5. Calculation of the unlevered and levered firm value.

本章重点与难点

1. 资本结构的基本概念。
2. 资本结构对公司价值的影响。
3. 公司价值的最大化与股东利益的最大化。
4. 资本结构相关理论。
5. 计算有负债公司和无负债公司的价值。

Self-Test Questions

Ⅰ. Single Choice Questions

1. Pecking order theory suggests which of the following? (　　)

A. Internal funds, debt, and external equity have the same risk-adjusted return.

B. Debt is preferred to external equity and internal funds.

C. External equity is preferred to debt which is preferred to internal funds.

D. Internal capital is preferred to debt which is preferred to external funds.

2. Which of the following does not make the firm more vulnerable to financial distress? ( )

A. High sensitivity of the company's revenues to the general level of economic activity.

B. High proportion of fixed to variable costs.

C. Physical capital assets which are relatively illiquid and difficult-to-market.

D. The tax shields.

3. Suppose a company's capital structure is composed of \$300 million debt and \$200 million equity. The company's cost of debt is 5%, its cost of equity is 15%. The tax rate is 40%. What is the firm's weighted average cost of capital? ( )

A. 7.8%

B. 9%

C. 10 %

D. 6%

Ⅱ. True (T) or False (F) Questions

1. The optimal capital structure is the structure of liabilities that can maximize the value of the company. ( )

2. When a company has debt, there will be conflicts of interest between stockholders and bondholders. ( )

3. MM Proposition I states that the value of the firm is always the same under different capital structures. ( )

4. MM theory implies that the cost of equity is negatively related to financial leverage. ( )

5. A company's capital structure decisions involves a trade-off between a tax subsidy and financial distress costs. ( )

6. Much debate exists about the real-world applications of the MM theory given its highly restrictive assumptions. ( )

Ⅲ. Calculation Questions

1. Hardy Corp. is currently an all-equity firm worth \$20 million with 500,000 shares of common stock outstanding. Hardy Corp. plans to issue debt and use the proceeds to repurchase common stock. After the sale of the bonds, it will maintain the new capital structure indefinitely. Corporate tax rate is 30 percent.

Given the following information:

Debt	\$ 10 million bonds with a coupon rate of 10 percent and a current price quote of 90; 10 years to maturity. \$ 1, 000 par value.
Annual pretax earnings	\$ 5 million; expected to remain constant in perpetuity.

Questions:

(1) What is the price per share of the firm's equity before the announcement of the debt issue?

(2) How many shares will the firm repurchase as a result of the debt issue? How many shares of common stock will remain after the repurchase?

(3) Construct the market value balance sheet after the restructuring.

(4) What is the required return on equity after the restructuring?

本章习题答案

Chapter 10 Dividend Policy （股利政策）

Learning Objectives

- Understand dividend types and how they are paid.
- Understand the issues surrounding dividend policy decisions.
- Understand why share repurchases are an alternative to dividends.
- Understand the difference between cash and stock dividends.

The term dividend usually refers to a cash distribution of earnings and mainly includes cash dividends and stock dividends. Cash dividends are the most common way to distribute. Firstly, there are four types of dividends and other payouts we will study, cash dividends, stock repurchases, stock dividends and stock splits. Next, for the process of payment of dividends, the right to pay dividends belongs to the general meeting of shareholders. The specific process is proposed by the board of directors and can be determined once approved by the shareholders' general meeting. In order to determine who can receive the dividend, some date boundaries must be determined before the dividend is paid. In addition, the irrelevance of dividend policy explains that the dividend policy does not have any impact on the value of the company. Finally, the realistic factors affecting dividend policy will also be introduced.

10.1 Dividends and Other Payouts

When a listed company distributes profits, it will distribute a certain amount of profit to shareholders. The distribution of profits is generally called a dividend, and the distribution of capital is called a liquidation dividend. Usually, any direct distribution by the company to shareholders can be considered part of the dividend. Dividend policy includes whether the company will pay dividends, how many dividends will be paid, and when. The main issue involved is the strategy of a company to distribute its earnings or retain them for reinvestment. In addition, there are multiple types of dividends.

10. 1. 1 Cash Dividends(现金股利)

The most common type of dividend is in the form of cash. When companies pay cash dividends, they usually pay regular cash dividends several times a year. The board of directors of the company has the decision-making power to pay dividends. Once the company declares dividends, it is an irrevocable liability.

The payment of cash dividend has standard process. There are four important dates in the payment of cash dividends. The distribution mechanism is shown in Figure 10-1.

1. **Declaration date(股利宣布日)**: The board of directors declares a payment of dividends.

On January 12 (the declaration date), the board of directors passes a resolution to pay a dividend of $1 per share on February 14 to all holders of record on January 28.

2. **Ex-dividend date(除息日)**: A share of stock becomes ex dividend on the date the seller is entitled to keep the dividend; under NYSE rules, shares are traded ex dividend on and after the second business day before the record date.

The procedure for the date of record would be unfair if efficient brokerage houses could notify the corporation by January 28 of a trade occurring on January 27, whereas the same trade might not reach the corporation until February 2 if executed by a less efficient house. To eliminate this problem, all brokerage firms entitle stockholders to receive the dividend if they purchased the stock three business days before the date of record. The second day before the date of record, which is January 26, in our example, is called the ex-dividend date. Before this date the stock is said to trade cum dividend.

3. **Record date(股权登记日)**: The declared dividends are distributable to shareholders of record on a specific date.

The corporation prepares a list on January 28 of all individuals believed to be stockholders as of this date. The word believed is important here: The dividend will not be paid to individuals whose notification of purchase is received by the company after January 28.

4. **Payment date（股利支付日）**: The dividend checks are mailed to shareholders of record.

The dividend checks are mailed to the stockholders on February 14.

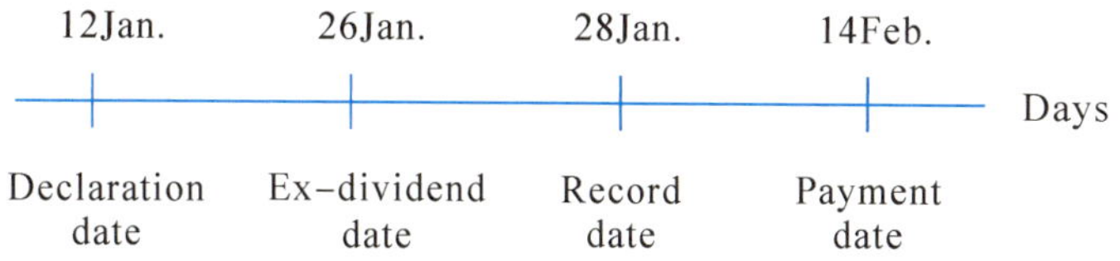

Figure 10-1 **A sample of procedure for dividend payment**

For investors, stocks purchased before the ex-dividend date receive current dividends, and stocks purchased on or after the ex-dividend date cannot receive current dividends. Assuming nothing else happens, the stock price falls on the ex-dividend date. At this point, a drop in stock price indicates that the market is efficient and that the market associates stock value with cash dividends. So, in an ideal world with no taxes and no transaction costs, the stock price decline equals the dividend.

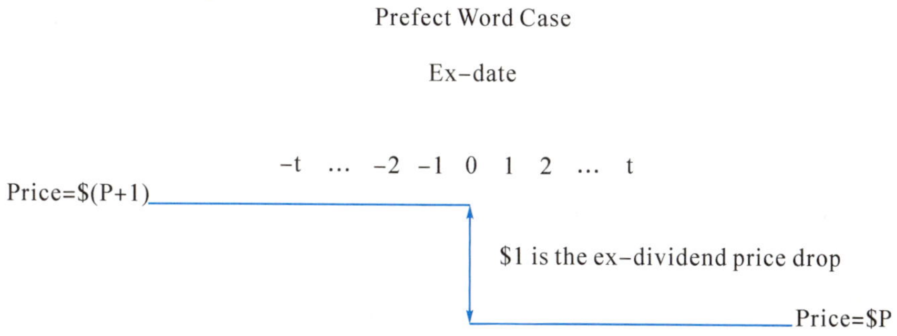

Figure10-2 **Price behavior around the ex-dividend date for a $1 cash dividend**

In a world without taxes, the stock price will fall by the amount of the dividend on the ex-date (time 0). If the dividend is $1 per share, the price will be equal to P on the ex-date.

The amount of the price drop may depend on tax rates. For example, consider the case with no capital gains taxes. On the day before a stock goes ex dividend, a purchaser must decide either: ① To buy the stock immediately and pay tax on the forthcoming dividend or ② To buy the stock tomorrow, thereby missing the dividend. If all investors are in the 17 percent tax bracket and the quarterly dividend is $1, the stock price should fall by $0.83 on the ex-dividend date. That is, if the stock price falls by this amount on the ex-dividend date, purchasers will receive the same return from either strategy.

【Example 10-1】

Ex-dividend date is November 15, 2020, and the dividend per share is \$4.40. Stock closed at \$26.09 on November 12 and opened at \$22.34 on November 15, with a known income tax rate of 15% on dividends. Calculate share price declines and dividends.

Answer:

Share price decline:

$$\$26.09-\$22.34=\$3.75$$

Dividend amount:

$$\$4.40\times85\%=\$3.74$$

So, the stock price decline and the dividend amount are basically equal.

10.1.2 Stock Repurchases(股票回购)

Listed companies use cash and other forms to buy back a certain amount of shares issued by the company from the market. In general, companies will cancel the shares after the repurchase is completed. In other cases, the companies retain the repurchased shares as treasury shares.

【Example 10-2】

Suppose a company has \$200,000 outstanding ordinary shares and the stock price is \$10 per stock. The company has two ways of distributing dividends: ① a cash dividend of \$1 per share; and ② a repurchase of 10% of the shares at a price of \$10 per share.

If the company decides to pay a cash dividend of \$1 per share, it needs to pay \$200,000 in cash, so the market value of the company's assets drops to \$1,800,000, and the stock price drops to \$9. If the company buys back 10% of the shares from the existing shareholders, with the decline in cash expenditure and the market value of the company's assets, the number of shares outstanding in common stock is reduced to 180,000 shares, and the decrease in the market value of the assets and the decrease in the number of shares outstanding cancel each other out, and the market price of the stock remains at the level of \$10 per share.

The above analysis shows that the cash dividend policy and the stock repurchase policy are the same. In both ways, the company needs to pay a certain amount of cash to the stock holders, whether it is in the form of cash dividends, or in the form of cash to buy back shares, the result is to reduce the company's total assets by \$200,000.

For investors, whether they receive a cash dividend or sell their shares for cash, the value of their wealth does not change. Suppose investor A holds 10, 000 shares of the company stock worth \$ 100, 000 before the dividend is distributed, and after the cash dividend is paid, he can get \$ 10, 000 in cash (dividends) and 10, 000 shares worth \$ 90, 000.

If the company adopts the method of stock repurchase, investor A holds 10, 000 shares of the company stock before the stock repurchase, accounting for 1% of the total number of shares in the company, and the investor sells 10% of the shares (1, 000 shares) to the company, the number of shares is still 1%, then he will receive \$ 10, 000 in cash and 9, 000 shares of the company shares worth \$ 90, 000.

Table 10-1 The impact of cash dividends and share repurchases on an investor's wealth

Types	Cash dividends	Stock repurchases
Before dividend distribution	\$ 10 per share × 10, 000 = \$ 100, 000	\$ 10 per share × 10, 000 = \$ 100, 000
After dividend distribution		
Cash	\$ 1 per share × 10, 000 = \$ 10, 000	\$ 10 per share × 1, 000 = \$ 10, 000
Stock market value	\$ 9 per share × 10, 000 = \$ 90, 000	\$ 10 per share × 9, 000 = \$ 90, 000

Regardless of taxation (stock repurchase proceeds are subject to capital gains tax, which is usually not equal to the dividend income tax rate), cash dividends and share repurchases do not affect the value of investors' wealth.

Companies may use cash to buy back their own shares instead of paying cash dividends. In recent years, stock repurchase has become an important form of profit distribution to shareholders. The methods of stock repurchase are:

(1) Ordinary Repurchases(普通回购): In the open market, companies buy their own shares at the market price of the stock, and the stock seller cannot tell whether the stock is sold back to the company or to other investors.

(2) Offer Repurchases(要约回购): The company announces to all shareholders that a certain amount of shares will be repurchased at a certain price. One method related to tender offers is Dutch auction. Companies no longer set prices uniformly, but instead organize auctions and bid on shares. The company will announce the number of shares that are willing to buy back at several different prices, and the shareholders will also give the number of shares they are willing to sell at different prices. The company finally selects the lowest price to achieve the set goal.

(3) **Targeted Repurchases(目标回购)**: The company repurchases a certain number of shares from specific shareholders. Companies engage in targeted repurchases for a variety of reasons. In some rare cases, a single large stockholder can be bought out at a price lower than that in a tender offer. The legal fees in a targeted repurchase may also be lower than those in a more typical buyback. In addition, the shares of large stockholders are often repurchased to avoid a takeover unfavorable to management.

Companies conduct stock repurchases mainly for the following purposes.

(1) Corporate mergers or acquisitions. In the case of an acquisition or merger, the payment method of the property exchange is cash purchase and the exchange of shares for shares. By exchanging the company's treasury shares for the shares of the acquired company, the company's cash expenditure can be reduced.

(2) Meet convertible terms and facilitate the exercise of warrants. Shares repurchased by a company can be exchanged for shares of an acquired or merged company. It can also be used to meet the needs of warrant holders to subscribe for the company's shares or convertible bondholders to convert the company's common stock.

(3) Establish a shareholding system for enterprise employees. The company uses the repurchased shares as a stock reserve to reward outstanding management personnel and transfer them to employees at a preferential price.

(4) Improve capital structure. The shares were repurchased in cash through debt borrowing, thereby rationalizing the capital structure.

(5) Allocate excess cash. Take the form of stock repurchases and distribute cash to shareholders.

(6) Stabilize stock price. Supporting the company's stock price by buying back shares is conducive to improving the company image.

10.1.3 Stock Dividends(股票股利)

Another type of dividend is paid out in shares of stock. This type of dividend is called a stock dividend. Stock dividends are dividends that a company distributes to investors in the form of shares. From an accounting perspective, stock dividends are simply transfers of capital between shareholder equity accounts, not the use of capital. That is, it merely transfers capital from retained earnings accounts to other owners' equity accounts, does not change the equity ratio of each shareholder, and does not increase the company's assets. The effect of a stock dividend is to increase the number of shares that each owner holds.

【Example 10-3】

Suppose a company announces a 10% stock dividend, and the market price of the stock is \$10 per share. The company issues 1,000 shares of its common stock. Shareholders receive 1 additional common stock for every 10 shares held, resulting in an additional 100 common shares issued for 1,100 new shares. With the payment of stock dividends, the common stock account increases by \$100 as the par (\$1) remains the same. The stock price of \$10 is \$9 higher than the par value because 100 new shares are added, resulting in an increase in the capital surplus of \$900 (\$9×100) and a decrease in retained earnings of 1,000 (\$10 ×100), while the total ownership equity of the company remains unchanged.

Table 10-2 **Owners' equity before and after the issuance of stock dividends unit: \$**

Before the stock dividends		After the stock dividends	
Common stock (\$1 par, 1,000 shares)	1,000	Common stock (\$1 par, 1,100 shares)	1,100
Capital surplus	10,000	Capital surplus	10,900
Retained earnings	50,000	Retained earnings	49,000
Total owners' equity	61,000	Total owners' equity	61,000

For corporate managements, the issuance of stock dividends may be motivated by the following motivations: First, in the case that profits and cash dividends are not expected to increase, the issuance of stock dividends can effectively reduce the price per share, thereby increasing investors' interest in investment; Second, the issuance of stock dividends allows shareholders to share in the company's earnings without distributing cash, which can retain more cash for reinvestment, which is conducive to the long-term healthy and stable development of the company.

10.1.4 Stock Split(股票分割)

An alternative to stock dividends is stock splitting, which refers to the exchange of shares with a higher denomination for several shares with lower denominations. When a split is declared, each share is split up to create additional shares. For example, in a three-for-one stock split, each old share is split into three new shares. From an accounting point of view, the stock split will not have any impact on the financial structure of the public company, generally only the number of shares issued and outstanding will increase, the par value per share will decrease, and thus the price of each stock will fall, while the balance of each account of owners' equity in the balance sheet will remain unchanged, and the total number of owners' equity will remain unchanged.

【Example 10-4】

Assuming the company decides to implement a stock split plan, shareholders will receive an additional 1 share for every 1 share they own, and the par value of the shares will be reduced from \$1 per share to \$0.5 per share. owners' equity remains unchanged before and after the stock split.

Table 10-3 **Owners' equity before and after the stock splits** unit: \$

Before the stock splits		After the stock splits	
Common stock (\$1 par, 1,000 shares)	1,000	Common stock (\$0.5 par, 2,000 shares)	1,000
Capital surplus	10,000	Capital surplus	10,000
Retained earnings	50,000	Retained earnings	50,000
Total owners' equity	61,000	Total owners' equity	61,000

Stock dividends and stock splits, except for accounting differences, are essentially the same: ① neither increases shareholder cash flow; ② both increase the number of shares outstanding in common stock and reduces the stock market price; and ③ neither changes the total amount of owners' equity, but the stock dividend changes internally in owners' equity and must pay dividends in current earnings or retained earnings, whereas stock splits are not subject to this restriction.

As far as the managers are concerned, the main purposes and motivations for stock splitting are: First, to reduce the market price of stocks. Generally speaking, the stock price is too high, which is not conducive to stock trading activities. Reduce the stock price through stock splitting, so that the company's stock is more widely dispersed into the hands of investors. Second, prepare for the issuance of new shares. The high price of the stock makes many potential investors too overwhelmed to invest easily in the company's stock. Before the issuance of new shares, the use of stock splits to reduce the stock price is conducive to improving the transfer ability of stocks and promoting market transactions, thereby increasing investors' interest in stocks and enabling newly issued shares to sell well. Lastly, it will help the company to implement the merger and consolidation policy. When a company merges or merges with another company, splitting the company's shares first can improve its attractiveness to the shareholders of the merged party.

10.2 The Irrelevance of Dividend Policy

The irrelevance of dividend policy theory (MM theory,股利无关理论) was first proposed by Miller and Modigliani (1961), which argues that dividend policies do not affect the value of companies under perfect capital market conditions. The value of a company is determined by the profitability and risk portfolio determined by the investment decisions, rather than by the way the company's surplus is divided (dividend distribution policy). Explanation of irrelevance of dividend policy theory as follows.

10.2.1 Theoretical Assumptions

The basic assumptions of MM theory is: ① all shareholders of the company have an accurate grasp of the company's situation, and investors and managers have the same information as managers for future investment opportunities; ② there is no personal income tax or corporate income tax, and there is no difference for investors whether they receive dividends or capital gains; ③ there is no stock issuance or transaction fee; and ④ the company's investment decisions are independent of dividend policy. MM theory holds that without changing the investment decision and target capital structure, no matter how much dividends are paid with the remaining cash flow, it will not affect shareholder wealth.

First, after the company meets the project investment needs, there is still a surplus cash N dollars to pay dividends, and before paying dividends, the shareholders have N dollars claims on the company's assets; After the payment of dividends, on the one hand, the amount of the company's "cash on hand" account and the "owners' equity" account is reduced equally, on the other hand, the shareholders also lose the corresponding claim to the company's assets after receiving N dollars cash.

Second, the company does not have enough cash to pay dividends, and before the dividends are paid, it must issue new shares equal to the amount of dividends paid, which can temporarily increase the value of the company; After the dividends are paid, the value of the company returns to the value it was before the issuance of the new shares.

Lastly, the company does not pay dividends, but existing shareholders want to receive cash dividends, which they can exchange for cash by finding and selling some of their shares to new investors. In exchange for cash, existing shareholders cede a portion of their shares to new investors.

Under sound market conditions, the price transfer that new shareholders are willing to pay for the purchase of shares must be consistent with the value of the company's shares. As a result, this behavior results in a transfer of value between new and old shareholders - the old shareholders transfer a portion of their own assets to the new shareholders, and the value of the company remains the same. This direct transaction (shareholders selling shares in exchange for cash) is called self-made dividends.

10.2.2 Current Dividend Policy vs Alternative Dividend Policy

1. Current Dividend Policy(现期股利政策)

Current dividend policy means that dividends set equal to cash flow. Under the current dividend policy, dividends at each point in time are set at \$5,000, and the value of the company can be calculated by dividends. The value of company is calculated as follows:

$$V_0 = \text{Div}_0 + \frac{\text{Div}_1}{1 + R_s}$$

where Div_0 and Div_1 are the cash dividend paid, and R_s is the discount rate. If the first dividend is paid immediately, no discount is required.

【Example 10-5】

If an all-equity firm that started 10 years ago. The current financial managers know at the present time (Date 0) that the firm will dissolve in one year (Date 1). At Date 0 the managers are able to forecast cash flows with perfect certainty. The managers know that the firm will receive a cash flow of \$5,000 immediately and another \$5,000 next year. The company has no additional positive NPV projects.

If the current dividend policy is in place and $R_s = 10\%$, the value of the company is:

$$\$9,545.45 = \$5,000 + \frac{\$5,000}{1.1}$$

If the number of outgoing shares is 100 shares, the value of per share is:

$$\$95.45 = \$50 + \frac{\$50}{1.1}$$

Suppose the Ex-dividend date and Payment date are the same day. Immediately after the dividend is paid, the stock price falls to:

$$\$95.45 - \$50 = \$45.45$$

2. Alternative Dividend Policy(备选股利政策)

Under alternative dividend policy, initial dividend is greater than cash flow. The distribution of the alternative policy is for the company to pay dividends of $5.5per share for a total of $5,500. With a cash flow of only $5,000, the shortfall of $500 had to be raised through other sources. If $100 of shares are issued at Date 0, and the new shareholder expects to receive sufficient cash flow at Date 1, the return on investment at Date 0 is 10%. Then the new shareholders ask for $550 in cash flow at Date1, and the old shareholders only have $4,450 left.

Table 10-4 The dividends to the old stockholders

	Date 0	Date 1
Aggregate dividends to old stockholders	$5,500	$4,450
Dividends per share	$55	$44.5

The present value of dividends per share is:

$$\$95.45 = \$55 + \frac{\$44.5}{1.1}$$

Since new shareholders are not eligible for spot dividends, they are willing to pay a share price of:

$$\$40.45 = \frac{\$44.50}{1.1}$$

The number of new shares to be issued is:

$$12.36 = \frac{\$500}{\$40.45}$$

Note that the values of per share in current dividend policy and alternative dividend policy are equal. This leads to the initially surprising conclusion that the change in dividend policy did not affect the value of a share of stock as long as all distributable cash flow is paid out. That is to say, neither increasing nor decreasing the current dividend can change the current value of the company. MM theory is premised on multiple assumptions that do not exist in real life, such as the transaction cost of stocks; The issuance of shares is subject to the issuance fee; Business managers usually have more information than outside investors; The government levies income tax on companies and individuals. Therefore, the irrelevance of dividend policy theory is not necessarily valid under real conditions.

10.2.3 Dividend vs Stock Repurchases

【Example 10-6】

Imagine that Telephonic Industries has excess cash of \$200,000 (\$2 per share) and is considering an immediate payment of this amount as an extra dividend. The firm forecasts that, after the dividend, earnings will be \$400,000 per year, or \$4.0 for each of the 100,000 shares outstanding. Because the price-earnings ratio is 5 for comparable companies, the shares of the firm should sell for \$20 (= \$4.0×5) after the dividend is paid. These figures are presented in the top half of Table 10.5. Because the dividend is \$2 per share, the stock would have sold for \$22 a share before payment of the dividend.

Alternatively, the firm could use the excess cash to repurchase some of its own stock. Imagine that a tender offer of \$22 per share is made. Here, 20,000 shares are repurchased so that the total number of shares remaining is 80,000. With fewer shares outstanding, the earnings per share will rise to \$5 (= \$400,000/80,000). The price-earnings ratio remains at 5 because both the business and financial risks of the firm are the same in the repurchase case as they were in the dividend case. Thus, the price of a share after the repurchase is \$25 (= \$5×5). These results are presented in the bottom half of Table 10.5.

Table 10-5 **Dividend versus stock repurchases** unit: \$

	Total	Per share
Extra Dividend		(100,000 shares outstanding)
Proposed dividend	200,000	2.00
Forecasted annual earnings after dividend	400,000	4.00
Market value of stock after dividend	2,000,000	20.00
Repurchase		(80,000 shares outstanding)
Forecasted annual earnings after repurchase	400,000	5.00
Market value of stock after repurchase	2,000,000	25.00

If commissions, taxes, and other incomplete factors are not taken into account, shareholders do not care whether dividends are paid or shares are repurchased. Because in the perfect capital market, the total value of shareholders under the two strategies of issuing dividends and recovering shares is exactly equal.

In fact, most firms that pay dividends also repurchase shares of stock. If some companies choose to repurchases instead of dividends, the common reasons are as follows:

(1) **Flexibility（弹性）**: Firms often view dividends as a commitment to their stockholders and are quite hesitant to reduce an existing dividend. Repurchases do not represent a similar commitment. Thus, a firm with a permanent increase in cash flow is likely to increase its dividend. Conversely, a firm whose cash flow increase is only temporary is likely to repurchase shares of stock.

(2) **Executive Compensation（管理层激励）**: As part of the overall compensation, management is often granted certain stock options. The price of shares after a share repurchase is generally higher than the dividend paid, so the value of the period right to repurchase the stock is higher.

(3) **Offset to Dilution（对冲稀释）**: After the exercise of stock options, the number of shares outstanding will increase, which will dilute the stock. To this end, companies often buy back their shares to hedge dilutions.

(4) **Undervaluation（价值低估）**: Many companies buy back stock because they believe that a repurchase is their best investment. and repurchases are especially likely to occur when management believes that the stock price is temporarily undervalued. The short-term reaction of the stock market after the announcement of share buybacks is often positive. There are also empirical studies that show that the stock prices of repurchased stock companies perform better in the long term than companies that do not repurchase shares.

(5) **Tax（税）**: Taxes on buying back shares are more favorable than dividends.

10.3 Real-World Factors

In reality, dividends are taxed on personal income. Financial managers might find ways to reduce dividends. In contrast, stock repurchases have many benefits, such as saving taxes. But why do companies still pay high dividends to their shareholders? Why do some companies prefer a low dividend policy? Why do others prefer a high dividend policy? What factors affect dividend policy?

10.3.1 Real-World Factors Favoring a Low Dividend Policy

1. Tax（税）

In the real world, the tax law is more complicated. The main feature of taxes is the tax treatment of dividend income and capital gains. For individual shareholders, the effective tax rate on dividend income is higher than capital gains. Dividends received by shareholders are treated as ordinary income when taxed, while capital gains are subject to lower tax rates. Capital gains tax can be deferred to the time the stock is sold. The present value of the tax is smaller, resulting in a lower effective rate of capital gains tax.

In the no-tax case, the entrepreneur receives the $100 in dividends that he gave to the firm when purchasing stock. The entire operation is called a wash; in other words, it has no economic effect. With taxes, the entrepreneur still receives $100 in dividends. However, assume he must pay $20 in taxes to the tax authority. The entrepreneur loses and the tax authority wins when a firm issues stock to pay a dividend.

Though the example is clearly contrived and unrealistic, similar results can be reached for more plausible situations. Thus, financial economists generally agree that in a world of personal taxes, firms should not issue stock to pay dividends. The direct costs of issuance will add to this effect. Investment bankers must be paid when new capital is raised. Thus, the net receipts due to the firm from a new issue are less than 100 percent of total capital raised. Because the size of new issues can be lowered by a reduction in dividends, we have another argument in favor of a low-dividend policy.

2. Issuing Cost(发行成本)

In the example of how dividend policy doesn't work, we see that if a company has to pay dividends, it can offer some new shares. The cost of offering new shares can be expensive. If the cost of issuance is included in our discussion, we will find that offering new shares will reduce the value of the shares.

Imagine two companies, except for one that distributes a higher percentage of its cash flow in the form of dividends, and is the same in every way. The other company retained more surpluses, so its equity grew faster. If the two companies remain the same, then companies with higher dividend payouts will have to offer new shares on a regular basis. Because it's expensive to do so, companies may gravitate toward lower dividend payout ratios.

3. Dividend Limits(股利限制)

In some cases, a company may face restrictions on its ability to pay dividends. For example, a common feature of bond contracts is that dividend payments in excess of a certain amount are prohibited. And, if the amount of a company's dividends exceeds the amount of retained earnings of the company, state law in the United States may prohibit it.

10.3.2 Real-World Factors Favoring a High Dividend Policy

1. Desire for Current Income(渴望现期收入)

Most investors prefer current income. For retirees and other people who live on a fixed income, who coax stock prices when dividends rise and suppress stock prices when dividends fall.

In fact, dividends are relevant because there will be gold and other transaction costs associated with selling low-dividend stocks, and these direct cash charges will not be incurred when investing in dividend stocks. In addition, the time required to sell shares motivates investors to buy high-dividend securities.

Besides, financial intermediaries such as mutual funds are able to complete these repackaging transactions for individual investors at a very low cost. These intermediaries buy stocks with low dividends, then realize the profits through certain measures, and then issue them to its investors at a higher payment rate.

2. Behavioral Finance(行为金融)

Behavioral finance also offers an alternative explanation for high dividends. A very important concept in psychology: self-control. Similarly, investors must deal with the issue of self-control. Suppose a retiree intends to spend \$20,000 a year from his savings, social security contributions, and pensions. He can either buy stocks with a high dividend yield of enough to distribute \$20,000 a year, or buy stocks that don't pay dividends and then sell \$20,000 a year to spend. Both methods have the same financial results, but the second method is much more flexible. Without self-control, he may sell too many stocks and leave fewer for later years. A better solution might be to invest in dividend-paying stocks and strictly adhere to the principle of never consuming principal.

Do behavioral financiers also favor increased share buybacks? The answer is no, because investors will sell shares that the company buys back. As mentioned earlier, selling stocks is more flexible, and investors may sell too many stocks at a time, resulting in fewer stocks left for later years.

3. Agency Costs(代理成本)

Although stockholders, bondholders, and managers start firms for mutually beneficial reasons, one party may later gain at the other's expense. For example, conflicts of interest often arise between bondholders and stockholders. Bondholders would like stockholders to leave as much cash as possible in the firm so that this cash would be available to pay the bondholders during times of financial distress.

Conversely, stockholders would like to keep this extra cash for themselves. In other words, a dividend can be viewed as a wealth transfer from bondholders to stockholders. Bondholders know about the propensity of stockholders to transfer money out of the firm. To protect themselves, bondholders frequently create loan agreements stating that dividends can be paid only if the firm has earnings, cash flow, and working capital above specified levels.

Although managers may be looking out for stockholders in any conflict with bondholders, managers may pursue selfish goals at the expense of stockholders in other situations. For example, the managers have high consumption, invest in projects with a negative net present value, or do not work hard. When a company has sufficient cash flow of its own, it is easier for managers to pursue their own interests.

10.3.3 The Clientele Effect(客户效应)

We pointed out that the existence of personal taxes favors a low-dividend policy, whereas other factors favor high dividends. The financial profession had hoped that it would be easy to determine which of these sets of factors dominates. However, one particular idea, known as **the clientele effect(客户效应)**, implies that the two sets of factors are likely to cancel each other out after all. To understand this idea, let's separate investors in high tax brackets from those in low tax brackets. Individuals in high tax brackets likely prefer either no or low dividends. Low tax bracket investors generally fall into three categories.

First, there are individual investors in low brackets. They are likely to prefer some dividends if they desire current income. Second, pension funds pay no taxes on either dividends or capital gains. Because they face no tax consequences, pension funds will also prefer dividends if they have a preference for current income. Finally, corporations can exclude at least 70% of their dividend income but cannot exclude any of their capital gains. Thus, corporations are likely to prefer high-dividend stocks, even without a preference for current income.

Suppose that 40 % of all investors prefer high dividends and 60 % prefer low dividends, yet only 20 % of firms pay high dividends while 80 % pay low dividends. Here, the high-dividend firms will be in short supply, implying that their stock should be bid up while the stock of low-dividend firms should be bid down. However, the dividend policies of all firms need not be fixed in the long run. In this example, we would expect enough low-dividend firms to increase their payout so that 40 % of the firms pay high dividends and 60 % of the firms pay low dividends. After this adjustment, no firm will gain from changing its dividend policy. Once payouts of corporations conform to the desires of stockholders, no single firm can affect its market value by switching from one dividend strategy to another.

Table 10-6 Clienteles are likely to form in the following way

Group	Stocks
Individuals in high tax brackets	Zero- to low-payout stocks
Individuals in low tax brackets	Low- to medium-payout stocks
Tax-free institutions	Medium-payout stocks
Corporations	High-payout stocks

As long as there are already enough high-dividend firms to satisfy dividend-loving investors, a firm will not be able to boost its share price by paying high dividends. A firm can boost its stock price only if an unsatisfied clientele exists.

10.3.4 The Information Content Effect(信息内涵效应)

The stock price of a firm generally rises when the firm announces a dividend increase and generally falls when a dividend reduction is announced.

Consider the following three positions on dividends:

1. From the homemade dividend argument of MM, dividend policy is irrelevant, given that future earnings (and cash flow) are held constant.

2. Because of tax effects, a firm's stock price is negatively related to the current dividend when future earnings (or cash flow) are held constant.

3. Because of stockholders' desire for current income, a firm's stock price is positively related to its current dividend, even when future earnings (or cash flow) are held constant.

At first glance, the empirical evidence that stock prices rise when dividend increases are announced may seem consistent with Position 3 and inconsistent with Position 1 and 2. In fact, many writers have said this. However, other authors have countered that the observation itself is consistent with all three positions. They point out that companies do not like to cut a dividend. Thus, firms will raise the dividend only when future earnings, cash flow, and so on are expected to rise enough so that the dividend is not likely to be reduced later to its original level. A dividend increase is management's signal to the market that the firm is expected to do well. It is the expectation of good times, and not only the stockholders' affinity for current income, that raises the stock price.

The rise in the stock price following the dividend signal is called **the information content effect**(**信息内涵效应**) of the dividend. To recapitulate, imagine that the stock price is unaffected or even negatively affected by the level of dividends, given that future earnings (or cash flow) are held constant. Nevertheless, the information content effect implies that the stock price may rise when dividends are raised—if dividends simultaneously cause stockholders to increase their expectations of future earnings and cash flow.

案例分析 10-1 《格力电器股利分配政策》

珠海格力电器股份有限公司成立于1991年,1996年11月在深交所挂牌上市。公司主营家用空调、中央空调、空气能热水器等产品,产业覆盖家用消费品和工业装备两大领域,产品远销190多个国家和地区。

格力电器2014年的股利分配方案是每10股派发现金30元,并用资本公积金转增股本,向所有股东每10股转增10股;2015年的股利分配方案是每10股派发现金股利15元;2016年的股利分配方案是每10股派发现金红利18元。这样的分配方案在国内来说是非常丰厚的,对于投资者来说是有极大吸引力的。格力电器对于股利分配政策的走势具有连续性、稳定性,在2007—2016年坚持每年进行现金分红,使得投资者对于长期持有该公司的股票有较大信心。2017年,该公司股利分配方案为"不发现金红利,不送红股,不以公积金转增股本"。新的股利分配方案激起市场巨大反应,引起大部分股民的负面情绪,对股价影响非常大。格力电器之所以能够实行高派现金股利政策,一方面是因为格力电器的销售获利能力、资本获利能力以及股本获利能力均高于行业均值,较好的盈利能力为格力电器赚取利润、积累资金提供前提条件。另一方面是因为相比于行业内部的平均值,格力电器的产权比率较高、短期偿债的流动比率较低,这说明格力电器长期偿债能力提高,短期偿债能力中的速运比率合理。该公司对借入资金的灵活运用能力,优秀的变现能力为其完成高派现分配制度提供了充足保障。

但是格力电器股利分配政策也存在一些问题。比如,股利支付率可以代表分配股利的总金额所占当年所有盈利的比重,能够最直观反映企业股利支付的能力。通过数据分析,发现格力电器股利支付率变动比较大,在2007—2012年间,该公司股利支付率维持在20%到30%之间;2012年以后,该公司股利支付率出现大幅提升,在2014—2016年间,格力电器的股利支付率甚至超过60%。根据中国证监会相关条例规定,格力公司股利支付水平高于该公司所处行业的平均值,其股利分配政策为高派现股利政策。虽然证监会有着强制性规定,但格力电器自2012年起现金分红的金额已经超过归属上市公司股东权益的净利润的40%，在2016年甚至达到了70.22%，足以看出股利分配已经占用了格力电器大部分的利润收入。这种做法虽然迎合了投资者对现金股利的偏好，但容易造成企业的短视行为。而在2017年格力电器突然公布不分配，也导致许多投资者的不满，因此，采用稳健的股利分配政策是最合理的选择。

企业股利分配政策是企业高质量发展的重要保障，建立一套合理的分红政策可以为企业的长远发展提供有效的支持。习近平总书记在党的二十大报告指出："完善中国特色现代企业制度，弘扬企业家精神，加快建设世界一流企业。"在推进中国式现代化的进程中，企业有必要制定合理的股利分配政策，进而保证市场稳定运行和企业长久发展。第一，企业分配股利，必须根据国家颁布的《中华人民共和国证券法》和《中华人民共和国公司法》，充分考虑影响股利分配政策的相关因素和市场反应。第二，公司在制定股利政策时，也应充分考虑股利政策的各种影响因素，从保护股东、公司本身和债权人的利益出发，才能使公司的收益分配合理化。第三，实施持续且稳定的股利分配政策。为了保证公司的吸引力，企业不能只把眼光放在大股东身上，也要保证小股东的利益，使用延续性的分配政策将会为小股东提供投资的信心。

资料来源：

[1]云苗苗.上市公司股利分配政策的案例分析：以格力电器为例.中外企业家，2020，(11)

[2]田方正，李铭宇，李永军.上市公司股利分配政策研究：以格力电器为例.河北企业，2022，(02)

Key Concepts and Skills

1. Dividend and other types of payouts.
2. Concepts of cash dividend and stock dividend.
3. Standard method of cash dividend payment.
4. Impact of stock repurchase and stock split.
5. Value of the firm $V_0 = \text{Div}_0 + \frac{\text{Div}_1}{1 + R_s}$.
6. The theoretical assumption and illustration of the Irrelevance of Dividend Policy.
7. Real-World factors favoring a low-dividend and high-dividend policy.
8. The clientele effect and information content.

本章重点与难点

1. 股利和其他支付政策的类型及其特点。
2. 现金股利和股票股利的概念。
3. 现金股利的发放程序。
4. 股票回购与股票分割对公司价值和投资者收益的影响。
5. 公司的价值：$V_0 = \mathrm{Div}_0 + \dfrac{\mathrm{Div}_1}{1 + R_s}$。
6. 股利政策无关论的假设条件、分析过程及结论。
7. 投资者偏爱低股利和高股利政策的影响因素。
8. 客户效应和信息内涵效应的含义。

Self-Test Questions

Ⅰ. True (T) or False (F) Questions

1. Share repurchases result in fewer common shares and higher earnings per share. (　　)

2. The less liquid a company is, the more likely it is to adopt a high dividend policy. (　　)

3. Share repurchases can lead to a reduction in owner's equity and change the company's capital structure. (　　)

4. After the stock dividend is paid, if the total earnings remain unchanged, it will cause the earnings per share to decline and the stock market price per share to rise. (　　)

5. If the company issues a total of 2 million common stocks, the par value of each share is ＄2. The company declares a two-for-one stock split. The new par value per share is ＄1. (　　)

Ⅱ. Single Choice Questions

1. What is the most common and most acceptable dividend payment method for investors? (　　)

A. Cash dividends

B. Stock dividends

C. Debt dividends

D. Property dividends

2. The price of stocks traded after the(　　) may decrease.

A. Declaration date

B. Ex-dividend date

C. Record date

D. Payment date

3. A company issued an announcement on March 16, 2021: the board of directors of the company decided at the meeting on March 15, 2021 to pay a dividend of $3 per share in 2020; On April 8, 2021, the company will pay the above dividends to those who have registered as shareholders of the company on Friday, March 26, 2021. Which one is correct for the following statement? (　　)

A. March 15, 2021 is the declaration date.

B. March 29, 2021 is the Ex-dividend date.

C. March 25, 2021 is the Ex-dividend date.

D. March 27, 2021 is the Ex-dividend date.

4. If the Ex-dividend date of a company's stock is November 15, 2004, and the dividend per share is $5.20. Stock closed at $36.95 on November 12 and opened at $32.51 on November 15, with a known income tax rate of 15% on dividends. What are the share prices declines and dividends ? (　　)

A. $4.43, $4.42

B. $4.42, $5.42

C. $4.42, $3.43

D. $4.43, $5.42

5. The company issued 2,000,000 ordinary shares with a par value of $1 each. The capital reserve is $1,000,000, the undistributed profit is $6,000,000, and the market price of the stock is $20. If stock dividends are issued at a rate of 10% and converted according to the market price, how much is the company's capital reserve? (　　)

A. $3,800,000

B. $4,000,000

C. $4,200,000

D. $4,800,000

Ⅲ. Calculation Questions

1. The owners' equity accounts for a company are shown here:

Common stock ($1 par value)	$50,000
Capital surplus	$120,000

Table(continue)

Retained earnings	$ 450, 500
Total owners' equity	$ 620, 500

Questions:

(1) If the company's stock currently sells for $ 30 per share and a 10 percent stock dividend is declared, how many new shares will be distributed? Show how the equity accounts would change.

(2) If the company declared a 20 percent stock dividend, how would the accounts change?

2. Companies with common stock accounts declare a 20% dividend on their shares at a price of $ 65 per share.

Common stock ($ 1 par value)	$ 10, 000
Capital surplus	$ 150, 000
Retained earnings	$ 330, 200
Total owners' equity	$ 580, 200

Questions:

(1) How will the issuance of stock dividends affect the company's owner's equity account?

(2) Suppose the company instead decides on a five-for-one stock split. The cash dividend per new share after the split was 40 cents, which represents a 10% increase in the cash dividend per share from last year's cash dividend on pre-split stock. How does this affect equity accounts? What was last year's dividend per share?

本章习题答案

Part Four
Short-Term Finance Management Decision
(短期营运管理决策)

Chapter 11 Short-Term Finance and Planning（短期财务和规划）

Learning Objectives

- Understand the components of the cash cycle and why it is important.
- Understand the pros and cons of the various short-term financing policies.
- Be able to prepare a cash budget.
- Understand the various options for short-term financing.

This chapter begins with a discussion of short-term finance, which focuses on the analysis of decisions affecting current assets and current liabilities. The difference between short-term finance and long-term finance mainly lies in the timing of cash flow. Short-term financial decisions mainly refer to the inflows and outflows of cash flow within a year. For example, companies ordering raw materials, paying cash, and selling products and receiving cash within a year all involve short-term financial decisions. In contrast, buying a special piece of equipment with a company that will reduce operating costs for years to come involves long-term financial decisions. What is a reasonable level of cash to keep on hand (in a bank) to pay bills? How much should the firm borrow in the short term? How much credit should be extended to customers? This chapter describes the basic elements of short-term financial decision-making. Firstly, this section will discuss the company's short-term business activities, followed by some other short-term financial policies. Finally, the basic elements of a short-term financial plan will be summarized and short-term financing instruments will be elaborated.

11.1 Tracing Cash and Net Working Capital

To begin, recall that current assets are cash and other assets that are expected to convert to cash within the year. Current assets are presented on the balance sheet in order of their accounting liquidity—the ease with which they can be converted to cash and the time it takes to convert them. Four of the most important items found in the current asset section of a balance sheet are cash and cash equivalents, marketable securities, accounts receivable, and inventories.

Analogous to their investment in current assets, firms use several kinds of short-term debt called current liabilities. Current liabilities are obligations that are expected to require cash payment within one year (or within the operating period if it is longer than one year). Three major items found as current liabilities are accounts payable, expenses payable (including accrued wages and taxes), and notes payable.

We can first define cash from other elements of the balance sheet. This allows us to isolate our cash accounts and explore the impact of our company's operational and financing decisions on cash. The identity of the basic balance sheet can be expressed as follows:

$$\text{Net working capital} + \text{Fixed assets} = \text{Long-term debt} + \text{Equity}$$

where **Net working capital (净营运资本)** is related to making short-term financial decisions. Short-term financial management is often referred to as working capital management. Net working capital is cash plus other current assets, less current liabilities, that is:

$$Net\ working\ capital = Cash + Other\ current\ assets - Current\ liabilities$$

If we substitute this for net working capital in the basic balance sheet identity, we see that cash is:

$$Cash = Long - term\ debt + Equity - Net\ working\ capital(excluding\ cash) - Fixed\ assets$$

This tells us in general terms that some activities naturally increase cash and some activities decrease it. We can list these various activities, along with an example of each, as follows:

Activities That Increase Cash (现金来源)

Increasing long-term debt (borrowing over the long term)

Increasing equity (selling some stock)

Increasing current liabilities (getting a 90-day loan)

Decreasing current assets other than cash (selling some inventory for cash)

Decreasing fixed assets (selling some property)

Activities That Decrease Cash (现金运用)

Decreasing long-term debt (paying off a long-term debt)

Decreasing equity (repurchasing some stock)

Decreasing current liabilities (paying off a 90-day loan)

Increasing current assets other than cash (buying some inventory for cash)

Increasing fixed assets (buying some property)

Broadly speaking, the increase or decrease in cash is related to the company's specific activities. Sources of cash include an increase in a liability (or equity) account or a decrease in an asset account. Increasing a liability means that you can raise money by borrowing or selling company ownership. A decrease in assets means the sale or liquidation of an asset.

Uses of cash are just the reverse. The use of cash includes reducing liabilities through liquidation, or it may also be to increase assets by purchasing something. Both activities require companies to pay cash.

11.2 The Operating Cycle and the Cash Cycle

Short-term finance involves the short-term operating activity of the company. The short-term business activities of a typical manufacturing company consist of the following series of events, such as buying raw material, paying cash, manufacturing the product, selling the product and collecting cash.

11.2.1 Defining the Operating and Cash Cycles

In this section, we will define the operating cycle and cash cycle by an example as follows.

【Example 11-1】

One day, we purchased $500 worth of inventory on credit. We pay the bill 30 days later, and, after 20 more days, someone buys the $500 in inventory for $700. Our buyer does not actually pay for another 45 days. We can summarize these events chronologically as follows:

Day	Activity	Cash Effect
0	Acquire inventory	None
30	Pay for inventory	- $500
50	Sell inventory on credit	None
95	Collect on sale	+ $700

1. Defining the Operating Cycle(经营周期)

Firstly, let's define the operating cycle through the above example. The operating cycle is the time it takes to purchase inventory, sell inventory, and collect payments. This cycle consists of two distinct parts, the first being the time to buy and sell inventory. This time is 50 days in our example, which is called the inventory period. The second part is the time to recover the sales proceeds, 45 days in our example. This is called the accounts receivable period.

Based on the definitions above, the operating cycle is obviously just the sum of the inventory and accounts receivable period:

$$\text{Operating cycle} = \text{Inventory period} + \text{Accounts receivable period}$$

$$95 \text{ days} = 50 \text{ days}$$

2. Defining the Cash Cycle(现金周期)

Cash flows and other events do not occur simultaneously. For example, we do not pay for goods until 30 days after the inventory is purchased. The intervening 30-day period is called the accounts payable period. Then, after we paid the cash on Day 30, we had to wait until Day 95 to get the payment back. So we had to manage to get \$500 in 95−30=65 days. This period is called the cash cycle.

In general, the cash cycle is the number of days in which we collect cash from sales from the day we actually pay for the inventory purchase. The cash cycle is equal to the difference between the operating cycle and the accounts payable period:

$$\text{Cash cycle} = \text{Operating cycle} - \text{Accounts payable period}$$

$$65 \text{ days} = 95 \text{ days} - 30 \text{ days}$$

Figure 11−1 depicts short-term operating activities and cash flows of a typical manufacturing company using a cash flow timeline. As it is shown, the cash flow time line graphically represents the operating cycle and the cash cycle. From the time gap between cash inflow and cash outflow, it can be seen that the company needs to carry out short-term financial management, which is related to the lengths of the operating cycle and accounts payable cycle.

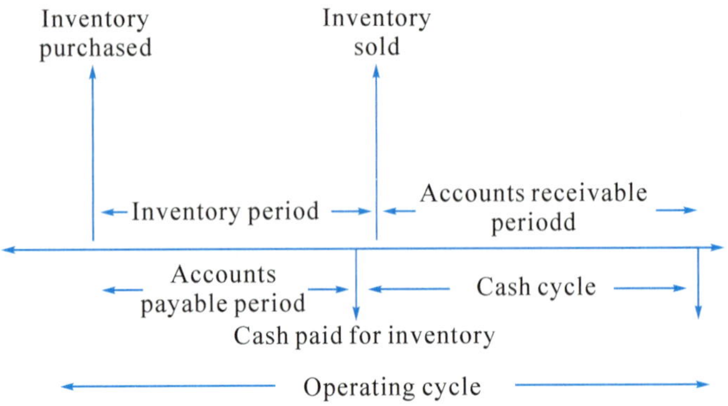

Figure 11-1 **Cash Flow Time Line and the Short-Term Operating Activities of a Typical Manufacturing Firm**

From the chart above, the time gap between short-term cash inflows and outflows, two approaches can generally be used. One approach could be by borrowing or holding liquidity reserve, such as cash or marketable securities. Another way is to shorten this time gap by changing the inventory, receivable, and payable periods.

11.2.2 Calculating the Operating and Cash Cycles

In this section we will show the use of financial statement information to calculate the operating cycle and cash cycle.

【Example 11-2】

In the beginning, we needed to find out the answers to questions such as how long it took on average to sell inventory and how long it took a company to collect receivables on average. We start by gathering balance sheet information as follows (in thousands):

Item	Beginning	Ending	Average
Inventory	$ 1,800	$ 2,800	$ 2,500
Accounts receivable	1,400	1,800	1,600
Accounts payable	800	900	875

Also, from the most recent income statement, we might have the following figures (in thousands):

Net sales	$ 12,500
Cost of goods sold	8,400

1. Calculating the Operating Cycle

First of all, we need the inventory period. We spent $8.4 million on inventory (our cost of goods sold). Our average inventory was $2.5 million. We thus turned our inventory over 8.4/2.5 times during the year:

Inventory turnover = Cost of goods sold/Average inventory
= 8.4/2.5 = 3.36 times

Loosely speaking, this tells us that we bought and sold off our inventory 3.36 times during the year. This means that, on average, we held our inventory for:

Inventory period = 365 days/Inventory turnover = 365/3.36 = 109 days

So, the inventory period is about 109 days. On average, in other words, inventory sat for about 109 days before it was sold.

Similarly, receivables averaged $1.6 million, and sales were $12.5 million. Assuming that all sales were credit sales, the accounts receivable turnover is:

Accounts receivable turnover = Credit sales/Average accounts receivable
= 12.5/1.6 = 7.8 times

If we turn over our receivables 6.4 times a year, then the is:

Accounts receivable period
= 365 days/accounts receivable turnover = 365/7.8
= 47 days

The receivables period is also called the days' sales in receivables, or the average collection period. Whatever it is called, it tells us that our customers took an average of 47 days to pay.

The operating cycle is the sum of the inventory and receivables periods:

Operating cycle = Inventory period + Accounts receivable period
= 109+47 = 156 days

This tells us that, on average, 156 days elapse between the time we acquire inventory and, having sold it, collect for the sale.

2. Calculating the Cash Cycle

We now need the accounts payable period. From the information given earlier, we know that average payable were $875,000 and cost of goods sold was $8.4 million. Our accounts payable turnover is:

Accounts payable turnover
= Cost of goods sold/Average accounts payable = 8.4/0.875
= 9.6 times

The accounts payable period is:

$$\text{Accounts payables period} = 365 \text{ days/Accounts payable turnover} = 365/9.6 = 38 \text{ days}$$

Thus, we took an average of 38 days to pay our bills.

Finally, the cash cycle is the difference between the operating cycle and the payables period:

$$\text{Cash cycle} = \text{Operating cycle} - \text{Accounts payable period} = 156-38 = 118 \text{ days}$$

So, on average, there is a 118-day delay between the time we pay for merchandise and the time we collect on the sale.

11.3 Some Aspects of Short-Term Financial Policy

The short-term financial policy adopted by a firm consists of at least two elements:

1. The size of the firm's investment in current assets: This is usually measured relative to the firm's level of total operating revenues. A flexible short-term financial policy will maintain a high ratio of current assets to sales. A restrictive short-term financial policy will maintain a low ratio of current assets to sales.

2. The financing of current assets: This is measured as the proportion of short-term debt to long-term debt. A restrictive short-term financial policy implies a high ratio of short-term debt to long-term financing, while a flexible policy means less short-term debt and more long-term debt.

11.3.1 The Size of the Firm's Investment in Current Assets

Flexible short-term finance policies（稳健型短期财务政策）would maintain a high ratio of current assets to sales which include:

1. Keeping large cash balances and investments in marketable securities
2. Large investments in inventory
3. Liberal credit term

Restrictive short-term finance policies（**激进型短期财务政策**）would maintain a low ratio of current assets to sales which include:

1. Keeping low cash balances, no investment in marketable securities
2. Making small investments in inventory

3. Allowing no credit sales (thus no accounts receivable)

Current assets management can be thought of as a trade-off between costs that rise with the level of investment and costs that fall with the level of investment. Costs that rise with the level of investment in current assets are called carrying costs（持有成本）. Costs that fall with rising investment levels in current assets are called shortage costs（短缺成本）.

There are generally two types of carrying costs: the first is the opportunity cost of holding liquid assets, because current assets have a low rate of return compared to other assets. The second category is the cost of maintaining the economic value of the asset, such as the cost of warehousing inventory, which belongs to this category.

Shortage costs occur when the level of investment in current assets is low. There are two types of shortage costs that fall with the level of current asset investment:

1. Trading or order, costs（交易或订购成本）: Order costs are the costs of placing an order for more cash, such as brokerage costs. Whereas, ordering cost is the cost of ordering inventory, such as production setup costs.

2. Costs related to safety reserves（与安全库存相关的成本）: These are the costs of lost sales, lost customer goodwill, and disruption of production schedules.

Figure 11-2 shows us the basic characteristics of carrying costs and shortage costs. The minimum point of the total cost curve (CA *) can reflect the optimal balance of current assets which are determined by the sum of the inventory cost and the shortage cost. This curve is generally quite flat at the optimum. It is difficult to find the exact optimal balance between the cost of shortage and the cost of inventory. We usually pick a little bit near the optimum.

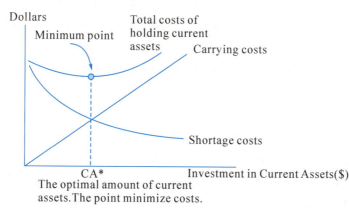

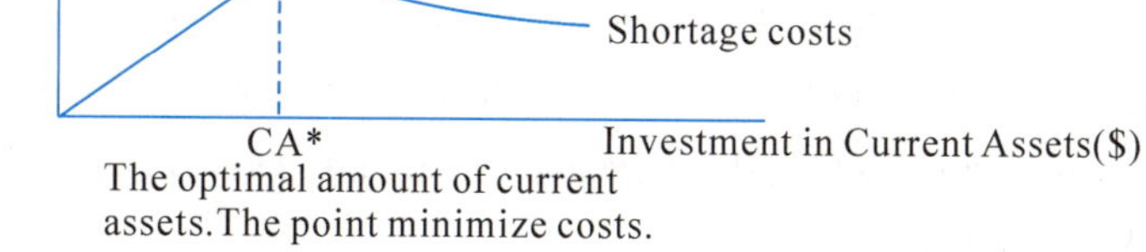

a)

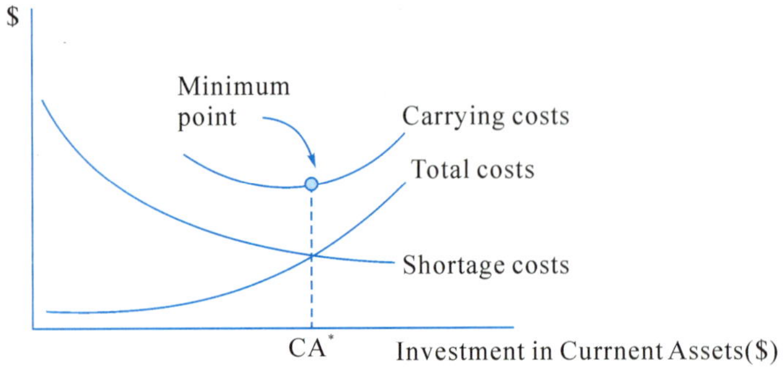

b) Flexible policy

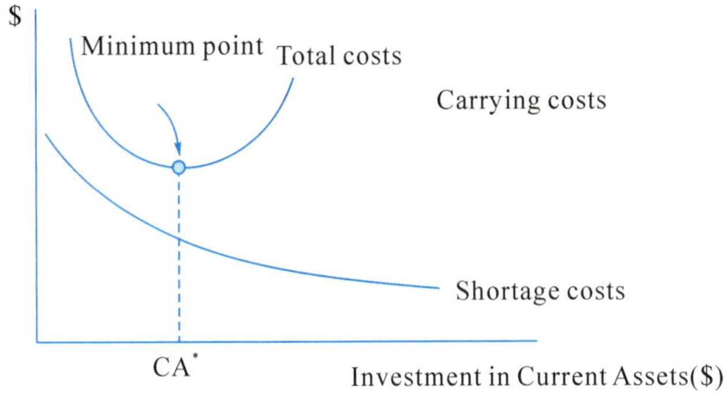

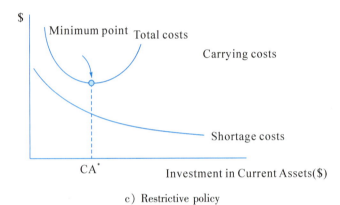

c) Restrictive policy

Figure 11-2 **Carrying Costs and Shortage Costs**

Carrying costs increase with the level of investment in current assets. They include both opportunity costs and the costs of maintaining the asset's economic value. Shortage costs decrease with increases in the level of investment in current assets. They include trading costs and the costs of running out of the current asset (e.g., being short on cash).

If carrying costs are low or shortage costs are high, the optimal policy requires holding a large amount of current assets. In other words, the optimal policy is a flexible one. That is illustrated in the middle graph of Figure 11-2b.

If carrying costs are high or shortage costs are low, the optimal policy is a restrictive one. That is, the optimal policy requires holding an appropriate amount of current assets. This is illustrated in the bottom graph of the figure.

11.3.2 Alternative Financing Policies for Current Assets

In an ideal world, short-term assets can always be financed with short-term debt; long-term assets can be financed with long-term debt and equity. In this economic environment, net working capital is always zero. Figure 11-3 can illustrate this situation.

In a real world, it is difficult for current assets to drop to zero because a long-term upward trend in sales levels leads to some permanent investment in current assets. It can be said that a growing firm has a permanent need for both current and long-term assets. This total asset requirement will exhibit balances over time reflecting:

1. A secular growth trend,

2. A seasonal variation around the trend

3. Unpredictable day-to-day and month-to-month fluctuations

This is depicted in Figure 11-4 (We have not tried to show the unpredictable day-to-day and month-to-month variations in the total asset requirement.)

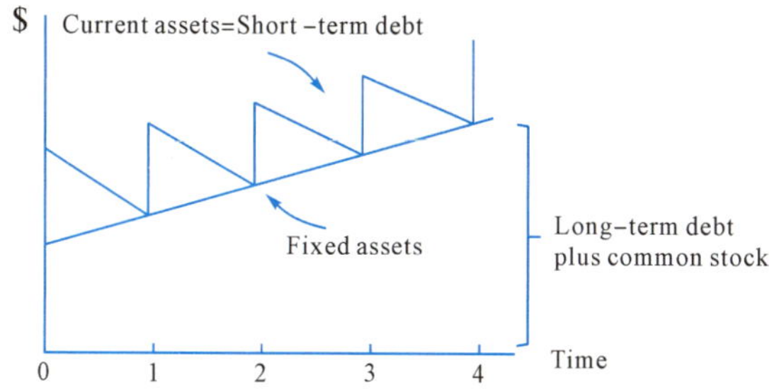

Figure 11-3 Financing Policy for an Ideal Economy

In an ideal world, net working capital is always zero because short-term assets are financed with short-term debt.

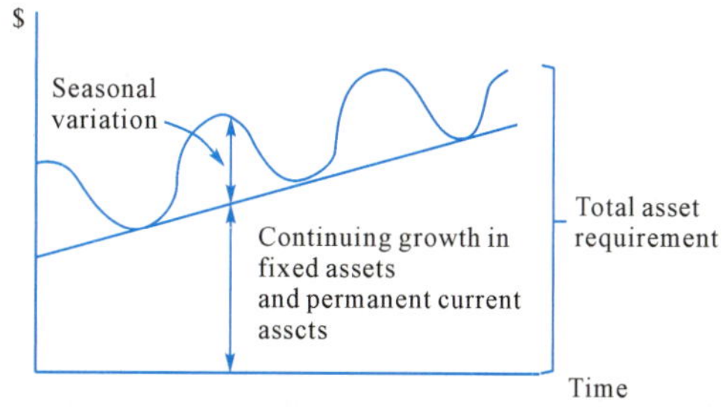

Figure 11-4 The Total Asset Requirement over Time

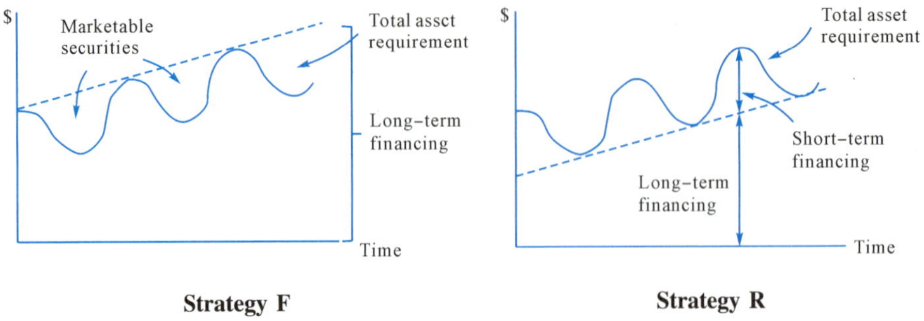

11-5 **Alternative Asset Financing Policies**

Strategy F always implies a short-term cash surplus and a large investment in cash and marketable securities. Strategy R uses long-term financing for continuing asset requirements only, and short-term borrowing for seasonal variations.

Now let us look at how this asset requirement is financed. First, consider the strategy in which long-term funding sources exceed total asset demand even during seasonal peaks (Strategy F in Figure 11-5). When total asset demand declines from its peak, firms have excess cash that can be used for investment in marketable securities. Since this approach implies that there is always a short-term cash surplus and a large investment in net working capital, it is considered a flexible strategy.

When long-term funding sources cannot meet total asset needs, firms must borrow short term to make up the deficit. This restrictive strategy is represented as strategy R in Figure 11-5.

What is best? Several considerations must be included in a proper analysis:

1. Cash reserves: The flexible financing strategy means excess cash and little short-term borrowing. This strategy reduces the likelihood that the company falling into financial distress. Companies don't need to worry too much about how to repay the ongoing short-term obligations. However, investments in cash and marketable securities are zero net present value investments at best.

2. Maturity hedging: Most firms finance inventories with short-term bank loans and fixed assets with long-term financing. Companies try to avoid using short-term borrowing to finance long-lived assets. This maturity mismatch strategy has to be funded frequently and is inherently risky because short-term interest rates are more volatile than long-term ones.

3. Term Structure: Short-term interest rates are normally lower than long-term interest rates. This means that, on average, it is more expensive to rely on long-term borrowing than short-term borrowing.

11.4 Cash Budget

Cash budget（现金预算）is a basic tool for short-term financial planning. It is the way of identifying the cash flow gap on the cash flow time line. The idea of the cash budget is simple: it records estimates of cash receipts and expenses.

11.4.1 Cash Receipts（现金回收）

We illustrate cash budgeting with the following example of company A.

【Example 11-3】

All of company A's cash inflows come from the sale of goods. Cash budgeting for company A starts with a sales forecast for the next year by quarter:

	First Quarter	Second Quarter	Third Quarter	Fourth Quarter
Sales($ in millions)	50	150	100	50

Company A sell the goods to department stores on credit, and the sales do not generate cash immediately, and the cash could not be recovered until 90 days later. That said, the company has a 90-day collection period. In other words:

Collections = Last quarter's sales

This relationship implies that:

Accounts receivable at end of last quarter = Last quarter's sales

We assume that sales in the fourth quarter of the previous fiscal year were $ 100 million. From the above formula, the cash collection from accounts receivable in the first quarter of the current fiscal year is $ 100 million. The first quarter sales of the current fiscal year of $ 50 million are added to the accounts receivable, but $ 100 million of collections are subtracted. The basic relationship is as follows:

Ending accounts receivable

= Starting accounts receivable + Sales collections

According to the above formula, we can predict the cash collections of company A for next four quarters, as shown in Table 11-1. Though collections are the only source of cash here, this need not always be the case. Other sources of cash could include sales of assets, investment income, and long-term financing.

Table 11-1 Sources of Cash ($ in millions)

	First Quarter	Second Quarter	Third Quarter	Fourth Quarter
Starting receivables	100	50	150	100
Sales	50	150	100	50
Cash collections	-100	-50	-150	-100
Ending receivables	50	150	100	50

Cash collections = Accounts receivable at end of last quarter

11.4.2 Cash outflow(现金流出)

Cash disbursements can be put into four basic categories, as shown in Table 11-2.

1. Payments of accounts payable: These are payments for goods or services, such as raw materials. These payments will generally be made after purchases. Purchases will depend on the sales forecast. In this example, assume that:

Payments = Last quarter's purchases

Purchases = 1/2 next quarter's sales forecast

2. Wages, taxes, and other expenses: This category includes all other normal costs of doing business that require actual expenditures, such as depreciation.

3. Capital expenditures: These are payments of cash for long-lived assets. company A plans a major capital expenditure in the fourth quarter.

4. Long - term financing: This category includes interest and principal payments on long-term outstanding debt and dividend payments to shareholders.

In this example, we assume that the purchase volume (amount) of company A from the supplier in each quarter is equal to 50% of the predicted sales revenue in the next quarter. And the supplier's accounts payable period is 90 days. For example, in the first quarter, company A ordered $0.5 \times 50 = 25$, namely \$25 million. The loan will actually be repaid in the first quarter of the next year.

Wages, taxes and other expenses are fixed at 20% of sales. Currently, interest and dividends are \$10 million per quarter. In addition, company A company plans to have a major plant expansion (capital expenditure) of US \$100 million in the fourth quarter. Putting these information above together, the total forecast outflow appears in the last line of Table 11-2.

Table 11-2 **Disbursement of Cash** (**$ in millions**)

	First Quarter	Second Quarter	Third Quarter	Fourth Quarter
Sales	50	150	100	50
Purchases	75	50	25	25
Uses of cash				
Payments of accounts payable	25	75	50	25
Wages, taxes, and other expenses	10	30	20	10
Capital expenditures	0	0	0	80
Long-term financing expenses: interest and dividends	10	10	10	10
Total uses of cash	45	115	80	125

11.4.3 The cash balance(现金余额)

The net cash balance is shown in Table 11-3. Significant net cash outflow is forecast in the second quarter. This large outflow is delayed collections on sales. This results in a cumulative cash shortage of $10 million in the second quarter.

Company A has established a minimum operating cash balance of $5 million to facilitate transactions, prevent unexpected contingencies and maintain compensating balances at its commercial banks. This means that company A has a cash shortage of $15 million in the second quarter.

The projected net cash inflow is the difference between cash collections and total uses of cash. What we can see is that there are cash balances in Q1 and Q3, and a cash deficit in Q2 and Q4.

	First Quarter	Second Quarter	Third Quarter	Fourth Quarter
Cash collections	100	50	150	100
Total uses of cash	45	115	80	125
Net cash flow	55	-65	70	-25

Company A has established a minimum operating cash balance of $5 million to facilitate transactions, prevent unexpected contingencies and maintain compensating balances at its commercial banks. During the quarter, the cash inflow was $55 million, resulting in a cash balance of $55 million at the end of the quarter. The $5 million is the minimum retention amount, so subtract that to get a cash surplus of $55 - 5 = 50$ *million* in Q1.

At the start of the second quarter, company A had \$55 million in cash (from last quarter's ending balance). Net cash inflow is -\$60 million, so the end of the quarter balance is $55 - 65 = -10$ *million*. And we need an additional \$5 million for urgent needs, so the total deficit is -\$15 million. The calculation process for all four quarters is shown in Table 11-3.

Table 11-3 **The Cash Balance ($ in millions)**

	First Quarter	Second Quarter	Third Quarter	Fourth Quarter
Cash balance at the beginning of the quarter	0	→ 55	→ -10	→ 60
Net cash flow	55	-65	70	-25
Cumulative excess cash balance	55	-10	60	35
Minimum cash balance	-5	-5	-5	-5
Cumulative finance surplus(deficit) requirement	50	-15	55	30

11.5 The Short-Term Financial Plan

Company A has a short-term financing problem. It cannot meet the forecast cash outflows in the second quarter from internal sources. Its financing options include unsecured loans, secured loans, and other sources.

11.5.1 Unsecured loans(无抵押贷款)

The most common way to finance a temporary cash deficit is a short-term unsecured bank loan. Firms that take advantage of short-term bank loans often require banks to grant non-committed or committed line of credit. A noncommitted line of credit is a non-positive arrangement in which a company can borrow within a pre-established limit without going through the formal paperwork. The line of credit loan interest rate is generally equal to the bank's prime lending rate plus an additional percentage.

Committed lines of credit are formal agreement with legal effect that usually involves a commitment fee paid by a company to a bank, which are different for large companies and small companies. For large companies, interest rates are generally pegged to the London Interbank Offered Rate (LIBOR) or the bank's cost of funds, rather than the prime rate. Smaller and midsized companies are often required to maintain compensating balances in banks.

11.5.2 Secured loans(抵押贷款)

Banks and other finance companies often require security for a loan. Security for short term loans usually consists of accounts receivable or inventories.

Under accounts receivable financing, receivables can be assigned or factored. By way of assignment of accounts receivable, the lender, as known as the factor, must not only have a right of retention in the receivables, but also have a right of recourse against the borrower.

Inventory loan uses inventory as collateral. Some common types of inventory loans are:

1. Blanket inventory lien: The blanket inventory lien gives the lender a lien against all the borrower's inventories.

2. Trust receipt: Under this arrangement, the borrower holds the inventory in trust for the lender. The document acknowledging the loan is called the trust receipt. Proceeds from the sale of inventory are remitted immediately to the lender.

3. Field warehouse financing: In field warehouse financing, a public warehouse company supervises the inventory for the lender.

11.5.3 Other Sources

A variety of other sources of short-term funds are employed by corporations. The most important of these are financing through banker's acceptance and the issuance of commercial paper.

A banker's acceptance (银行承兑汇票) is an agreement by which a bank promises to pay a sum of money. When the seller delivers the bill or draft to the customer, the customer's bank accepts the bill of exchange and notes the acceptance on it, which constitutes an obligation of the bank. In this way, firms that purchase goods from suppliers can effectively arrange for banks to pay the outstanding bills. Of course, bank charges the customer a fee for this service.

Commercial paper (商业票据) is a short-term note issued by a large company with a high rated firm. Typically, these notes are short in maturity, up to 270 days (beyond that limit the firm must file a registration statement with the SEC).

案例分析 11-1 《短期财务规划与供应链金融——基于亚马逊与长安集团案例分析》

亚马逊自 1995 年 7 月建立以来，迄今已 20 余年，商品已涉足百万种品类，除图书外，还包括电子产品、家居用品、家用电器、服装、化妆品、婴幼儿用品、音像制品等。经过多年发展，亚马逊现已成为全球第二大互联网公司，是电商行业的标杆。亚马逊将精益思想根植于企业文化中多年，其供应链体系建设完善，运营成熟。自亚马逊成立以来，“成为全球最以客户为中心的公司”便是亚马逊的使命。此案例将对以下亚马逊价值链上的资金运营成本进行分析，其展现的短期财务计划体现了亚马逊精益管理的中心思想，即杜绝浪费，并为客户提供最实惠的价格。

（1）现金循环周期分析。亚马逊的现金循环周期（存货周转天数+应收账款周转天数-应付账款周转天数）一直都保持的-20～-40 天左右，营业周期（存货周转天数+应收账款周转天数）远低于应付账款周转期，从而导致现金循环周期成负数。具体针对亚马逊的短期财务计划进行分析，亚马逊一般在进货 90 天以上才向供应商付款，而客户往往在 20 天内就要向亚马逊付款，可见亚马逊在企业上下游供应链中具有较强的议价能力。供应商实际上垫付了亚马逊经营所需的流动资金，亚马逊利用自身的规模与渠道优势，以滚动的方式占用供应商资金，类似于获得无成本或低成本的短期融资，降低了资金成本，提高了资金使用效率。

（2）支付环节成本分析。亚马逊为了缩短企业的应收账款周期，加快了资金回收，提升了自身资金使用效率。亚马逊支持多种支付方式，包含网银在线、第三方支付平台支付、货到付款等。这样一方面能给消费者的资金支付予以安全保障，另一方面有利于加快资金周转，减少资金占用的机会成本，节约支付环节的交易成本。

可见，在短期财务计划方面，亚马逊主要通过以下方法来延长应收账款周期，缩短应付账款周期，提升资金使用效率。第一，资金流成本方面，亚马逊通过与供应商的博弈来延缓应付账款周转期，通过高效的仓储管理降低存货的资金占用。第二，简化支付流程以加快应收账款的回收，达到提升资金周转效率、降低资金成本的目的。第三，企业通过与多方合作，为顾客提供多种支付方式，提升顾客满意度，缩减了支付环节的交易成本。

通过上述案例，亚马逊之所以有良好的资金使用效率，离不开亚马逊高水平的议价能力和良好的企业声誉。但大部分企业，特别是小微企业，经常会因为过度投资、过度负债、过度运营和过度赊销等原因而出现资金短缺的情况，严重威胁到企业的生存与发展。对此，为稳住市场主体，中国政府出台了一系列的扶持政策，多措并举支持中小微企业的发展，例如灵活运用多种货币政策工具，出台减税降费等一系列政策以及持续优化营商环境等。值得注意的是，近些年来，随着金融科技的不断发展，基于网络的供应链金融，立足于广域网技术，将供应链的资金流、信息流、商流与物流等数据进行共享共治，对中小企业融资起到了重要补充作用。针对供应链金融，党和国家也出台了一系列政策文件，例如：党的二十大报告明确提出“着力提升产业链供应链韧性和安全水平”“供应链金融是支持实体经济发展的有效工具”；2022 年 1 月，商务部发布《“十四五”国内贸易发展规划》，指出要稳步推进供应链金融发展，丰富供应链金融服务产品，规范发展供应链存货、仓单和订单融资，开展供应链金融资产证券化，提高中小微企业应收账款融资效率；7 月，银保监会发布《关于进一步推动金融服务制造业高质量发展的通知》，提出积极稳妥发展供应链金融服务，依托制造业产业链核心企业，在有效控制风险的基础上，加强数据和信息共享，运用应收账款、存货与仓单质押融资等方式，为产业链上下游企业提供方便快捷的金融服务。

在相关供应链金融的政策引导下，一种“类金融模式”在国内企业中流行起来，即利用企业自身议价能力占用上游供应商短期资金，并通过账期管理对资金进行长期滚动使用。长安汽车是国内汽车行业龙头，近年来在疫情、汛情等灾害中捐资捐款，主动承担社会责任，为企业赢得了良好声誉。长安集团的营运资本管理具有以下特点：

(1)关联方资金融通。近年来凭借自身在业内的地位和信誉，长安集团拆入资金和吸收存款及同业存放占流动负债比重分别在 10%和 15%处浮动，降低了企业关联方获取短期资金的难度。也就是说，长安集团的金融机构在供应链中充当了一个商业银行的角色，利用信誉吸收存款为关联方融通低成本、低风险的资金。

(2)供应商融资。类金融模式企业的显著特征是低成本应付款项在流动负债占较大比例，近年来长安集团的应付款项在流动负债中的占比基本维持在 35%水平以上，也是流动负债中占比最大的项目，可见长安集团是凭借自身议价能力，占用上游短期资金，利用低成本的短期资金来支撑自身运营的。

(3)资金用途。类金融模式的最终目的是通过账期管理使得资金滚动用于企业的经营活动。长安集团募得的资金一方面要满足内部的生产经营、研发投入等，另一方面可由自身金融机构进行集约化管理，用于贷款和投资业务，实现集团内供应链的整合。

此种类金融融资模式对长安集团的营运资金管理有着显著的改善作用，这一点可以通过分析长安集团的营运资金周转期而知。长安集团数年来现金周转期为负，且绝对值越来越大，截至 2020 年缩短为-24.11 天，这表示应付账款周转效率高于存货与应收账款的周转效率之和，意味着长安集团在完成了采购、生产、销售环节并收清货款之后，但在偿还供应商的应付资金之前，仍在24.11天内使用这部分资金来开展自身业务活动，使其在短期内获得一定资金优势。现金周转期为负也是类金融模式最核心的特征。

资料来源：

[1]齐祥芹，钱丹蕾，尤诗翔.电商企业的精益供应链成本管理研究：以亚马逊为例[J].财会月刊，2019，No.858(14)：57-64.

[2]李彬彬王虹. 类金融模式下S集团营运资金管理绩效评价研究：基于“要素-供应链”双视角的多案例[J]. 财会通讯，2022(22)：121-126.

Key Concepts and Skills

1. Operating and cash cycle.
2. Sources and uses of cash.
3. Types of short-tern financial policies and their determinants.
4. Cash budgeting, cash outflow, and cash balance.
5. Types of the short-term financial plan.

本章重点与难点

1. 经营周期与现金周期。
2. 现金的来源与运用。
2. 短期财务决策的类型及影响因素。
3. 现金预算、现金流出与现金余额。
4. 短期融资计划的基本类型。

Self-Test Questions

Ⅰ. True (T) or False (F) Questions

1. Increasing fixed assets (selling some property) can increase cash. ( )

2. The situation when accounts payable go up by $50 indicates a source. ( )

3. Increasing accounts receivable turnover is a way to reduce the operating cycle. ( )

4. The speculative motive is the need to hold cash in order to be able to take advantage of additional investment opportunities. ( )

5. The time elapsed from the acquisition of inventory to the collection of receivables from the sale of inventory is called the accounts receivable period. ( )

Ⅱ. Single Choice Questions

1. If you pay the supplier 4 days early, which of the following is likely to happen? ( )

A. Cash cycle will decrease

B. Operating cycle will increase

C. Average accounts payable will decrease

D. Accounts payable turnover will decrease

2. A company has an inventory turnover rate of 17.5 and its accounts payable turnover rate of 11. The accounts receivable period is 36 days. How long is the cash cycle? (365 days a year) ( )

A. 41.42

B. 23.68

C. 58.81

D. 52.00

3. A company has an accounts payable period of 30 days. The company expects sales for each quarter of the year to be 1,100, 1,400, 1,600, and 2,100 million. The amount of goods purchased in the current quarter is 68% of the next quarter's sales. At the beginning of the year, the company's accounts payable balance was 550 million. based on the company's estimate, how much cash does it expect to have available to pay its accounts payable in the third quarter? (Consider one year as 360 days and only the current quarter's advance purchases for the next quarter are credit purchases, the rest are cash purchases, and assume the advance purchases occur on average in the current quarter.) ( )

A.1,315million

B.1,337million

C. 1,195million

D. 1,208million

4. The company expects sales for each quarter of the year to be 700, 800, 900, and 1,000 million. Suppose the amount of goods purchased in the current quarter is 35% of the next quarter's sales. When having an accounts payable period of 60 days, how much cash does the company expect to have available to pay its accounts payable in the second quarter? (Consider one year as 360 days and only the current quarter's advance purchases for the next quarter are credit purchases,

the rest are cash purchases, and assume the advance purchases occur on average in the current quarter. ( )

A. 356.67 million

B. 212.67 million

C. 351.33 million

D. 291.67 million

5. A company has an accounts receivable period of 90 days. Data shows that the company's turnover in the first quarter is the lowest of the year and the one in the fourth quarter is the highest. What's more, the maximum value of the previous year's turnover is more than the minimum value of the current year's turnover. And the cash expenses do not vary much from quarter to quarter. Based on this, determine in which quarter the company is most likely to run out of cash (assuming 30 days for each of the 12 months). ( )

A. Q1

B. Q2

C. Q4

D. The probability of cash shortage is the same for each quarter.

Ⅲ. Calculation Questions

1. Calculating Cycles Consider the following financial statement information for the Company B. Calculate the operating and cash cycles. How do you interpret your answer?

Item	Beginning	Ending
Inventory	$ 17,385	$ 19,108
Accounts receivable	13,182	13,973
Accounts payable	15,385	16,676
Net sales	$ 216,384	
Costs of goods sold	165,763	

本章习题答案

Chapter 12 Cash Management（现金管理）

Learning Objectives

- Understand the importance of float and how it affects the cash balance.
- Understand how to accelerate collections and manage disbursements.
- Understand the advantages and disadvantages of holding cash and some of the ways to invest idle cash.

This chapter is about how firms manage cash. The basic objective of cash management is to keep the investment in cash as low as possible while still keeping the firm operating efficiently and effectively. This goal usually reduces to the dictum, "Collect early and pay late." Accordingly, we discuss ways of accelerating collections and managing disbursements. In addition, firms must invest temporarily idle cash in short-term marketable securities. There are different types of these so-called money market securities, and we discuss a few of the most important ones.

12.1 Reasons for Holding Cash

John Maynard Keynes, in his classic work The General Theory of Employment, Interest, and Money, identified three motives for liquidity: The speculative motive, the precautionary motive, and the transaction motive. We discuss these next.

12.1.1 Speculative Motive(投机动机)

The speculative motive is the need to hold cash in order to be able to take advantage of, for example, bargain purchases that might arise, attractive interest rates, and favorable exchange rate fluctuations. For most firms, reserve borrowing ability and marketable securities can be used to satisfy speculative motives. Thus, there might be a speculative motive for maintaining liquidity, but not necessarily for holding cash.

12.1.2 Precautionary Motive(预防动机)

The precautionary motive is the need for a safety supply to act as a financial reserve. Once again, there probably is a precautionary motive for maintaining liquidity. However, given that the value of money market instruments is relatively certain and that instruments such as T-bills are extremely liquid, there is no real need to hold substantial amounts of cash for precautionary purposes.

12.1.3 Transaction Motive(交易动机)

The transaction motive is the need to have cash on hand to pay bills. Transaction-related needs come from the normal disbursement and collection activities of the firm. Cash is collected from product sales, the selling of assets, and new financing. The cash inflows (collections) and outflows (disbursements) are not perfectly synchronized, and some level of cash holdings is necessary to serve as a buffer.

12.1.4 Costs of Holding Cash

When a firm holds cash in excess of some necessary minimum, it incurs opportunity costs. To determine the appropriate cash balance, the firm must trade off between opportunity cost of holding cash relative to the transaction cost of converting marketable securities to cash for transactions.

12.2 Understanding Float

The cash balance that a firm shows on its books is called the firm's *book, or ledger, balance*. The balance shown in its bank account as available to spend is called its *available, or collected, balance*. The difference between the available balance and the ledger balance, called the float (浮差), represents the net effect of checks in the process of clearing (moving through the banking system).

12.2.1 Kinds of Float

1. Disbursement Float

Checks written by a firm causes a decrease in the firm's book balance but no change in its available balance, which generate disbursement float.

$$\text{Available balance at bank} - \text{book balance} > 0$$

2. Collection Float

Checks received by the firm create collection float. Collection float increases book balances but does not immediately change available balances.

$$\text{Available balance at bank} - \text{book balance} < 0$$

3. Net Float

In general, a firm's payment (disbursement) activities generate disbursement float, and its collection activities generate collection float. The sum of the total collection and disbursement floats is the net float.

$$\text{Net float} = \text{disbursement float} + \text{collection float}$$

A firm should be concerned with its net float and available balance more than with its book balance.

【Example 12-1】

You have \$3,000 in your checking account. You just deposited \$2,000 and wrote a check for \$2,500.

What is the disbursement float?

What is the collection float?

What is the net float?

What is your book balance?

What is your available balance?

Answer:

The disbursement float = \$2,500

The collection float = \$2,000

The net float = \$4,500

The book balance = \$2,500

The available balance = \$3,000

12.2.2 Float Management

Float management involves controlling the collection and disbursement of cash. The objective of cash collection and disbursement are below.

Table 12-1 The objective of float management

	Objective
Cash collection	Speed up collections and reduce the lag between the time customers pay their bills and the time the cash becomes available.
Cash disbursement	Control payments and minimize the firm's costs associated with making payments.

Total collection or disbursement times can be broken down into three parts: Mailing time, processing delay, and availability delay:

Table 12-2 Components of float management

Parts	Meaning
Mailing time	The time required for check in the postal system.
Processing delay	The time of the check receiver to process the payment and deposit it in a bank.
Availability delay	The time required to clear a check through the banking system.

$$\text{Delay} = \text{mailing time} + \text{processing delay} + \text{availability delay}$$

Speeding up collections involves reducing one or more of these components. Slowing up disbursements involves increasing one of them.

1. Measuring Float

The size of the float depends on both the dollars and the time delay involved.

$$\text{Average daily float} = \frac{\text{Total float}}{\text{Total days}}$$

$$\text{Average daily float} = \text{Average daily receipts} \times \text{Weighted average delay}$$

$$= \frac{\text{Total receipts}}{\text{Total days}} \times \text{Weighted average delay}$$

【Example 12-2】

Suppose you mail a check each month for $1,000 and it takes 3 days to reach its destination, 1 day to process, and 1 day before the bank makes the cash available. What is the average daily float (assuming 30-day months)?

Answer:

Method 1:

$$\text{The total delay} = 3+1+1 = 5 \text{ days}$$

$$\text{The total float} = 5 \times 1,000 = 5,000$$

$$\text{Average daily float} = (5 \times 1,000 + 25 \times 0)/30 = 166.67$$

Method 2:

$$\text{Average daily float} = 1,000 \times 5/30 + 0 \times 25/30 = 166.67$$

This means that, on an average day, your book balance is \$166.67 less than your available balance.

2. Cost of the Float

The basic cost of collection float to the firm is simply the opportunity cost of not being able to use the cash. At a minimum, the firm could earn interest on the cash if it were available for investing.

【Example 12-3】

Suppose the average daily float is \$3 million with a weighted average delay of 5 days. What is the total amount unavailable to earn interest? What is the NPV of a project that could reduce the delay by 3 days if the cost is \$ 8million?

Answer:

$$\text{The total float} = 5 \times \$3\text{million} = \$15 \text{ million}$$

$$\text{Immediate cash flow} = 3 \times \$3\text{million} = \$9 \text{ million}$$

$$\text{NPV} = \$9\text{million} - \$8\text{million} = \$1 \text{ million}$$

12.3 Cash Collection and Concentration

We know that collection delays work against the firm. So, a firm will adopt procedures to speed up collections. In addition, even after cash is collected, firms need procedures to funnel, or concentrate, that cash where it can be best used. We discuss some common collection and concentration procedures next.

12.3.1 Components of Collection Time

As Figure 12-1 illustrates, the total time in this process is made up of mailing time, check-processing delay, and the bank's availability delay. The amount of time depends on where the firm's customers and banks are located and how efficient the firm is in collecting cash. One of the goals of float management is to try to reduce the collection delay. There are several techniques that can reduce various parts of the delay.

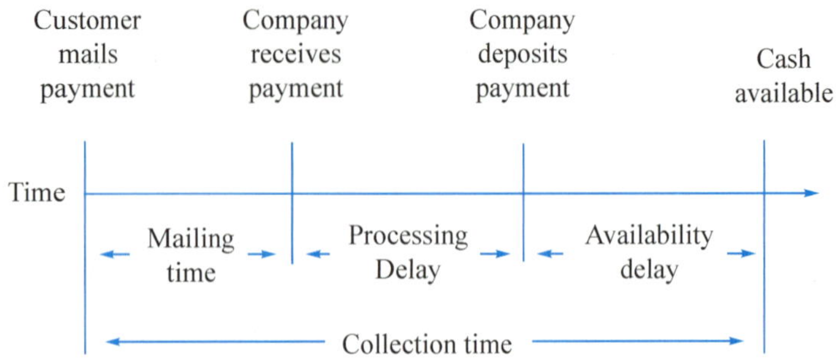

Figure12-1 **Cash collection time**

12.3.2 Cash Collection

There are two common ways to collect cash as follows.

1. The Preauthorized Payment Arrangement(集中银行法)

With this arrangement, the payment amounts and payment dates are fixed in advance. When the agreed-upon date arrives, the amount is automatically transferred from the customer's bank account to the firm's bank account, which sharply reduces or even eliminates collection delays.

2. Lockboxes(锁箱法)

When a firm receives its payments by mail, it must decide where the checks will be mailed and how the checks will be picked up and deposited. Careful selection of the number and locations of collection points can greatly reduce collection times. Many firms use special post office boxes called lockboxes to intercept payments and speed up cash collection. Figure 12-2 illustrates a lockbox system.

【Example 12-4】

Your company does business nationally, and currently, all checks are sent to the headquarters in Tampa, FL. You are considering a lock-box system that will have checks processed in Phoenix, St. Louis and Philadelphia. The Tampa office will continue to process the checks it receives in house.

Collection time will be reduced by 2 days on average

Daily interest rate on T-bills =0.01%

Average number of daily payments to each lockbox is 5,000

Average size of payment is \$500

The processing fee is \$0.10 per check plus \$10 to wire funds to a centralized bank at the end of each day.

Average daily collections = 3×5,000×500 = 7,500,000

Increased bank balance = 2(7,500,000) = 15,000,000

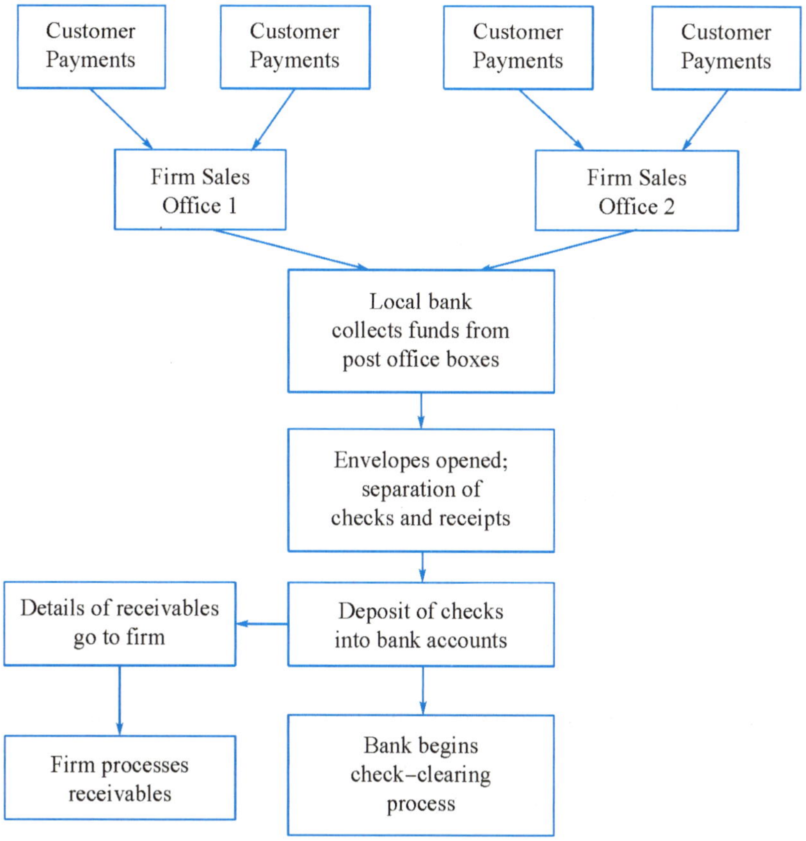

Figure 12-2 **Overview of Lockbox**

Daily cost = 0.1×15,000 + 3×10 = 1,530

Present value of daily cost = 1,530/0.0001 = 15,300,000

NPV = 15,000,000 − 15,300,000 = −300,000

The company should not accept this lock-box proposal.

12.3.3 Cash Concentration

A firm will commonly have many cash collection points. The procedures that the firm move the cash from different cash collection points into its main accounts is called cash concentration. Concentration systems are often used in conjunction with lockbox systems. By cash concentration, the firm will have a larger pool of funds available, which is good for negotiation and obtaining a better rate on any short-term investments. The firm can greatly simplifies its cash concentration by reducing the number of accounts that must be tracked.

12.4 Cash Disbursements and Idle Cash Investment

From the firm's point of view, disbursement float is desirable, so the goal in managing disbursement float is to slow down disbursements. To do this, the firm may take measures to increase mail float, processing float, and availability float. Beyond this, firms have developed procedures for minimizing cash held for payment purposes.

However, if a firm has a temporary cash surplus, it can invest in short-term securities. The maturity of short-term financial assets that trade in the money market is one year or less. Most large firms manage their own short-term financial assets, carrying out transactions through banks and dealers.

12.4.1 Increasing Disbursement Float

Slowing down payments depends on the time involved in mail delivery, check processing, and collection of funds. Disbursement float can be increased by writing a check on a geographically distant bank.

However, the strategy of maximizing the float in cash payments is morally and economically controversial. On the one hand, payment terms frequently offer a substantial discount for early payment, which is usually much larger than float. On the other hand, suppliers are not likely to be fooled by attempts to slow down disbursements. The negative consequences of poor relations with suppliers can be costly.

12.4.2 Controlling Disbursements

In addition to maximizing cash payment float, the company can also reduce cash retention by establishing an effective system for managing cash disbursements to maximize profits. There are two approaches to accomplishing this goal.

1. Zero-Balance Accounts

With a zero-balance account system, the firm maintains a master account and a set of subaccounts. When a check written on one of the subaccounts must be paid, the necessary funds are transferred in from the master account. Under this system, the firm can maintain safe cash holdings only in a master account and transfer the funds to the subsidiary accounts as needed, which frees up cash to be used elsewhere.

2. Controlled Disbursement Accounts

With a controlled disbursement account system, almost all payments that must be made in a given day are known in the morning. The bank informs the firm of the total, and the firm transfers (usually by wire) the amount needed.

12.4.3 Temporary Cash Surpluses

Firms have temporary cash surpluses for various reasons. Two of the most important are the financing of seasonal or cyclical activities of the firm and the financing of planned or possible expenditures.

1. Seasonal or Cyclical Activities

Some firms have a predictable cash flow pattern. They have surplus cash flows during part of the year and deficit cash flows the rest of the year, such as toy retail enterprise. These firm may buy marketable securities when surplus cash flows occur and sell marketable securities when deficits occur. Of course, bank loans are another short-term financing device.

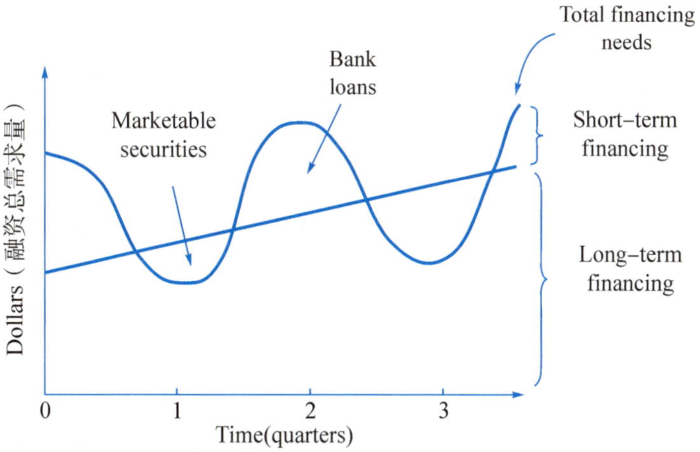

Figure 12-3 **Seasonal Cash Demands**

2. Planned or Possible Expenditures

Firms frequently accumulate marketable securities in anticipation of upcoming expenses. Thus, firms may issue bonds and stocks before the cash is needed, investing the proceeds in short-term marketable securities and then selling it to finance the expenditures. Also, firms may face the possibility of having to make a large cash outlay. An example is the possibility of losing a large lawsuit. Firms may build up cash surpluses against such a contingency.

12.4.4 Characteristics of Short-Term Securities

The most important characteristics of short-term marketable securities are their maturity, default risk, marketability, and taxes.

1. Maturity(到期日)

The prices of longer-maturity securities will change more than those of shorter maturity securities, which is called interest rate risk. As a consequence, firms that invest in long-term securities are accepting greater risk. Firms often limit their investments in marketable securities to those maturing in less than 90 days to avoid the interest rate risk.

2. Default Risk(违约风险)

Default risk refers to the probability that interest and principal will not be paid in the promised amounts on the due dates (or will not be paid at all). Of course, some securities have negligible default risk, such as Treasury bills. Given the purposes of investing idle corporate cash, firms should avoid investing in marketable securities with high default risk.

3. Marketability(市场流动性)

Market ability refers to how easy it is to convert an asset to cash; so marketability and liquidity mean much the same thing.

4. Taxes(税收)

Firms should consider different tax characteristics when making a decision.

延伸阅读 12-1 《企业集团多银行现金管理》

一、企业现金管理的重要意义

现金流是企业的生命线，许多企业倒闭的重要原因就是现金流断裂。二十大报告中强调要“坚持把发展经济的着力点放在实体经济上”，要保障企业资金链的安全。对于各种实体企业来说，现金则是一直是关乎其生死的关键因素。因此，加强企业现金管理、提高创现能力具有十分重要的现实意义。

一方面，现金是企业持续经营的重要来源。企业在生产经营活动中，如果扣除非付现成本后(包括折旧和摊销等)，经营性净现金流量为正，标志着企业经营活动创造现金的能力较强，该企业是一个经营运行质量较高的企业，企业的持续生产经营就有了保障，将来进一步发展也有可靠的资金来源。另一方面，现金是企业资金链条不发生断链的重要保证。在企业正常的生产经营活动中，如果不注意偿债能力管理，或不能按照现金—资产—现金(增值)的良性循环，不断地获取现金，增加资产，那么股东、债权人就可能对企业失去信心，企业就难以得到维持经营的资金支持，一旦不能到期按时还债，发生债务危机，就会发生资金断链现象，诱发严重后果。

二、案例背景

河南煤业化工集团注册资本金122亿元人民币，2016年企业资产总额达1 109.31亿元，在职员工20万人。除总部外在全国还有多家成员单位，涉及煤炭、钼金属、铝矿资源及上下游各类附属产品生产等产业，因业务运作相对独立，各家下属单位根据业务的需要，已经分别在不同的银行开户。各商业银行提供的现金管理产品及网上银行等服务系统互相独立，该集团公司常常遇到以下困难：其一，河南煤业化工集团在国内的合作银行不止一家，各银行账户管理、资金收付以及对应的账务处理等以手工为主，工作负荷偏高；其二，资金头寸信息不清楚、不及时，资金预算和计划管控流于形式，资金风险偏高；其三，资金使用、安排不够精细，资金流动性的管理主要依靠过往经验，资金成本偏高。

三、解决方案

某商业银行联合第三方软件厂商，合作研发了多银行资金管理系统(MBS)，提供给河南煤业化工集团公司针对该系统的全方位服务。一方面，该系统通过多银行数据服务平台实现了企业与各家银行的直联，支持账户管理、支付结算等基本业务；另一方面，该系统是一套企业内部的资金管理系统，实现了对资金预算、流量分析的管理，并支持与企业财务、办公等系统对接。多银行现金管理系统的逻辑架构(以用友ERP-NC资金管控平台为例，如图1所示)。通过与第三方软件厂商的网银适配器可实现与多家银行的对接。

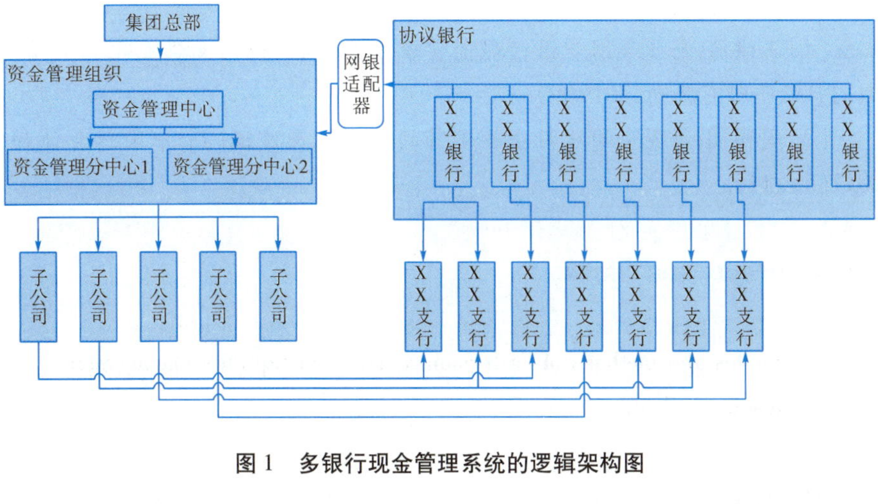

图1　多银行现金管理系统的逻辑架构图

(1)通过多银行现金管理系统账户管理平台，河南煤业化工集团可以通过资金管理中心自主设定和维护需要管理的所有银行账户，按照自身的组织构架来定义账户结构，并可以在总部层面实时查询和掌握所有成员机构在各银行的资金余额和交易状况，所有信息按层级分别显示，余额自动汇总，整体资金情况一目了然。

(2)通过平台的资金结算划拨模块，河南煤业化工集团能够对各银行账户进行收付结算处理，并支持根据自身财务制度灵活设置各种资金交易的审批流程。资金交易可以通过手动或自动方式发起，系统及时反馈交易信息。与 ERP 相连后，还可以联动记账，生成财务凭证。同时，所有资金交易均支持单笔录入或批量导入。此外，还可以通过特殊对账码实现自动对账，并生成余额调节表，减少人工操作。

(3)通过其中的计划预算管控平台，河南煤业化工集团可以建立全面的资金计划管理体系，包括制定统一的资金计划政策和模块，资金计划审批、执行、调整和控制等。企业也可以根据实际收支情况，自动提交计划执行情况，实现资金计划考核和资金风险防范。

(4)通过资金流量分析平台，河南煤业化工集团可以结合收支计划和当前资金存量计算下一计划周期的资金盈缺，为集团提供资金管理的考核及决策依据，同时将资金流量计划汇总到集团，对集团资金做出平衡试算，并能据此做出资金安排和投融资决策。

多银行资金管理系统既是一种集团企业资金管理系统，也是一种先进商业模式，为企业集团提供了高附加值的财资管理服务，有效地帮助河南煤业化工集团提升资金效率与效益，实现资金风险自由可控，强化资金管控能力。这种银行与软件企业联手的商业模式开启了中国集团企业资金管理未来模式，指引了银行现金管理服务模式和资金管理软件行业的发展方向。

资料来源：

[1]王洪涛.企业集团多银行现金管理方案分析：以河南煤业化工集团为例[J].经济研究导刊，2019(9).

[2]周园园.论现金管理对企业运营的重要性及建议[J].中国总会计师，2017(5)：113.

Key Concepts and Skills

1. Motives and methods of cash management and liquidity management.
2. Measuring float.

本章重点与难点

1. 现金和流动资金管理的动机和手段。
2. 浮差的计算方法。

Self-Test Questions

Ⅰ. True (T) or False (F) Questions

1. The primary advantages of holding T-bills are the generally higher yields compared to alternative money market investments. ( )

2. The firm can make use of a variety of procedures to manage the collection and disbursement of cash. Some methods to speed up the disbursement are the use of lockboxes, concentration banking, and wire transfers. ( )

3. Net disbursement float is more desirable because the bank thinks the firm has more money than it actually does, and the firm is, therefore, receiving interest on funds it has already spent. ( )

4. Because of seasonal and cyclical activities, to help finance planned expenditures, or as a contingency reserve, firms temporarily hold a cash surplus. ( )

5. The main drawback of the commercial paper market are the higher default risk characteristics of the security and the lack of an active secondary market which may excessively restrict the flexibility of corporations to meet their liquidity adjustment needs. ( )

Ⅱ. Single Choice Questions

1. In a typical month, the Corporation A receives 140 checks totaling \$113,500. These are delayed four days on average. Please calculate the average daily float. ( )

A. \$15,133.33

B. \$3,783.33

C. \$15,163.33

D. \$3,763.33

2. Company A receives an average of \$13,800 in checks per day. The delay in clearing is typically four days. The current interest rate is .01 8percent per day. What is the highest daily fee the company should be willing to pay to eliminate its float entirely? ( )

A. \$4.97

B. \$9.94

C. \$7.45

D. \$2.48

3. Derek goes to the post office once a month and picks up two checks, one

for ＄9, 700 and one for ＄2, 600. The larger check takes four days to clear after it is deposited; the smaller one takes five days. Assuming 30 days in a month. What is the weighted average delay? ( )

A. 1. 06 days

B. 3. 15days

C. 4. 21 days

D. 6. 12 days

4. Firm A is a mail-order firm. It processes 5, 450 checks per month, of which 70% are ＄55 checks and 30% are ＄80 checks. The ＄55 checks are delayed two days on average; the ＄80 checks are delayed three days on average. How much should the firm A be willing to pay to eliminate the float? ( )

A. ＄27, 068

B. ＄28, 068

C. ＄27, 880

D. ＄28, 880

5. Company A pays a check every two weeks for an average of ＄62, 000 and takes seven days to clear. How much interest can the company earn annually if it delays transfer of funds from an interest-bearing account that pays 0. 015 percent per day for these seven days? Ignore the effects of compounding interest. ( )

A. ＄1, 692. 6

B. ＄1, 684. 41

C. ＄1, 664. 34

D. ＄1, 650. 41

Ⅲ. Calculation Questions

1. Firm A has an average receipt size of ＄120. B bank has approached you concerning a lockbox service that will decrease total collection time by two days. Firm A typically receive 5, 600 checks per day. The daily interest rate is 0. 015 percent. If the bank charges a fee of ＄160 per day, should the lockbox project be accepted? What is the net annual savings if this service is used?

2. Company A has determined that a majority of its customers are located in City B. It therefore is considering using a lockbox system offered by a bank located in City C. The bank has estimated that use of the system will reduce collection time by two days. Based on the following information, should the lockbox system be adopted?

Average number of payments per day	850
Average value of payment	$ 630
Variable lockbox fee (per transaction)	$ 0. 20
Annual interest rate on money market securities	7%

本章习题答案

Chapter 13 Credit and Inventory Management（信用和库存管理）

Learning Objectives

- Understand the key issues related to credit management.
- Understand the impact of cash discounts.
- Be able to evaluate a proposed credit policy.
- Understand the components of credit analysis.
- Understand the major components of inventory management.
- Be able to use the EOQ model to determine optimal inventory ordering.

This chapter is about how firms manage credit and inventory. The advantage of granting credit is that it will increase sales. However, the disadvantage is that customers may not pay and the company has to bear the costs of carrying the receivables. The basic objective of credit management is to keep carrying cost as low as possible while still keep benefits of increased sales. Accordingly, we discuss key issues of terms of sale, credit policy and credit analysis. In addition, inventories represent a significant investment for many firms. We thereby introduce the EOQ approach, to show how to determine optimal inventory ordering for a firm.

13.1 Credit and Receivables

The advantage of granting credit is that it will increase sales. However, the disadvantage is that customers may not pay and the company has to bear the costs of carrying the receivables. The credit policy decision thus involves a trade-off between the benefits of increased sales and the costs of granting credit.

13. 1. 1 Components of Credit Policy

If a firm decides to grant credit to its customers, then it must establish procedures for extending credit and collecting. In particular, the firm will have to deal with the following components of credit policy:

1. Terms of Sale(销售条件)

The terms of sale establish how the firm proposes to sell its goods and services. The terms of sale will specify (perhaps implicitly) the credit period, the cash discount and discount period, and the type of credit instrument.

2. Credit Analysis(信用分析)

In granting credit, firms use a number of devices and procedures to determine the probability that customers will not pay.

3. Collection Policy(收账政策)

Firms have the potential problem of collecting the cash, for which it must establish a collection policy.

13. 1. 2 The Cash Flows from Granting Credit

The accounts receivable period as the time it takes to collect on a sale. Some of the events that occur during this period generate cash flows related to the granting of credit.

As figure 13-1 illustrates, the typical sequence of events when a firm grants credit is as follows: ① The credit sale is made, ② the customer sends a check to the firm, ③ the firm deposits the check, and ④ the firm's account is credited for the amount of the check.

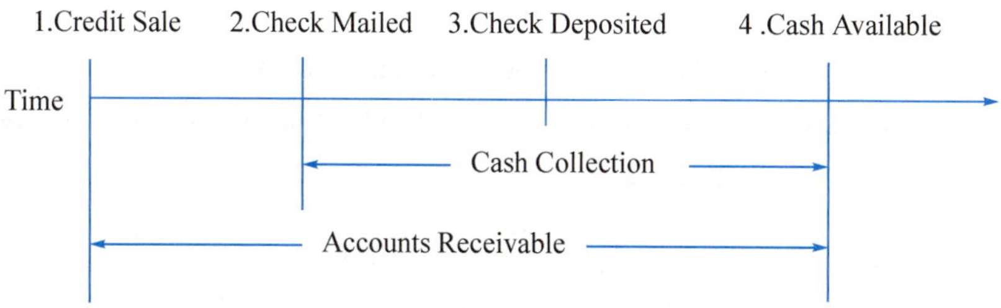

Figure 13-1 The Cash Flows from Granting Credit

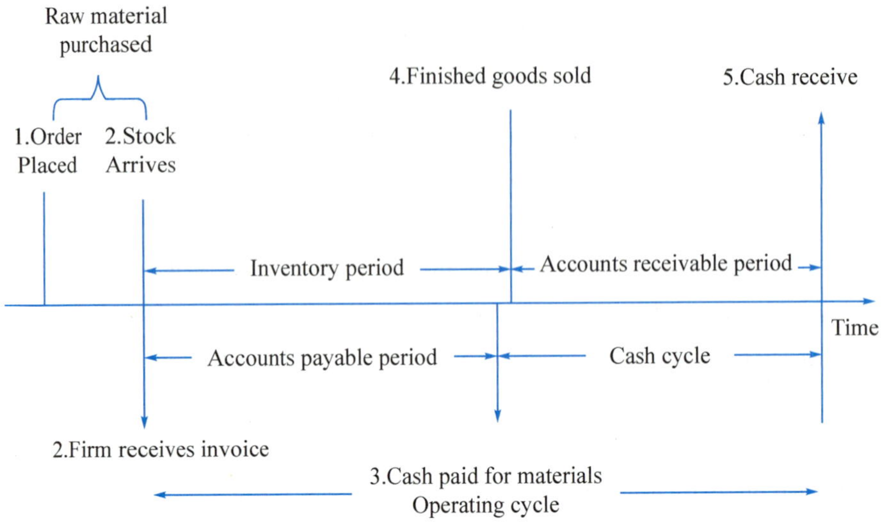

Figure 13-2 **Cash Flow Time Line and the Short Term Operating Activities of a Typical Manufacturing Firm**

13.1.3 The Investment in Receivables

The investment in accounts receivable for any firm depends on the amount of credit sales and the average collection period. For example, if a firm's average collection period, ACP, is 30 days. Then, there are 30 days at any given time when the corresponding sales are not collected. If credit sales run \$1,000 per day, the firm's accounts receivable will then be equal to 30 days × \$1,000 per day = \$30,000, on average.

A firm's receivables generally will be equal to its average daily sales multiplied by its average collection period:

$$\text{Accounts receivable} = \text{Average daily sales} \times \text{ACP}$$

Thus, a firm's investment in accounts receivable depends on factors that influence credit sales and collections.

13.2 Terms of Sale

The terms of a sale are made up of three distinct elements:

1. The period for which credit is granted (the credit period).
2. The cash discount and the discount period.
3. The type of credit instrument.

13.2.1 The Basic Form

In general, credit terms are interpreted in the following way: take this discount off the invoice price/if you pay in this many days, or pay the full invoice amount in this many days

Terms such as 2/10, net 45 are common. This means that total amount due in 45 days if discount not taken. However, if payment is made within 10 days, a 2 percent cash discount can be taken.

If you buy $500 worth of merchandise with the credit terms given above. You should pay $490 if you pay in 10 days, or pay $500 if you pay in 45 days.

13.2.2 The Credit Period(信用期限)

The credit period is the basic length of time for which credit is granted. The credit period varies widely from industry to industry, but it is almost always between 30 and 120 days. If a cash discount is offered, then the credit period has two components: The net credit period and the cash discount period.

The net credit period is the length of time the customer has to pay. The cash discount period is the time during which the discount is available. With 2/10, net 30, for example, the net credit period is 30 days and the cash discount period is 10 days.

Several factors influence the length of the credit period. Two important ones are the buyer's inventory period and operating cycle. There are a number of other factors that influence the credit period and operating cycle. Among the most important are these:

1. Perishability and Collateral Value Perishable items have relatively rapid turnover and relatively low collateral value. Credit periods are thus shorter for such goods.

2. Consumer Demand Products that are well established generally have more rapid turnover. Newer or slow-moving products will often have longer credit periods associated with them to entice buyers.

3. Cost, Profitability, and Standardization Relatively inexpensive goods tend to have shorter credit periods. However, there are exceptions. Auto dealers, for example, generally pay for cars as they are received.

4. Credit Risk The greater the credit risk of the buyer, the shorter the credit period is likely to be (if credit is granted at all).

5. Size of the Account If an account is small, the credit period may be shorter because small accounts cost more to manage, and the customers are less important.

6. Competition When the seller is in a highly competitive market, longer credit periods may be offered as a way of attracting customers.

7. Customer Type A single seller might offer different credit terms to different buyers.

13.2.3 Cash Discounts(现金折扣)

One reason discounts are offered is to speed up the collection of receivables. This will have the effect of reducing the amount of credit being offered, and the firm must trade this off against the cost of the discount. Another reason for cash discounts is that they are a way of charging higher prices to customers that have had credit extended to them. In this sense, cash discounts are a convenient way of charging for the credit granted to customers.

1. Cost of the Credit

With 2/10, net 30, for example, early payment gets the buyer only a 2 percent discount. It might seem that the cash discounts are rather small. However, the implicit interest rate is extremely high.

【Example 13-1】

Suppose the order is for \$1,000. The buyer can pay \$980 in 10 days or wait another 20 days and pay \$1,000. It's obvious that the buyer is effectively borrowing \$980 for 20 days and that the buyer pays \$20 in interest on the "loan." What's the interest rate?

Answer:

Credit terms of 2/10 net 30

Period rate : $r = 2/98 = 2.040,8\%$

Period : $P = (30 - 10) = 20$ days

$365/20 = 18.25$ periods per year

EAR $= (1.020,408)^{18.25} - 1 = 44.59\%$

The company benefits when customers choose to forgo discounts. This is an expensive source of financing.

2. Trade Discounts

Trade discount is also called commercial discount. Trade discount refers to the discount given by a certain percentage according to the order quantity, relationship and other factors.

3. The Cash Discount and the ACP

To the extent that a cash discount encourages customers to pay early, it will shorten the receivables period and reduce the firm's investment in receivables.

【Example 13-2】

Suppose a firm currently has terms of net 30 and an average collection period (ACP) of 30 days. If it offers terms of 2/15, net 35, then perhaps 50 percent of its customers (in terms of volume of purchases) will pay in 15 days. The remaining customers will still take an average of 35 days to pay.

What will the new ACP be? If the firm's annual sales are \$15 million (before discounts), what will happen to the investment in receivables?

Answer:

$$\text{NEW ACP} = 0.5 \times 15 \text{ days} + 0.5 \times 35 \text{ days} = 25 \text{ days}$$

The ACP thus falls from 30 days to 25 days. Average daily sales are \$15 million/365 = \$41,096 per day. Receivables will thus fall by \$41,096 × 15 = \$616,440.

13.2.4 Credit Instruments(信用工具)

The credit instrument is the basic evidence of indebtedness. Most trade credit is offered on open account. This means that the only formal instrument of credit is the invoice, which is sent with the shipment of goods and which the customer signs as evidence that the goods have been received. Afterward, the firm and its customers record the exchange on their books of account.

Promissory notes are not common, but they can eliminate possible controversies later about the existence of debt. One problem with promissory notes is that they are signed after delivery of the goods.

A commercial draft can obtain the customer's credit commitment before delivery. Typically, the firm draws up a commercial draft calling for the customer to pay a specific amount by a specified date. The draft is then sent to the customer's bank with the shipping invoices. If immediate payment is required on the draft, it is called a **sight draft**. If immediate payment is not required, then the draft is a **time draft**.

When the draft is presented and the buyer "accepts" it, meaning that the buyer promises to pay it in the future, then it is called a **trade acceptance**. If a bank accepts the draft, meaning that the bank is guaranteeing payment, then the draft becomes a **banker's acceptance**.

13.3 Credit Policy

In this section, we will analyze the factors affecting credit granting decisions in more detail. Granting credit makes sense only if the NPV from doing so is positive. We thus need to look at the NPV of the decision to grant credit and calculate the optimal credit line based on this. In principle, the optimal amount of credit is determined by the point at which the incremental cash flows from increased sales are exactly equal to the incremental costs of carrying the increase in investment in accounts receivable.

13.3.1 Credit Policy Effects

In evaluating credit policy, there are five basic factors to consider:

Revenue Effects. If the firm grants credit, then there will be a delay in revenue collections. However, the firm may be able to charge a higher price if it grants credit and it may be able to increase the quantity sold. Total revenues may thus increase.

Cost Effects. Although the firm may experience delayed revenues if it grants credit, it will still incur the costs of sales immediately.

1. The cost of sale: Cost of the sale is still incurred even though the cash from the sale has not been received.

2. The cost of debt: When the firm grants credit, it must arrange to finance the resulting receivables.

3. The probability of nonpayment: If the firm grants credit, some percentage of the credit buyers will not pay.

4. The cash discount: When the firm offers a cash discount as part of its credit terms, some customers will choose to pay early to take advantage of the discount.

13.3.2 Evaluating a Proposed Credit Policy

To illustrate how credit policy can be analyzed, we will start with a relatively simple case.

【Example 13-3】

Your company is evaluating a switch from a cash only policy to a net 30 policy. The price per unit is \$100, and the variable cost per unit is \$40. The company currently sells 1, 000 units per month. Under the proposed policy, the company expects to sell 1, 050 units per month. The required monthly return is 1. 5%.

(1) What is the NPV of the switch?

(2) Should the company offer credit terms of net 30?

(3) What is the break-even sales increase?

Answer:

P = Price per unit

v = Variable cost per unit

Q = Current quantity sold per month

Q' = Quantity sold under new policy

R = Monthly required return

$$\begin{aligned}\text{NPV} &= -[PQ + v(Q' - Q)] + [(P - v)(Q' - Q)]/R \\ &= -[100 \times 1,000 + 40 \times (1,050 - 1,000)] + [(100 - 40)(1,050 - 1,000)]/1.5\% \\ &= 98,00\end{aligned}$$

Therefore, the switch is very profitable. The company should offer credit terms of net 30.

A Break-Even Application We can calculate the break-even point explicitly by setting the NPV equal to zero and solving for $(Q' - Q)$:

$$\text{NPV} = 0 = -[PQ + v(Q' - Q)] + [(P - v)(Q' - Q)]/R$$

$$Q' - Q = PQ/[(P - v)/R - v]$$

The break-even sales increase is thus:

$$Q' - Q = 100 \times 1,000/[(100 - 40)/.015 - 40] = 25.25$$

This tells us that the switch is a good idea as long as Your company is confident that it can sell at least 25. 25 more units per month.

13. 3. 3 The Total Credit Cost Curve

To begin, the carrying costs associated with granting credit come in three forms:

1. The required return on receivables.
2. The losses from bad debts.
3. The costs of managing credit and credit collections. The cost of managing credit consists of the expenses associated with running the credit department.

The opportunity costs refer to lost sales due to a restrictive credit policy.

The sum of the carrying costs and the opportunity costs of a particular credit policy is called the total credit cost. As Figure 13-3 illustrates, there is a point where the total credit cost is minimized. This point corresponds to the optimal amount of credit or, equivalently, the optimal investment in receivables.

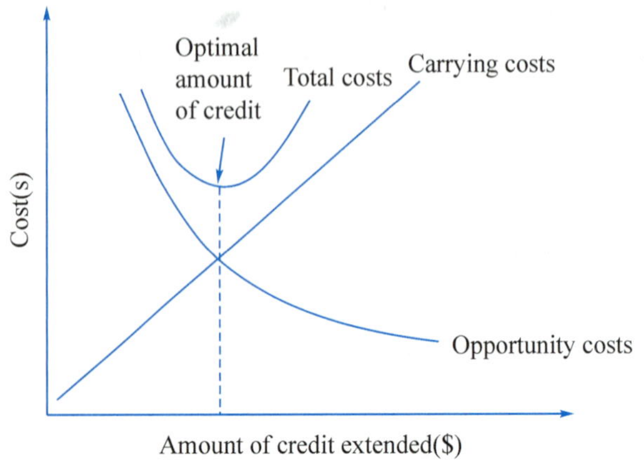

Figure 13-3 **The Costs of Granting Credit**

If the firm extends more credit than this minimum, the additional net cash flow from new customers will not cover the carrying costs of the investment in receivables. If the level of receivables is below this amount, then the firm is forgoing valuable profit opportunities.

13.4 Credit Analysis

Credit analysis refers to the process of deciding whether to extend credit to a particular customer. It usually involves two steps: Gathering relevant information and determining creditworthiness.

13.4.1 When Should Credit be Granted?

We will use some special cases to illustrate when should credit be granted.

1. A One-Time Sale

A new customer wishes to buy one unit on credit at a price of P per unit. If credit is refused, the customer will not make the purchase. If credit is granted, the customer will either pay up or default in one month. The probability of the second of these events is Π. Our business does not have repeat customers, so this is strictly a one-time sale. Finally, the required return on receivables is R per month, and the variable cost is v per unit.

If the firm refuses credit, then the incremental cash flow is zero. If it grants credit, then it spends v (the variable cost) this month and expects to collect $(1-\pi)P$ *next month. The NPV* of granting credit is:

$$NPV = -v + (1-\pi)P/(1+R)$$

【Example 13-4】

Your company is considering granting credit to a new customer. The variable cost per unit is \$50; the current price is \$110; the probability of default is 15%; and the monthly required return is 1%.

What is the NPV? What is the break-even probability?

Answer:

$$NPV = -v + (1-\pi)P/(1+R)$$
$$= -50 + (1-0.15) \times 110/1.01 = 42.57$$

The break-even probability in this case can be determined by setting the NPV equal to zero and solving for π :

$$NPV = 0 = -50 + (1-\pi) \times 110/1.01$$
$$\pi = 54.09\%$$

The firm should extend credit when there is a 1 − 0.540,9 = 45.91% chance or better of collecting. This explains why firms with higher markups tend to have looser credit terms. This percentage (54.09 percent) is the maximum acceptable default probability for a new customer.

2. Repeat Business

A very important factor to keep in mind is the possibility of repeat business. Assuming that a new customer who does not default the first time around will remain a customer forever and never default.

Assuming that the default probability is π . With probability $(1-\pi)$, however, the firm will have a permanent new customer. The value of a new customer is equal to the present value of $(P-v)$ every month forever. The NPV of extending credit is therefore:

$$NPV = -v + (1-\pi)(P-v)/R$$

【Example 13-5】

In the previous example, what is the NPV if we are looking at repeat business?

Answer:

$$NPV = -50 + (1-0.15)(110-50)/0.01 = 5,050$$

13.4.2 Credit Information

Information sources commonly used to assess creditworthiness include the following:

1. Financial Statements

The company calculates financial ratios according to customers' financial statements and makes decisions based on them.

2. Payment History with the Company

The most obvious way to obtain information about the likelihood of customers not paying is to examine whether they have settled past obligations (and how quickly).

3. Credit Reports with Customer's Payment History to Other Firms

Quite a few organizations sell information about the credit strength and credit history of business firms. Companies can evaluate customer credit based on the information.

4. Banks

Banks will generally provide some assistance to their business customers in acquiring information about the creditworthiness of other firms.

13.4.3 Credit Evaluation and Scoring

Credit scoring is the process of calculating a numerical rating for a customer based on information collected; credit is granted or refused based on the result. In very general terms, the classic **five Cs of credit** are the basic factors to be evaluated:

1. **Character(品德)**: The customer's willingness to meet credit obligations.
2. **Capacity(能力)**: The customer's ability to meet credit obligations out of operating cash flows.
3. **Capital(资本)**: The customer's financial reserves.
4. **Collateral(担保)**: An asset pledged in the case of default.
5. **Conditions(条件)**: General economic conditions in the customer's line of business.

13.5 Collection Policy

Collection policy involves monitoring receivables to spot trouble and obtaining payment on past-due accounts.

13.5.1 Monitoring Receivables

First of all, a firm will normally keep track of its average collection period

(ACP) through time. If a firm is in a seasonal business, the ACP will fluctuate during the year.

The **aging schedule** is a second basic tool for monitoring receivables. To prepare one, the credit department classifies accounts by age. Firms usually use aging schedule to determine percentage of payments that are being made late.

13.5.2 Collection Effort

A firm usually goes through the following sequence of procedures for customers whose payments are overdue:

1. **Delinquency Letter** It sends out a delinquency letter informing the customer of the past-due status of the account.

2. **Telephone Call** It makes a telephone call to the customer.

3. **Collection Agency** It employs a collection agency.

4. **Legal Action** It takes legal action against the customer.

At times, a firm may refuse to grant additional credit to customers until arrearages are cleared up. This may antagonize a normally good customer, which points to a potential conflict between the collections department and the sales department.

13.6 Inventory Management

Inventory can be a large percentage of a firm's assets. There can be significant costs associated with carrying too much inventory. There can also be significant costs associated with not carrying enough inventory. Inventory management tries to find the optimal trade-off between carrying too much inventory versus not enough (trade-off). The goal of inventory management is usually framed as cost minimization. There are some techniques are discussed in this section.

13.6.1 Inventory Types

For a manufacturer, inventory is normally classified into one of three categories.

1. Raw Materials (原材料)

This is whatever the firm uses as a starting point in its production process, such as iron ore for a steel manufacturer or disk drives for a computer manufacturer.

2. Work-in-Progress (Unfinished Product, 在产品)

How big this portion of inventory is depends in large part on the length of the production process.

3. Finished Goods(产成品)

Keep in mind two things concerning inventory types. First, remember that one firm's "raw material" may be another firm's "finished goods". The second thing to keep in mind is that the various types of inventory can be quite different in terms of their liquidity, which normally depends on the nature of the product.

13.6.2 Inventory Costs(存货成本)

As we all know, carrying costs and shortage cost are associated with current assets in general and with inventory in particular.

Carrying Costs(持有成本) represent all of the direct and opportunity costs of keeping inventory on hand. These include:

1. Storage and tracking costs.
2. Insurance and taxes.
3. Losses due to obsolescence, deterioration, or theft.
4. The opportunity cost of capital on the invested amount.

The sum of these costs can be substantial, ranging roughly from 20 to 40 percent of inventory value per year.

Shortage Costs (短缺成本) are costs associated with having inadequate inventory on hand. These include:

1. Restocking costs: Depending on the firm's business, restocking costs are either the costs of placing an order with suppliers or the costs of setting up a production run.

2. Lost sales or lost customers

A basic trade-off exists in inventory management because carrying costs increase with inventory levels, whereas shortage or restocking costs decline with inventory levels. The basic goal of inventory management is thus to minimize the sum of these two costs.

13.6.3 The ABC Approach

The ABC approach is a simple approach to inventory management in which the basic idea is to classify inventory by cost, demand, and need. The underlying rationale is that a small portion of inventory in terms of quantity might represent a large portion in terms of inventory value. Firms generally maintain smaller quantities of expensive items and a substantial supply of less expensive basic materials. Figure 13 - 4 illustrates an ABC comparison of items in terms of the percentage of inventory value represented by each group versus the percentage of items represented.

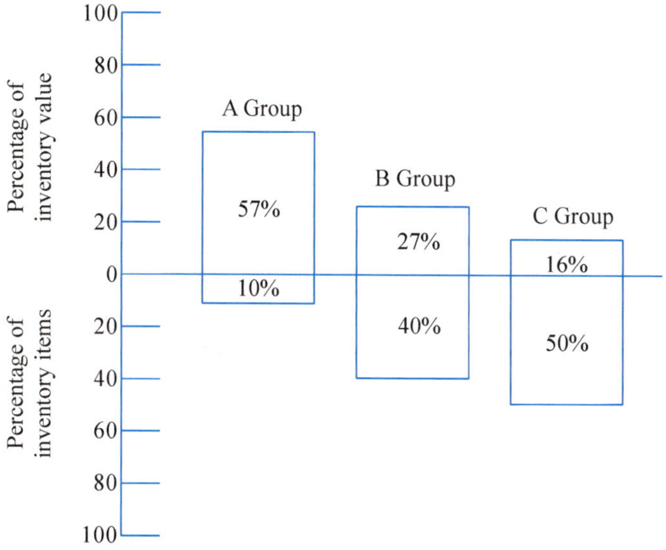

Figure 13-4　**ABC Inventory Analysis**

13.6.4　The Economic Order Quantity Model(经济订购量模型)

The economic order quantity (EOQ) model is the best-known approach for explicitly establishing an optimal inventory level. As Figure 13-5 shown, inventory carrying costs rise and restocking costs decrease as inventory levels increase. With the EOQ model, we will attempt to specifically locate the minimum total cost point, Q^*. What we are analyzing here is how much the firm should have on hand at any particular time. More precisely, we are trying to determine what order size the firm should use when it restocks its inventory.

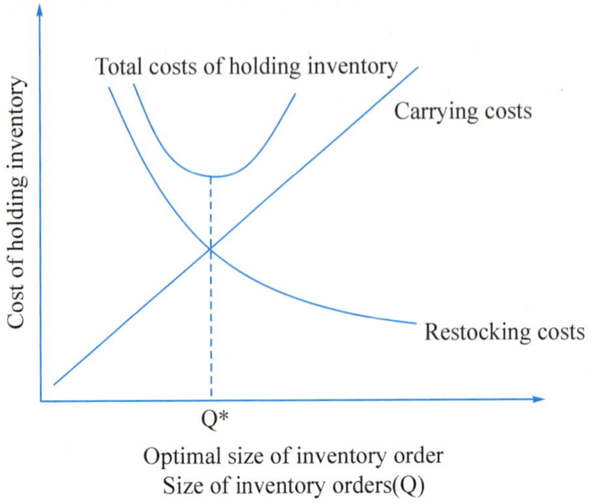

Figure 13-5 **Costs of Holding Inventory**

1. Inventory Depletion

To develop the EOQ, we will assume that the firm's inventory is sold off at a steady rate until it hits zero. At that point, the firm restocks its inventory back to some optimal level.

【Example 13-6】

Suppose the Eyssell Corporation starts out today with 3, 600 units of a particular item in inventory. Annual sales of this item are 46, 800 units, which is 900 per week (52weeks). If Eyssell sells 900 units of inventory each week, all the available inventory will be sold after 4 weeks, and Eyssell will restock by ordering (or manufacturing) another 3, 600 and start over. Please calculate the average inventory of Eyssell company.

As the figure 13-6 shows, Eyssell always starts with 3, 600 units in inventory and ends up at zero. On average, then, inventory is half of 3, 600, or 1, 800 units.

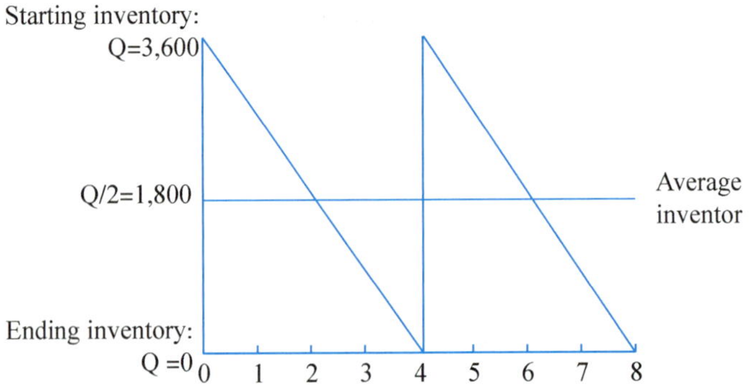

Figure 13-6 **Inventory Holdings for the Eyssell Corporation**

2. The Carrying Costs

3. As Figure 13-5 illustrates, carrying costs are normally assumed to be directly proportional to inventory levels. Suppose Q is the quantity of inventory and CC is the carrying cost per unit per year. Total carrying costs will be:

$$\text{Total carrying costs} = \text{Average inventory} \times \text{Carrying costs per unit} = (Q/2) \times \text{CC}$$

In Eyssell's case, if carrying costs were \$.75 per unit per year, total carrying costs will be:

$$\text{Total carrying costs} = (3,600/2) \times .75 = 1,350$$

3. The Restocking Costs

4. Restocking costs are normally assumed to be fixed. Suppose F is the restocking cost and T is the firm's total unit sales per year. If the firm orders Q units each time, then it will need to place a total of T/Q orders.

$$\text{Total restocking costs} = \text{Fixd cost per oder} \times \text{Number of oders} = F \times (T/Q)$$

For Eyssell, if the fixed cost per order is \$50, the total restocking cost for the year would be:

$$\text{Total restocking costs} = 50 \times 46,800/3,600 = 650$$

4. The Total Costs

5. The total costs associated with holding inventory are the sum of the carrying costs and the restocking costs:

$$\text{Total costs} = \text{Carrying costs} \times \text{Restocking costs} = (Q/2) \times \text{CC} + F \times (T/Q)$$

5. The Minimum Total Cost Point

As Figure illustrates, the minimum point occurs right where the two lines cross. At this point, carrying costs and restocking costs are the same. So we can find the minimum point just by setting these costs equal to each other and solving for Q^* :

$$\text{Carrying costs} = \text{Restocking costs}$$

$$(Q^*/2) \times \text{CC} = F \times (F/Q^*)$$

$$Q^* = \sqrt{\frac{2T \times F}{\text{CC}}}$$

This reorder quantity, which minimizes the total inventory cost, is called **the economic order quantity (EOQ)**. For the Eyssell Corporation, the EOQ is:

$$Q^* = \sqrt{\frac{(2 \times 46,800) \times 50}{0.75}} = 2,498 \text{ units}$$

【Example 13-7】

Consider an inventory item that has carrying cost= $1.50 per unit. The fixed order cost is $50 per order, and the firm sells 100,000 units per year. What is the economic order quantity?

Answer:

$$Q^* = \sqrt{\frac{2T \times F}{CC}} = \sqrt{\frac{(2 \times 100,000) \times 50}{1.50}} = 1,766 \text{ units}$$

案例分析 13-1 《小米公司"零库存管理"》

一、企业库存管理的重要意义

作为国家"六保"任务中的重要组成部分，切实保障产业链、供应链的稳定既是畅通国民经济循环的基础，又是中国经济转向高质量发展的必然要求。党的二十大报告中着重强调了要"着力提升产业链供应链韧性和安全水平"。"十四五"规划纲要中更明确指出了要以高水平双向投资高效利用全球资源要素和市场空间，完善产业链、供应链保障机制，推动产业竞争力提升。

企业的存货管理体系在保障产业链、供应链的稳定中发挥着关键作用。伴随生产分工的精细化发展及物流效率的提升，社会把降低存货视为企业管理运营能力提升的现实表现。不可否认，良好的库存管理是企业降低成本、优化生产、提升市场价值的重要途径，一定程度上决定了企业是否能够实现长远的发展。因此，企业在发展的同时，应加强库存管理。

二、小米公司存货管理状况

小米之所以能够吸引很多消费者，在手机市场占有一定的份额，是因为它每一代手机都拥有最新旗舰型高端配件，但是销售价格却很亲民，这是小米手机每一代产品都能够取得巨大成功的原因。在2015年4月9日，小米还破了一项吉尼斯世界纪录，在世界单一网络平台上，24小时内小米销售的手机数量最多。而小米备受关注有以下两个原因。其一，良好的营销手段。其二，小米公司在采购、生产、信息管理、销售渠道等诸多方面上对成本的控制，导致它可以高配置、低价格地销售产品。小米公司最典型的存货管理方法就是"零库存管理"。

"零库存"并不是指在企业仓库里产品的储存量真的是零，而是指在经过特殊的手段和办法之后，仓库内产品在不影响企业运作的同时，可以存在的最小量。所以"零库存"管理的内涵是在企业运作和发展不受到影响的同时，仓库产品数量不需要不断地进行补充，只要保持在一定的最小数量。小米手机的生产模式可称为"类PC生产"，这是一种"按需定制"的生产模式。小米手机用户通过网络下单，企业获得市场需求，然后通过供应链采购零部件，比如向夏普采购屏幕，向高通采购芯片，向索尼采购摄像头，再通过其他厂商采购其他零部件。零件供应商→代工工厂→线上销售→配送中心→买家。“零库存”可以进一步降低库存成本给企业带来的竞争压力，但是低库存也会带来风险。“零库存”的风险包括买方缺货、供应源单一单链、可能断裂的供应链、可能产生连锁放大的效应、不合理转嫁运作、供应链配送成本增加、供应链上下游企业合作、相关信息泄露等，对企业的生产、销售、供应链都可能造成影响。一般情况下，公司会根据自身情况，针对零库存模式设置不同的控制措施，尽可能减少零库存供应造成的风险。

三、小米公司存货管理机制与其他企业的对比

1. 小米公司与中兴公司对比

中兴公司进入手机市场很早，采用传统的存货管理模式，库存较大，其产品一开始也并未采用线上销售模式，导致市场不明确，不仅增加了存货成本，产品定价也不能符合广大消费者预期，并且因为缺乏线上的市场调研，产品信息与市场不对称。以上种种导致这个老牌的通讯厂商未能在手机行业走得更远。中兴与小米公司对比异常明显。由于零库存模式成本的降低，加上饥饿营销在消费者心中的冲击，因此小米的产品质量与市场知名度相较于中兴有大幅提高，更重要的是由于采用线上销售模式，小米公司对于市场动向与产品定位的把握更准确。结果显而易见，最终以小米公司的不断壮大和中兴这类老牌厂商的落幕结束。

2. 小米公司与苹果公司对比

苹果公司作为国际性的大公司，其存货管理与小米公司有很大不同。苹果公司由于其全球覆盖的销售以及供应商众多等缘故，其库存管理成本一度高达 7 亿美金，产品库存周转率不到 13 次，与小米的大规模产品涉及覆盖不同，苹果公司采用了其他手段降低库存成本：

第一，减少供应商的数量。苹果公司将原来庞大而复杂的供应商数量减少为更多的中央供应商，并开始更频繁地与他们进行沟通，以便他们能共同应对可能的突发库存风险。苹果公司经常向供应商发送预测信息，以共同应对各种原因造成的库存爆炸风险。然而，苹果公司也对供应商提出了一系列相对苛刻的要求。无论何时，一个项目，苹果公司都会要求供应商在 12 小时内完成其根本要求，如果它不符合要求的话，将很难与苹果公司继续合作。

第二，减少产品种类。这是整个改革进程中最基本的部分。苹果只保留了 4 种基本的产品风格。其余 9 种产品已从中减去，使得他们使用的部件更加标准化，从而减少不必要的浪费并降低能耗。例如，iPod nano 减少了元件准备所需的时间和库存量，因为所有通用 IC 都在为其提供服务。2007 年，苹果实现了快速的库存周转和高速增长。

第三，提供更多的虚拟产品以降低成本。到目前为止，苹果在需求预测和

库存管理方面投入仍十分巨大，但问题也依然很多。然而，苹果推出 iTunes 音乐商店服务吸引消费者并建立零库存的商品供应链，最终完成近 20 亿美元的销售量。苹果的在线 iTunes 音乐商店也已经成为继沃尔玛和百思买之后的全球第三大音乐零售商。

资料来源：

[1]杨柳.小米公司存货管理研究[J].商场现代化，2023(2).

[2]李磊，刘泽寰.对外直接投资能够提高企业的精益存货管理水平吗：基于中国微观企业的研究[J].山西大学学报(哲学社会科学版)，2023，46(3)：135-147.

延伸阅读 13-2 《企业信用管理研究》

一、企业信用管理的重要意义

信用已经成为日常生活中不可或缺的一部分，并且在企业的日常经营管理中起到了重要的作用。党的十八大提出加强政务诚信、商务诚信、社会诚信以及司法公信建设；党的二十大报告中也强调要“完善产权保护、市场准入、公平竞争、社会信用等市场经济基础制度，优化营商环境”；同时国务院出台了相关行政法规要求明确推进企业诚信建设，并且鼓励企业建立信用管理模式；除此之外，国务院还要求鼓励企业将客户的信用记录纳入相对应的信用体系当中，从而更好地帮助企业加强自身管理。由此可见，我国十分重视企业信用管理体系的建设，信用管理对保障企业平稳发展和维护资本市场稳定有着举足轻重的作用。随着我国经济市场的发展，信用销售逐渐成为公司之间交易的主要方式，然而因为我国目前并没有建立十分完善的信用体制，导致企业在使用信用销售的过程中需要面临信用风险。

二、案例背景

Y 企业是一家大型纺织企业集团，诞生于 20 世纪 80 年代。Y 企业 2006 年 6 月末信用规模余额为 4.78 亿元(见表 1)，其中信用输入(信用需求)余额为 3.7 亿元，信用输出(信用供给)余额为 1.04 亿元；2003—2006 年上半年累计实现信用输入 31.8 亿元，实现信用输出 15.21 亿元。从动态看，信用总量呈逐年增长的趋势，2004—2006 年(折合年率)环比增长率分别为 7.53%、83.07%和 146.54%，其中信用输入分别增长-1.97%、89.36%和 144.48%，信用输出分别增长 53.98%、63.51%和 153.62%。

表 1 Y 企业信用输入与信用输出情况（万元）

项目	存量					流量				
	平均余额	2003 年	2004 年	2005 年	2006 年	合计	2003 年	2004 年	2005 年	2006 年 6 月
合计	47 838	29 571	31 799	58 216	71 764	470 356	104 371	90 258	154 120	121 607
1. 信用输入	37 479	24 549	24 066	45 572	55 730	318 220	74 319	55 815	103 819	84 267
银行贷款	20 237	12 398	13 254	25 524	29 771	105 252	16 200	15 513	35 135	38 404
应付票据	965	1 270	250	1 838	500	14 311	6 041	2 595	4 675	1 000
信用证	603	600	450	720	640	37 168	13 408	5 968	12 448	5 344
应付账款	3 673	4 000	2 177	4 207	4 306	109 811	32 000	23 453	36 097	18 261
预收账款	1 443	778	702	1 809	2 483	7 438	1 167	1 053	1 990	3 228
他方担保	3 500	1 500	1 500	3 000	8 000	16 000	1 500	1 500	5 000	8 000
职工集资	7 060	4 003	5 733	8 474	10 030	28 240	4 003	5 733	8 474	10 030
2. 信用输出	10 358	5 022	7 733	12 644	16 034	152 136	30 052	34 443	50 301	37 340
信用证	763	800	650	900	700	92 152	22 208	22 448	28 056	19 440
应收账款	3 168	1 545	2 287	3 476	5 362	30 524	4 924	6 200	11 700	7 700
预付账款	1 353	477	1 996	1 768	1 172	6 660	720	2 595	1 945	1 400
对外担保	5 075	2 200	2 800	6 500	8 800	22 800	2 200	3 200	8 600	8 800

注：1. 按企业账面数据整理所得；

2. 商业汇票、信用证额度为敞口部分；

3. 职工集资流量数据难以采集，担保流量变化不大，均以存量代替

三、信用风险

第一，信用管理意识不强，管理体系不健全。Y 企业虽然对信用管理有了一定的认识，但认识程度还不够。在信用标准和信用额度方面，企业没有统一、规范的标准和控制额度，全凭销售部经理随机掌握。在信用调查与风险控制方面，对客户选择没有规范的制度，流程交易前不调查、不评估，往往只注重人际关系等表面现象，较少关注客户财务数据，虽然设有客户档案，但资料相当缺乏，从未购买信息产品，基本上是凭主观判断进行风险评估和预测交易。中期不监控，对客户信用只了解静态情况，很少进行动态监测。交易管理不系统，使客户容易出现机会主义倾向。虽然设有账龄表，但对风险的事后控制不够有力，往往形成拖欠后才进行催收，延长了应收账款回收时间，增大了坏账可能性，管理水平有待提高。

第二，信用需求大于供给，结构失衡问题突出。从表 1 可以看出，Y 企业信用供需结构具有明显的不平衡性。一是信用需求始终大于信用供给。尽管从年均增速看，43%的信用输入增长率低于 59%的信用输出增长率，但由于前者基数大、后者基数小，从存量看前者对后者的比率始终保持在 2.1 倍以上，并且不论是存量还是流量，其差额近三年均呈逐渐扩大的趋势。二是信用输入突出表现为金融机构融资性输入。2003—2006 年 6 月末，银行借款和商业汇票、信用证（敞口）部分的平均存量占比达到 58.17%，累计流量占比虽然仅

有49.26%，但近两年有上升的趋势。三是信用采购交易量明显大于信用销售交易量。从存量看，除2006年上半年外，一年末应付账款均大于应收账款。从动态看，2003—2006年6月末应付账款的累计流量达到10.98亿元，比应收账款高出7.93亿元，是应收账款的3.6倍。这种信用需求大于信用供给的现状，必然会加剧社会信用供求失衡，因为社会信用供求总量是社会所有单个企业信用供求的加总。

第三，信用销售规模较小，对企业成长贡献度低。该企业没有充分重视信用交易在企业发展中的作用，使得信用销售对企业的成长贡献较低，主营业务收入的增长速度低于信用销售额增长速度，信用销售对主营业务收入增长没有起到倍乘作用。

第四，对客户信息掌握不及时、不全面，内外部信用风险偏高。企业信用风险具有双向性，即包括企业面临的信用风险和企业对其客户（或银行）的信用风险两方面。通过对Y企业掌握的客户信息状况的调查（包括客户的基本情况、重大事项、产品市场、财务状况、信用状况等）发现，该企业对其客户的一些重要信息和资料掌握得不及时、不全面，存在较为严重的信息不对称，面临着较大的信用风险。

四、解决方案

通过分析Y企业的信用管理政策，本文提出加强我国企业信用建设的建议：

1. 加强对企业信用管理重要性的认识

前世界银行首席经济学家斯蒂格里茨认为，在市场经济运作中，资源配置并非完全取决于价格因素，有时更多取决于企业信誉。加强企业信用管理，是企业积聚信誉、加快发展的必然选择，也是社会文明程度提高的需要。全社会都应当进一步提高对信用管理重要性的认识。

2. 营造企业信用管理的微观基础

企业是社会重要的基础部门，也是社会信用主体，其信用管理状况和微观机制再造对社会信用体系建设具有极其重要的基础作用。从对Y企业的调查看，当前应重点采取以下措施继续规范公司治理结构，制定明晰、完善的信用管理政策，进一步发挥个人信用价值的作用，努力改善财务状况，降低资产负债率。

3. 完善并充分发挥社会信用中介组织的作用

要加强企业信用管理，必须充分发挥社会中介组织的作用。中介组织通过对信用信息的搜集、加工、传递、评价，能有效地发挥其约束和降低社会交易费用等作用，这对于建立惩戒机制、加强企业信用管理和社会信用体系建设具有巨大的推动作用。

4. 充分发挥政府在社会信用体系建设中的作用

企业信用管理作为社会信用体系的重要组成部分，依赖于社会信用体系的完善，而社会信用体系建设又是一个复杂的系统工程。从各国情况看，政府在社会信用管理体系中都发挥着重要的作用，特别是在我国目前体制下，这一特点更加突出。

资料来源：

[1]庞建敏.企业信用管理研究：基于企业的案例分析[J].金融研究，2007(11)

[2]纪家权，谷沁芮，魏晔.中国企业信用管理体系构建[J].中国市场，2021(17)：91-93.

Key Concepts and Skills

1. Components of credit policy; credit analysis.
2. Calculation of break-even point.
3. Credit policy evaluation and collection policy.
4. Components and calculation of inventory costs.
5. The economic order quantity (EOQ) model.

本章重点与难点

1. 信用政策的组成，将信用政策用于净现值分析的方法。
2. 盈亏平衡点的计算。
3. 信用政策评估与收账政策。
4. 存货成本的构成及计算方法。
5. EOQ 模型计算经济订购数量。

Self-Test Questions

Ⅰ. True (T) or False (F) Questions

1. The NPV of granting credit depends on five factors: Revenue effects, cost effects, the cost of debt, the probability of nonpayment, and the cash discount. (　　)

2. A sight draft is an IOU that the customer signs. (　　)

3. A time draft is a commercial draft that does not require immediate payment. (　　)

4. Trade credit is usually granted on open account. ( )

5. A trade acceptance is when a bank guarantees the future payment of a commercial draft. ( )

Ⅱ. Single Choice Questions

1. Company A place an order for 300 units of inventory at a unit price of $120. The supplier offers terms of 1/10, net 30. If company A do take the discount, how much should it remit? ( )

A. $35, 640

B. $45, 540

C. $45, 640

D. $35, 540

2. You place an order for 500 units of inventory at a unit price of $130. The supplier offers terms of 1/10, net 30. If you don't take the discount, how much interest are you paying implicitly? ( )

A. $450

B. $550

C. $650

D. $750

3. Company A has weekly credit sales of $32, 000, and the average collection period is 30 days. What is the average accounts receivable figure? ( )

A. $130, 085. 71

B. $137, 142. 86

C. $137, 085. 71

D. $130, 142. 86

4. A firm has an average collection period of 32 days. Its average daily investment in receivables is $62, 000. What are annual credit sales? ( )

A. $707, 187. 5

B. $658, 073. 53

C. $685, 757. 58

D. $754, 333. 33

5. The ABC Corporation sells on credit terms of net 30. Its accounts are, on average, 6 days past due. Its annual credit sales are $ 8million. What is the company's balance sheet amount in accounts receivable? ( )

A. $858, 219. 18

B. $860, 576. 92

C. $789, 733. 46

D. $ 789, 040. 23

Ⅲ. Calculation Questions

1. A firm has annual sales of $ 30 million. The average collection period is 25 days. What is the average investment in accounts receivable as shown on the balance sheet?

2. Company A uses 1, 860 units of material B per week and then reorders another 1, 860. If the relevant carrying cost per material B is $ 7, and the fixed order cost is $ 750, is the company's inventory policy optimal? Please explain why?

3. Company A has an all-cash credit policy. It intends to change its credit policy by going to terms of net 30 days. The required return is .95 percent per month. Based on the following information, please give your suggestions.

	Current Policy	New Policy
Price per unit	$ 289	$ 296
Cost per unit	$ 226	$ 229
Unit sales per month	1, 105	1, 125

本章习题答案

References

[1]冯连福等. 公司治理[M]. 第 2 版. 中国人民大学出版社,2020.

[2]李薇. 公司金融(双语版)[M]. 厦门大学出版社,2008. 斯蒂芬 A. 罗斯. 伦道夫 W. 威斯特菲尔德. 杰弗利 F. 杰富. 布拉德福德 D.乔丹. 公司理财[M]. 英文版・原书第 11 版. 机械工业出版社,2018.

[3]刘广斌. 梁慧媛. 公司理财理论与案例[M]. 化学工业出版社,2015.

[4]刘曼红. 李朝晖. 公司理财[M]. 第 4 版. 中国人民大学出版社,2016。

[5]张良财. 企业理财案例分析实训[M]. 中国物质出版社,2007.

[6]朱叶. 公司金融[M]. 第 4 版. 复旦大学出版社,2018.

[7]Baker, H. K., Singleton, J. C., Veit, E. T. Dividends and Dividend Policy[M]. John Wiley, 2010.

[8]Banks, E. The Credit Risk of Financial Instruments[M]. Palgrave Macmillan London,1993.

[9]Berk, J. B., DeMarzo, P. M. Corporate Finance[M]. Pearson Education, 2007.

[10]Brealey, R. A., Myers, S. C., Allen, F. Principles of Corporate Finance[M]. McGraw-hill, 2014.

[11]Brooks, R. M. Financial Management: Core Concepts[M]. Pearson, 2016.

[12]Donald, D. V., Imai, K. Credit Risk Models and the Basel Accords [M]. John Wiley & Sons (Asia), 2003.

[13]Frankfurter, G., Wood, B. G., Wansley, J. Dividend Policy: Theory and Practice[M]. Elsevier, 2003.

[14]Keith, J. Inventory Management for Competitive Advantage: Including a Practical and Effective Purchasing Strategy for Managers[M]. Routledge, 2020.

[15]Keynes, J. M. The General Theory of Employment, Interest, and Money [M]. Palgrave Macmillan Cham, 2018.

[16]Petty, J. W., Titman, S., Keown, A. J., Martin, P., Martin, J. D. & Burrow, M. Financial Management: Principles and Applications[M]. Pearson Higher Education AU, 2015.

[17]Ross, S. A., Westerfield, R. W., Jordan, B. D. Essentials of Corporate Finance[M]. McGraw-Hill, 2017.

[18]Tirole, J. The Theory of Corporate Finance[M]. Princeton University Press, 2010.

[19]Van Horne, J. C. Financial Management & Policy, 12/E[M]. Pearson Education India, 2002.

附录

附录 1　复利终值系数表

期数	利率								
	1%	2%	3%	4%	5%	6%	7%	8%	9%
1	1. 0100	1. 0200	1. 0300	1. 0400	1. 0500	1. 0600	1. 0700	1. 0800	1. 0900
2	1. 0201	1. 0404	1. 0609	1. 0816	1. 1025	1. 1236	1. 1449	1. 1664	1. 1881
3	1. 0303	1. 0612	1. 0927	1. 1249	1. 1576	1. 1910	1. 2250	1. 2597	1. 2950
4	1. 0406	1. 0824	1. 1255	1. 1699	1. 2155	1. 2625	1. 3108	1. 3605	1. 4116
5	1. 0510	1. 1041	1. 1593	1. 2167	1. 2763	1. 3382	1. 4026	1. 4693	1. 5386
6	1. 0615	1. 1262	1. 1941	1. 2653	1. 3401	1. 4185	1. 5007	1. 5869	1. 6771
7	1. 0721	1. 1487	1. 2299	1. 3159	1. 4071	1. 5036	1. 6058	1. 7138	1. 8280
8	1. 0829	1. 1717	1. 2668	1. 3686	1. 4775	1. 5938	1. 7182	1. 8509	1. 9926
9	1. 0937	1. 1951	1. 3048	1. 4233	1. 5513	1. 6895	1. 8385	1. 9990	2. 1719
10	1. 1046	1. 2190	1. 3439	1. 4802	1. 6289	1. 7908	1. 9672	2. 1589	2. 3674
11	1. 1157	1. 2434	1. 3842	1. 5395	1. 7103	1. 8983	2. 1049	2. 3316	2. 5804
12	1. 1268	1. 2682	1. 4258	1. 6010	1. 7959	2. 0122	2. 2522	2. 5182	2. 8127
13	1. 1381	1. 2936	1. 4685	1. 6651	1. 8856	2. 1329	2. 4098	2. 7196	3. 0658
14	1. 1495	1. 3195	1. 5126	1. 7317	1. 9799	2. 2609	2. 5785	2. 9372	3. 3417
15	1. 1610	1. 3459	1. 5580	1. 8009	2. 0789	2. 3966	2. 7590	3. 1722	3. 6425
16	1. 1726	1. 3728	1. 6047	1. 8730	2. 1829	2. 5404	2. 9522	3. 4259	3. 9703
17	1. 1843	1. 4002	1. 6528	1. 9479	2. 2920	2. 6928	3. 1588	3. 7000	4. 3276
18	1. 1961	1. 4282	1. 7024	2. 0258	2. 4066	2. 8543	3. 3799	3. 9960	4. 7171
19	1. 2081	1. 4568	1. 7535	2. 1068	2. 5270	3. 0256	3. 6165	4. 3157	5. 1417
20	1. 2202	1. 4859	1. 8061	2. 1911	2. 6533	3. 2071	3. 8697	4. 6610	5. 6044
21	1. 2324	1. 5157	1. 8603	2. 2788	2. 7860	3. 3996	4. 1406	5. 0338	6. 1088
22	1. 2447	1. 5460	1. 9161	2. 3699	2. 9253	3. 6035	4. 4304	5. 4365	6. 6586
23	1. 2572	1. 5769	1. 9736	2. 4647	3. 0715	3. 8197	4. 7405	5. 8715	7. 2579
24	1. 2697	1. 6084	2. 0328	2. 5633	3. 2251	4. 0489	5. 0724	6. 3412	7. 9111
25	1. 2824	1. 6406	2. 0938	2. 6658	3. 3864	4. 2919	5. 4274	6. 8485	8. 623
30	1. 3478	1. 8114	2. 4273	3. 2434	4. 3219	5. 7435	7. 6123	10. 063	13. 268
35	1. 4166	1. 9999	2. 8139	3. 9461	5. 5160	7. 6861	10. 677	14. 785	20. 414
40	1. 4889	2. 2080	3. 2620	4. 8010	7. 0400	10. 286	14. 974	21. 725	31. 409
45	1. 5648	2. 4379	3. 7816	5. 8412	8. 9850	13. 765	21. 002	31. 920	48. 327
50	1. 6446	2. 6916	4. 3839	7. 1067	11. 467	18. 420	29. 457	46. 902	74. 358
55	1. 7285	2. 9717	5. 0821	8. 6464	14. 636	24. 650	41. 315	68. 914	114. 41
60	1. 8167	3. 2810	5. 8916	10. 520	18. 679	32. 988	57. 946	101. 26	176. 03

（FVIF 表）

利率										
10%	12%	14%	15%	16%	18%	20%	24%	28%	32%	36%
1.1000	1.1200	1.1400	1.1500	1.1600	1.1800	1.2000	1.2400	1.2800	1.3200	1.3600
1.2100	1.2544	1.2996	1.3225	1.3456	1.3924	1.4400	1.5376	1.6384	1.7424	1.8496
1.3310	1.4049	1.4815	1.5209	1.5609	1.6430	1.7280	1.9066	2.0972	2.3000	2.5155
1.4641	1.5735	1.6890	1.7490	1.8106	1.9388	2.0736	2.3642	2.6844	3.0360	3.4210
1.6105	1.7623	1.9254	2.0114	2.1003	2.2878	2.4883	2.9316	3.4360	4.0075	4.6526
1.7716	1.9738	2.1950	2.3131	2.4364	2.6996	2.9860	3.6352	4.3980	5.2899	6.3275
1.9487	2.2107	2.5023	2.6600	2.8262	3.1855	3.5832	4.5077	5.6295	6.9826	8.6054
2.1436	2.4760	2.8526	3.0590	3.2784	3.7589	4.2998	5.5895	7.2058	9.2170	11.703
2.3579	2.7731	3.2519	3.5179	3.8030	4.4355	5.1598	6.9310	9.2234	12.166	15.917
2.5937	3.1058	3.7072	4.0456	4.4114	5.2338	6.1917	8.5944	11.806	16.060	21.647
2.8531	3.4785	4.2262	4.6524	5.1173	6.1759	7.4301	10.657	15.112	21.199	29.439
3.1384	3.8960	4.8179	5.3503	5.9360	7.2876	8.9161	13.215	19.343	27.983	40.037
3.4523	4.3635	5.4924	6.1528	6.8858	8.5994	10.699	16.386	24.759	36.937	54.451
3.7975	4.8871	6.2613	7.0757	7.9875	10.147	12.839	20.319	31.691	48.757	74.053
4.1772	5.4736	7.1379	8.1371	9.2655	11.974	15.407	25.196	40.565	64.359	100.71
4.5950	6.1304	8.1372	9.3576	10.748	14.129	18.488	31.243	51.923	84.954	136.97
5.0545	6.8660	9.2765	10.761	12.468	16.672	22.186	38.741	66.461	112.14	186.28
5.5599	7.6900	10.575	12.375	14.463	19.673	26.623	48.039	85.071	148.02	253.34
6.1159	8.6128	12.056	14.232	16.777	23.214	31.948	59.568	108.89	195.39	344.54
6.7275	9.6463	13.743	16.367	19.461	27.393	38.338	73.864	139.38	257.92	468.57
7.4002	10.804	15.668	18.822	22.574	32.324	46.005	91.592	178.41	340.45	637.26
8.1403	12.100	17.861	21.645	26.186	38.142	55.206	113.57	228.36	449.39	866.67
8.9543	13.552	20.362	24.891	30.376	45.008	66.247	140.83	292.30	593.20	1178.7
9.8497	15.179	23.212	28.625	35.236	53.109	79.497	174.63	374.14	783.02	1603.0
10.835	17.000	26.462	32.919	40.874	62.669	95.396	216.54	478.90	1033.6	2180.1
17.449	29.960	50.950	66.212	85.850	143.37	237.38	634.82	1645.5	4142.1	10143.
28.102	52.800	98.100	133.18	180.31	328.00	590.67	1861.1	5653.9	16599.	47191.
45.259	93.051	188.88	267.86	378.72	750.38	1469.8	5455.9	19427.	66521.	*
72.890	163.99	363.68	538.77	795.44	1716.7	3657.3	15995.	66750.	*	*
117.39	289.00	700.23	1083.7	1670.7	3927.4	9100.4	46890.	*	*	*
189.06	509.32	1348.2	2179.6	3509.0	8984.8	22645.	*	*	*	*
304.48	897.60	2595.9	4384.0	7370.2	20555.	56348.	*	*	*	*

注：* 表示系数大于 99999。

附录2　复利现值系数表

期数	利率								
	1%	2%	3%	4%	5%	6%	7%	8%	9%
1	0.9901	0.9804	0.9709	0.9615	0.9524	0.9434	0.9346	0.9259	0.9174
2	0.9803	0.9612	0.9426	0.9246	0.9070	0.8900	0.8734	0.8573	0.8417
3	0.9706	0.9423	0.9151	0.8890	0.8638	0.8396	0.8163	0.7938	0.7722
4	0.9610	0.9238	0.8885	0.8548	0.8227	0.7921	0.7629	0.7350	0.7084
5	0.9515	0.9057	0.8626	0.8219	0.7835	0.7473	0.7130	0.6806	0.6499
6	0.9420	0.8880	0.8375	0.7903	0.7462	0.7050	0.6663	0.6302	0.5963
7	0.9327	0.8706	0.8131	0.7599	0.7107	0.6651	0.6227	0.5835	0.5470
8	0.9235	0.8535	0.7894	0.7307	0.6768	0.6274	0.5820	0.5403	0.5019
9	0.9143	0.8368	0.7664	0.7026	0.6446	0.5919	0.5439	0.5002	0.4604
10	0.9053	0.8203	0.7441	0.6756	0.6139	0.5584	0.5083	0.4632	0.4224
11	0.8963	0.8043	0.7224	0.6496	0.5847	0.5268	0.4751	0.4289	0.3875
12	0.8874	0.7885	0.7014	0.6246	0.5568	0.4970	0.4440	0.3971	0.3555
13	0.8787	0.7730	0.6810	0.6006	0.5303	0.4688	0.4150	0.3677	0.3262
14	0.8700	0.7579	0.6611	0.5775	0.5051	0.4423	0.3878	0.3405	0.2992
15	0.8613	0.7430	0.6419	0.5553	0.4810	0.4173	0.3624	0.3152	0.2745
16	0.8528	0.7284	0.6232	0.5339	0.4581	0.3936	0.3387	0.2919	0.2519
17	0.8444	0.7142	0.6050	0.5134	0.4363	0.3714	0.3166	0.2703	0.2311
18	0.8360	0.7002	0.5874	0.4936	0.4155	0.3503	0.2959	0.2502	0.2120
19	0.8277	0.6864	0.5703	0.4746	0.3957	0.3305	0.2765	0.2317	0.1945
20	0.8195	0.6730	0.5537	0.4564	0.3769	0.3118	0.2584	0.2145	0.1784
21	0.8114	0.6598	0.5375	0.4388	0.3589	0.2942	0.2415	0.1987	0.1637
22	0.8034	0.6468	0.5219	0.4220	0.3418	0.2775	0.2257	0.1839	0.1502
23	0.7954	0.6342	0.5067	0.4057	0.3256	0.2618	0.2109	0.1703	0.1378
24	0.7876	0.6217	0.4919	0.3901	0.3101	0.2470	0.1971	0.1577	0.1264
25	0.7798	0.6095	0.4776	0.3751	0.2953	0.2330	0.1842	0.1460	0.1160
30	0.7419	0.5521	0.4120	0.3083	0.2314	0.1741	0.1314	0.0994	0.0754
35	0.7059	0.5000	0.3554	0.2534	0.1813	0.1301	0.0937	0.0676	0.0490
40	0.6717	0.4529	0.3066	0.2083	0.1420	0.0972	0.0668	0.0460	0.0318
45	0.6391	0.4102	0.2644	0.1712	0.1113	0.0727	0.0476	0.0313	0.0207
50	0.6080	0.3715	0.2281	0.1407	0.0872	0.0543	0.0339	0.0213	0.0134
55	0.5785	0.3365	0.1968	0.1157	0.0683	0.0406	0.0242	0.0145	0.0087
60	0.5504	0.3048	0.1697	0.0951	0.0535	0.0303	0.0173	0.0099	0.0057

（PVIF 表）

利率										
10%	12%	14%	15%	16%	18%	20%	24%	28%	32%	36%
0.9091	0.8929	0.8772	0.8696	0.8621	0.8475	0.8333	0.8065	0.7813	0.7576	0.7353
0.8264	0.7972	0.7695	0.7561	0.7432	0.7182	0.6944	0.6504	0.6104	0.5739	0.5407
0.7513	0.7118	0.6750	0.6575	0.6407	0.6086	0.5787	0.5245	0.4768	0.4348	0.3975
0.6830	0.6355	0.5921	0.5718	0.5523	0.5158	0.4823	0.4230	0.3725	0.3294	0.2923
0.6209	0.5674	0.5194	0.4972	0.4761	0.4371	0.4019	0.3411	0.2910	0.2495	0.2149
0.5645	0.5066	0.4556	0.4323	0.4104	0.3704	0.3349	0.2751	0.2274	0.1890	0.1580
0.5132	0.4523	0.3996	0.3759	0.3538	0.3139	0.2791	0.2218	0.1776	0.1432	0.1162
0.4665	0.4039	0.3506	0.3269	0.3050	0.2660	0.2326	0.1789	0.1388	0.1085	0.0854
0.4241	0.3606	0.3075	0.2843	0.2630	0.2255	0.1938	0.1443	0.1084	0.0822	0.0628
0.3855	0.3220	0.2697	0.2472	0.2267	0.1911	0.1615	0.1164	0.0847	0.0623	0.0462
0.3505	0.2875	0.2366	0.2149	0.1954	0.1619	0.1346	0.0938	0.0662	0.0472	0.0340
0.3186	0.2567	0.2076	0.1869	0.1685	0.1372	0.1122	0.0757	0.0517	0.0357	0.0250
0.2897	0.2292	0.1821	0.1625	0.1452	0.1163	0.0935	0.0610	0.0404	0.0271	0.0184
0.2633	0.2046	0.1597	0.1413	0.1252	0.0985	0.0779	0.0492	0.0316	0.0205	0.0135
0.2394	0.1827	0.1401	0.1229	0.1079	0.0835	0.0649	0.0397	0.0247	0.0155	0.0099
0.2176	0.1631	0.1229	0.1069	0.0930	0.0708	0.0541	0.0320	0.0193	0.0118	0.0073
0.1978	0.1456	0.1078	0.0929	0.0802	0.0600	0.0451	0.0258	0.0150	0.0089	0.0054
0.1799	0.1300	0.0946	0.0808	0.0691	0.0508	0.0376	0.0208	0.0118	0.0068	0.0039
0.1635	0.1161	0.0829	0.0703	0.0596	0.0431	0.0313	0.0168	0.0092	0.0051	0.0029
0.1486	0.1037	0.0728	0.0611	0.0514	0.0365	0.0261	0.0135	0.0072	0.0039	0.0021
0.1351	0.0926	0.0638	0.0531	0.0443	0.0309	0.0217	0.0109	0.0056	0.0029	0.0016
0.1228	0.0826	0.0560	0.0462	0.0382	0.0262	0.0181	0.0088	0.0044	0.0022	0.0012
0.1117	0.0738	0.0491	0.0402	0.0329	0.0222	0.0151	0.0071	0.0034	0.0017	0.0008
0.1015	0.0659	0.0431	0.0349	0.0284	0.0188	0.0126	0.0057	0.0027	0.0013	0.0006
0.0923	0.0588	0.0378	0.0304	0.0245	0.0160	0.0105	0.0046	0.0021	0.0010	0.0005
0.0573	0.0334	0.0196	0.0151	0.0116	0.0070	0.0042	0.0016	0.0006	0.0002	0.0001
0.0356	0.0189	0.0102	0.0075	0.0055	0.0030	0.0017	0.0005	0.0002	0.0001	*
0.0221	0.0107	0.0053	0.0037	0.0026	0.0013	0.0007	0.0002	0.0001	*	*
0.0137	0.0061	0.0027	0.0019	0.0013	0.0006	0.0003	0.0001	*	*	*
0.0085	0.0035	0.0014	0.0009	0.0006	0.0003	0.0001	*	*	*	*
0.0053	0.0020	0.0007	0.0005	0.0003	0.0001	*	*	*	*	*
0.0033	0.0011	0.0004	0.0002	0.0001	*	*	*	*	*	*

注：* 表示系数小数点后 4 位为 0。

附录3 年金终值系数表

期数	利率								
	1%	2%	3%	4%	5%	6%	7%	8%	9%
1	1.0000	1.0000	1.0000	1.0000	1.0000	1.0000	1.0000	1.0000	1.0000
2	2.0100	2.0200	2.0300	2.0400	2.0500	2.0600	2.0700	2.0800	2.0900
3	3.0301	3.0604	3.0909	3.1216	3.1525	3.1836	3.2149	3.2464	3.2781
4	4.0604	4.1216	4.1836	4.2465	4.3101	4.3746	4.4399	4.5061	4.5731
5	5.1010	5.2040	5.3091	5.4163	5.5256	5.6371	5.7507	5.8666	5.9847
6	6.1520	6.3081	6.4684	6.6330	6.8019	6.9753	7.1533	7.3359	7.5233
7	7.2135	7.4343	7.6625	7.8983	8.1420	8.3938	8.6540	8.9228	9.2004
8	8.2857	8.5830	8.8923	9.2142	9.5491	9.8975	10.260	10.637	11.028
9	9.3685	9.7546	10.159	10.583	11.027	11.491	11.978	12.488	13.021
10	10.462	10.950	11.464	12.006	12.578	13.181	13.816	14.487	15.193
11	11.567	12.169	12.808	13.486	14.207	14.972	15.784	16.645	17.560
12	12.683	13.412	14.192	15.026	15.917	16.870	17.888	18.977	20.141
13	13.809	14.680	15.618	16.627	17.713	18.882	20.141	21.495	22.953
14	14.947	15.974	17.086	18.292	19.599	21.015	22.550	24.215	26.019
15	16.097	17.293	18.599	20.024	21.579	23.276	25.129	27.152	29.361
16	17.258	18.639	20.157	21.825	23.657	25.673	27.888	30.324	33.003
17	18.430	20.012	21.762	23.698	25.840	28.213	30.840	33.750	36.974
18	19.615	21.412	23.414	25.645	28.132	30.906	33.999	37.450	41.301
19	20.811	22.841	25.117	27.671	30.539	33.760	37.379	41.446	46.018
20	22.019	24.297	26.870	29.778	33.066	36.786	40.995	45.762	51.160
21	23.239	25.783	28.676	31.969	35.719	39.993	44.865	50.423	56.765
22	24.472	27.299	30.537	34.248	38.505	43.392	49.006	55.457	62.873
23	25.716	28.845	32.453	36.618	41.430	46.996	53.436	60.893	69.532
24	26.973	30.422	34.426	39.083	44.502	50.816	58.177	66.765	76.790
25	28.243	32.030	36.459	41.646	47.727	54.865	63.249	73.106	84.701
30	34.785	40.568	47.575	56.085	66.439	79.058	94.461	113.28	136.31
35	41.660	49.994	60.462	73.652	90.320	111.43	138.24	172.32	215.71
40	48.886	60.402	75.401	95.026	120.80	154.76	199.64	259.06	337.88
45	56.481	71.893	92.720	121.03	159.70	212.74	285.75	386.51	525.86
50	64.463	84.579	112.80	152.67	209.35	290.34	406.53	573.77	815.08
55	72.852	98.587	136.07	191.16	272.71	394.17	575.93	848.92	1260.1
60	81.670	114.05	163.05	237.99	353.58	533.13	813.52	1253.2	1944.8

(FVIFA 表)

利率										
10%	12%	14%	15%	16%	18%	20%	24%	28%	32%	36%
1.0000	1.0000	1.0000	1.0000	1.0000	1.0000	1.0000	1.0000	1.0000	1.0000	1.0000
2.1000	2.1200	2.1400	2.1500	2.1600	2.1800	2.2000	2.2400	2.2800	2.3200	2.3600
3.3100	3.3744	3.4396	3.4725	3.5056	3.5724	3.6400	3.7776	3.9184	4.0624	4.2096
4.6410	4.7793	4.9211	4.9934	5.0665	5.2154	5.3680	5.6842	6.0156	6.3624	6.7251
6.1051	6.3528	6.6101	6.7424	6.8771	7.1542	7.4416	8.0484	8.6999	9.3983	10.146
7.7156	8.1152	8.5355	8.7537	8.9775	9.4420	9.9299	10.980	12.136	13.406	14.799
9.4872	10.089	10.730	11.067	11.414	12.142	12.916	14.615	16.534	18.696	21.126
11.436	12.300	13.233	13.727	14.240	15.327	16.499	19.123	22.163	25.678	29.732
13.579	14.776	16.085	16.786	17.519	19.086	20.799	24.712	29.369	34.895	41.435
15.937	17.549	19.337	20.304	21.321	23.521	25.959	31.643	38.593	47.062	57.352
18.531	20.655	23.045	24.349	25.733	28.755	32.150	40.238	50.398	63.122	78.998
21.384	24.133	27.271	29.002	30.850	34.931	39.581	50.895	65.510	84.320	108.44
24.523	28.029	32.089	34.352	36.786	42.219	48.497	64.110	84.853	112.30	148.47
27.975	32.393	37.581	40.505	43.672	50.818	59.196	80.496	109.61	149.24	202.93
31.772	37.280	43.842	47.580	51.660	60.965	72.035	100.82	141.30	198.00	276.98
35.950	42.753	50.980	55.717	60.925	72.939	87.442	126.01	181.87	262.36	377.69
40.545	48.884	59.118	65.075	71.673	87.068	105.93	157.25	233.79	347.31	514.66
45.599	55.750	68.394	75.836	84.141	103.74	128.12	195.99	300.25	459.45	700.94
51.159	63.440	78.969	88.212	98.603	123.41	154.74	244.03	385.32	607.47	954.28
57.275	72.052	91.025	102.44	115.38	146.63	186.69	303.60	494.21	802.86	1298.8
64.002	81.699	104.77	118.81	134.84	174.02	225.03	377.46	633.59	1060.8	1767.4
71.403	92.503	120.44	137.63	157.41	206.34	271.03	469.06	812.00	1401.2	2404.7
79.543	104.60	138.30	159.28	183.60	244.49	326.24	582.63	1040.4	1850.6	3271.3
88.497	118.16	158.66	184.17	213.98	289.49	392.48	723.46	1332.7	2443.8	4450.0
98.347	133.33	181.87	212.79	249.21	342.60	471.98	898.09	1706.8	3226.8	6053.0
164.49	241.33	356.79	434.75	530.31	790.95	1181.9	2640.9	5873.2	12941.	28172.
271.02	431.66	693.57	881.17	1120.7	1816.7	2948.3	7750.2	20189.	51869.	*
442.59	767.09	1342.0	1779.1	2360.8	4163.2	7343.9	22729.	69377.	*	*
718.90	1358.2	2590.6	3585.1	4965.3	9531.6	18281.	66640.	*	*	*
1163.9	2400.0	4994.5	7217.7	10436.	21813.	45497.	*	*	*	*
1880.6	4236.0	9623.1	14524.	21925.	49910.	*	*	*	*	*
3034.8	7471.6	18535.	29220.	46058.	*	*	*	*	*	*

注：* 表示系数大于 99999。

附录 4　年金现值系数表

期数	利率								
	1%	2%	3%	4%	5%	6%	7%	8%	9%
1	0.9901	0.9804	0.9709	0.9615	0.9524	0.9434	0.9346	0.9259	0.9174
2	1.9704	1.9416	1.9135	1.8861	1.8594	1.8334	1.8080	1.7833	1.7591
3	2.9410	2.8839	2.8286	2.7751	2.7232	2.6730	2.6243	2.5771	2.5313
4	3.9020	3.8077	3.7171	3.6299	3.5460	3.4651	3.3872	3.3121	3.2397
5	4.8534	4.7135	4.5797	4.4518	4.3295	4.2124	4.1002	3.9927	3.8897
6	5.7955	5.6014	5.4172	5.2421	5.0757	4.9173	4.7665	4.6229	4.4859
7	6.7282	6.4720	6.2303	6.0021	5.7864	5.5824	5.3893	5.2064	5.0330
8	7.6517	7.3255	7.0197	6.7327	6.4632	6.2098	5.9713	5.7466	5.5348
9	8.5660	8.1622	7.7861	7.4353	7.1078	6.8017	6.5152	6.2469	5.9952
10	9.4713	8.9826	8.5302	8.1109	7.7217	7.3601	7.0236	6.7101	6.4177
11	10.3676	9.7868	9.2526	8.7605	8.3064	7.8869	7.4987	7.1390	6.8052
12	11.2551	10.5753	9.9540	9.3851	8.8633	8.3838	7.9427	7.5361	7.1607
13	12.1337	11.3484	10.6350	9.9856	9.3936	8.8527	8.3577	7.9038	7.4869
14	13.0037	12.1062	11.2961	10.5631	9.8986	9.2950	8.7455	8.2442	7.7862
15	13.8651	12.8493	11.9379	11.1184	10.3797	9.7122	9.1079	8.5595	8.0607
16	14.7179	13.5777	12.5611	11.6523	10.8378	10.1059	9.4466	8.8514	8.3126
17	15.5623	14.2919	13.1661	12.1657	11.2741	10.4773	9.7632	9.1216	8.5436
18	16.3983	14.9920	13.7535	12.6593	11.6896	10.8276	10.0591	9.3719	8.7556
19	17.2260	15.6785	14.3238	13.1339	12.0853	11.1581	10.3356	9.6036	8.9501
20	18.0456	16.3514	14.8775	13.5903	12.4622	11.4699	10.5940	9.8181	9.1285
21	18.8570	17.0112	15.4150	14.0292	12.8212	11.7641	10.8355	10.0168	9.2922
22	19.6604	17.6580	15.9369	14.4511	13.1630	12.0416	11.0612	10.2007	9.4424
23	20.4558	18.2922	16.4436	14.8568	13.4886	12.3034	11.2722	10.3711	9.5802
24	21.2434	18.9139	16.9355	15.2470	13.7986	12.5504	11.4693	10.5288	9.7066
25	22.0232	19.5235	17.4131	15.6221	14.0939	12.7834	11.6536	10.6748	9.8226
30	25.8077	22.3965	19.6004	17.2920	15.3725	13.7648	12.4090	11.2578	10.2737
35	29.4086	24.9986	21.4872	18.6646	16.3742	14.4982	12.9477	11.6546	10.5668
40	32.8347	27.3555	23.1148	19.7928	17.1591	15.0463	13.3317	11.9246	10.7574
45	36.0945	29.4902	24.5187	20.7200	17.7741	15.4558	13.6055	12.1084	10.8812
50	39.1961	31.4236	25.7298	21.4822	18.2559	15.7619	13.8007	12.2335	10.9617
55	42.1472	33.1748	26.7744	22.1086	18.6335	15.9905	13.9399	12.3186	11.0140
60	44.9550	34.7609	27.6756	22.6235	18.9293	16.1614	14.0392	12.3766	11.0480

(PVIFA 表)

利率										
10%	12%	14%	15%	16%	18%	20%	24%	28%	32%	36%
0.9091	0.8929	0.8772	0.8696	0.8541	0.8475	0.8333	0.8065	0.7813	0.7576	0.7353
1.7355	1.6901	1.6467	1.6257	1.5848	1.5656	1.5278	1.4568	1.3916	1.3315	1.2760
2.4869	2.4018	2.3216	2.2832	2.2107	2.1743	2.1065	1.9813	1.8684	1.7663	1.6735
3.1699	3.0373	2.9137	2.8550	2.7476	2.6901	2.5887	2.4043	2.2410	2.0957	1.9658
3.7908	3.6048	3.4331	3.3522	3.2089	3.1272	2.9906	2.7454	2.5320	2.3452	2.1807
4.3553	4.1114	3.8887	3.7845	3.6057	3.4976	3.3255	3.0205	2.7594	2.5342	2.3388
4.8684	4.5638	4.2883	4.1604	3.9475	3.8115	3.6046	3.2423	2.9370	2.6775	2.4550
5.3349	4.9676	4.6389	4.4873	4.2424	4.0776	3.8372	3.4212	3.0758	2.7860	2.5404
5.7590	5.3282	4.9464	4.7716	4.4972	4.3030	4.0310	3.5655	3.1842	2.8681	2.6033
6.1446	5.6502	5.2161	5.0188	4.7176	4.4941	4.1925	3.6819	3.2689	2.9304	2.6495
6.4951	5.9377	5.4527	5.2337	4.9085	4.6560	4.3271	3.7757	3.3351	2.9776	2.6834
6.8137	6.1944	5.6603	5.4206	5.0740	4.7932	4.4392	3.8514	3.3868	3.0133	2.7084
7.1034	6.4235	5.8424	5.5831	5.2178	4.9095	4.5327	3.9124	3.4272	3.0404	2.7268
7.3667	6.6282	6.0021	5.7245	5.3428	5.0081	4.6106	3.9616	3.4587	3.0609	2.7403
7.6061	6.8109	6.1422	5.8474	5.4517	5.0916	4.6755	4.0013	3.4834	3.0764	2.7502
7.8237	6.9740	6.2651	5.9542	5.5466	5.1624	4.7296	4.0333	3.5026	3.0882	2.7575
8.0216	7.1196	6.3729	6.0472	5.6295	5.2223	4.7746	4.0591	3.5177	3.0971	2.7629
8.2014	7.2497	6.4674	6.1280	5.7019	5.2732	4.8122	4.0799	3.5294	3.1039	2.7668
8.3649	7.3658	6.5504	6.1982	5.7652	5.3162	4.8435	4.0967	3.5386	3.1090	2.7697
8.5136	7.4694	6.6231	6.2593	5.8208	5.3527	4.8696	4.1103	3.5458	3.1129	2.7718
8.6487	7.5620	6.6870	6.3125	5.8695	5.3837	4.8913	4.1212	3.5514	3.1158	2.7734
8.7715	7.6446	6.7429	6.3587	5.9122	5.4099	4.9094	4.1300	3.5558	3.1180	2.7746
8.8832	7.7184	6.7921	6.3988	5.9498	5.4321	4.9245	4.1371	3.5592	3.1197	2.7754
8.9847	7.7843	6.8351	6.4338	5.9830	5.4509	4.9371	4.1428	3.5619	3.1210	2.7760
9.0770	7.8431	6.8729	6.4641	6.0121	5.4669	4.9476	4.1474	3.5640	3.1220	2.7765
9.4269	8.0552	7.0027	6.5660	6.1144	5.5168	4.9789	4.1601	3.5693	3.1242	2.7775
9.6442	8.1755	7.0700	6.6166	6.1705	5.5386	4.9915	4.1644	3.5708	3.1248	2.7777
9.7791	8.2438	7.1050	6.6418	6.2022	5.5482	4.9966	4.1659	3.5712	3.1250	2.7778
9.8628	8.2825	7.1232	6.6543	6.2205	5.5523	4.9986	4.1664	3.5714	3.1250	2.7778
9.9148	8.3045	7.1327	6.6605	6.2314	5.5541	4.9995	4.1666	3.5714	3.1250	2.7778
9.9471	8.3170	7.1376	6.6636	6.2380	5.5549	4.9998	4.1666	3.5714	3.1250	2.7778
9.9672	8.3240	7.1401	6.6651	6.2421	5.5553	4.9999	4.1667	3.5714	3.1250	2.7778